The Boreal Feast

The Boreal Feast

A CULINARY JOURNEY
THROUGH THE NORTH

Michele Genest

Photographs by Cathie Archbould
Illustrations by Laurel Parry

LOST MOOSE

Lost Moose is an imprint of Harbour Publishing Co. Ltd.
P.O. Box 219, Madeira Park, BC, Canada, V0N 2H0
www.harbourpublishing.com

Illustrations by Laurel Parry
Food styled by Tara Kolla-Hale
Edited by Anna Comfort O'Keeffe and Nicola Goshulak
Proofread by Cheryl Cohen
Indexed by Iva Cheung
Cover and text design by Diane Robertson

Printed and bound in Canada on chlorine-free paper
made with 10% post-consumer waste

Additional photo credits: Michele Genest, pp viii, 2,
16, 17, 18, 19, 20, 32 (left), 39, 101, 102, 106 (top and
bottom), 108, 112 (bottom), 121, 122, 137, 139, 140,
141, 142, 158, 172, 174, 177, 183 (bottom right), 197, 209
(right), 238 (bottom left and right); David MacKenzie,
p. 120; Laperla_foto/Thinkstock, p. 85; Hanna Dewey/
Thinkstock, p. 201; Lesyy/Thinkstock, p. 206.

Canada Council
for the Arts
Conseil des Arts
du Canada

BRITISH COLUMBIA
ARTS COUNCIL
An agency of the Province of British Columbia

Harbour Publishing acknowledges financial support
from the Government of Canada through the Canada
Book Fund and the Canada Council for the Arts, and
from the Province of British Columbia through the
BC Arts Council and the Book Publishing Tax Credit.

Cataloguing Data available from Library
and Archives Canada

ISBN 978-1-55017-627-8 (paperback)

ISBN 978-1-55017-629-2 (ebook)

For the
Edström family.

Contents

The Boreal Feast: An Introduction

I knew from the start I wanted to call this cookbook *The Boreal Feast*, and embarked on a search for the meaning of "feast" through dictionary, thesaurus and the gastronomic canon, trying to corral all the rich and plummy associations contained in that word into one, all-inclusive definition. I found feast-associated words like *celebrate, ritual, sumptuous, delight, banquet, holiday, religion, blow-out, village*. These were helpful. I made up a working definition for myself: a sumptuous meal or banquet requiring days of planning and preparation when a diverse selection of delicious foods is prepared with love and care, then consumed over many hours with friends, family or ceremonial guests.

But that definition quickly became too limiting. Sometimes a feast can be a spontaneous gathering based on a lucky catch, a windfall or a new ingredient in the supermarket. A feast can be seasonal or it can happen any time, it can be community-wide or particular to one family, steeped in tradition or newly conceived, given in community halls, cultural centres, dining rooms, around the kitchen table or on a campsite out on the land. A feast can be as elaborate as a 12-course tasting menu with

A pilgrim's wood supply and kettle for an overnight stay in a hut on a section of St. Olavsleden, or St. Olav's Way, along the Indalsälven River in Jämtland. Modern-day pilgrims can walk the whole route from Selånger on the Bothnian coast to Trondheim in Norway. The route is known as Sweden's and Norway's version of the Camino.

wine pairings in a fine restaurant or as simple and satisfying as a pot of Labrador tea and a piece of bannock on a hillside during a berry-picking expedition. Clearly, there's more to a feast than a banquet.

Here is the crux of the matter: whether elaborate or simple, a feast celebrates and strengthens our connection to each other and to the place we live—this field, forest, town, city, region, country, this earth—through good food and, let us not forget, fun. The food upon which we feast is at the centre, both a celebration in itself and the medium through which we celebrate, the connector to each other and to what sustains us. So, *The Boreal Feast* is a celebration of boreal food and the boreal forest.

Without the forest, there would be no feast. The boreal forest stretches in a green cape around the upper third of the globe, over Canada, Alaska, Siberia, parts of Asia, Russia and Scandinavia, a mantle of 12 million square kilometres. It's the largest biome on earth, home to thousands of species of birds, animals, fish, insects, trees and plants, and a vital source of oxygen and fresh water. The trees and minerals of the forest provide the raw materials that contribute to the economies of Canada, America, Sweden, Finland, Norway and Russia. We need the boreal forest, and yet our attitude towards it can be ambivalent, even contradictory. We too easily destroy what sustains us. We over-harvest; we leave a mess.

Many organizations, such as Canadian Parks and Wilderness Society, Yukon Conservation Society, the

Sámi coffee cups, or guksi, are a favourite vessel for a favourite drink: strong, boiling hot coffee. Now we just need a bit of suovas, or a piece of coffee cheese...

Canadian Boreal Initiative, and the David Suzuki Foundation, work with indigenous peoples, industry, government non-profit organizations to raise awareness of the importance of conserving the boreal forest for the longevity of the planet. Books like J. David Henry's *Canada's Boreal Forest*, Beverley Gray's *The Boreal Herbal*, Andy MacKinnon, et al.'s *Edible & Medicinal Plants of Canada* and numerous field guides and cookbooks help us get to know the forest as a source of sustenance, healing and nutrition. This is good: the more we get to know the boreal forest, the better we'll appreciate it, and the harder we'll work to conserve it.

My first cookbook, *The Boreal Gourmet,* and now *The Boreal Feast* are, I hope, small steps in that same direction. I hope that by encouraging readers and cooks to spend time in the boreal forest, to harvest wild food with care and attention, and then to have fun experimenting in the kitchen to prepare delicious dishes, the amount of love available for the forest will grow exponentially, and so will our efforts to preserve it.

Experimentation and culinary adventure were the cornerstones of *The Boreal Gourmet*. I learned as I went, and hoped that readers would too. That's still true. Like many in the Canadian north, I turn to books such as *Edible & Medicinal Plants of Canada* and *The Boreal Herbal*, to field guides such as David Arora's *All That the Rain Promises and More*, and ethno-botanical guides such as Alestine Andre and Alan Fehr's *Gwich'in Ethnobotany*, paying special attention to the "Food Uses" sections, to gain clues to the culinary possibilities of plants I'm just beginning to know.

In the fall of 2012 my husband, Hector, and I went on a tour through Sweden, Norway and Finland to learn about what other northern peoples did with the same wild ingredients that live and grow in the Canadian boreal forest. That was an eye-opener. There is a rich culinary tradition in each of those countries, and a lively population of adventurous chefs who are producing imaginative food based on indigenous hunted, foraged and cultivated foods. For several years in a row Scandinavian chefs have won the global gastronomic competition, Bocuse d'Or. René Redzepi and his restaurant Noma, and now Magnus Nilsson and Fäviken, are household names synonymous with foraging and fierce experimentation. Home cooks are proud of their regional culinary traditions, and eager to share them.

The more we get to know the boreal forest, the better we'll appreciate it, and the harder we'll work to conserve it.

In Sweden, the government has launched an initiative called Sweden: The New Culinary Nation, and supports small artisanal producers through grant programs, marketing and culinary tourism promotion. Slow Food Sápmi encourages Sámi chefs to develop recipes and new culinary directions based on traditional Sámi foods and food customs. The Finnish government has launched programs to support local food production and culinary tourism. The Norwegian government's Innovation Norway has developed Norwegian Foodprints, a branding program that identifies restaurants that serve local food cooked from scratch.

I have been influenced! Whereas *The Boreal Gourmet* cast its eye southward, creating northern–southern fusion dishes, *The Boreal Feast* scans the northern latitudes, including Alaska, for inspiration. But influences are not exclusively northern. One of the big differences between the Old and New Worlds is the pace of settlement in the New: fast, furious and recent. Canadian culinary traditions reflect the original peoples and those who have settled here over the past 450 years. As the north becomes more culturally diverse, it is common to find German, Somalian, Southeast Asian and Filipino interpretations of the wild foods we're accustomed to. And with our interest in becoming more self-sufficient, we have also seen a return to homesteading traditions. *The Boreal Feast* reflects some of these interests, without being exhaustive. The bibliography of suggested titles at the back of the book provides sources of more information.

The Boreal Feast is divided into five chapters. The first four chapters gather a few menus for each season, starting in the first days of winter–spring and ending with a matryoshka doll painting party in January. The final chapter, "The Boreal Pantry," is based on seasonal gatherings of wild ingredients, with some cultivated items included. This chapter includes recipes for pantry items such as jellies, jams, syrups, infused oils and liqueurs, useful in preserving the harvest and putting together a basic northern pantry. I hope the complementary sections contribute to your enjoyment of cooking with the wild and cultivated foods of the boreal latitudes.

I wish you all the best in your deepening relationship with the boreal forest, and hope that your love and affection for this beautiful place grows with each delicious feast you prepare.

Michele Genest
Whitehorse, March 2014

A NOTE ON MEASUREMENTS AND INGREDIENTS

The recipes in this book were composed using volume measurements based on the American teaspoon, tablespoon and cup for both dry and liquid ingredients. Their rounded metric equivalents are included in each recipe. In these recipes, olive oil is always extra-virgin, vegetables are washed and organic wherever possible and butter is salted unless stated otherwise.

Acknowledgements

I couldn't have completed this book without the help of many kind and generous people in Canada and Scandinavia who shared their knowledge, their recipes, their home, their kitchens and their encouragement.

My heartfelt thanks to Margaret Huber, Canada's Chief of Protocol from 2010 to 2013, who has been a tremendous support and champion. Special thanks to His Excellency Teppo Tauriainen, Ambassador of Sweden to Canada from 2010 to 2014, who, with his staff, assisted with travel ideas, introductions, menu suggestions and recipes. Many thanks to Mr. Kenneth Macartney, Ambassador of Canada to Sweden, to the staff at the Embassy of Canada in Sweden, and to chef Göran Amnegård for a wonderful dinner at the embassy. Thanks to Bjørn Petter Hernes at the Embassy of Canada in Norway, whom we didn't manage to meet in person but who never stopped offering suggestions and made sure that a copy of the excellent *Taste of National Tourist Routes* found its way to me in Whitehorse. Thanks to Deb Bartlette for being the courier.

My husband Hector and I were bowled over by the hospitality and enthusiasm of those we met on our travels. My sister-in-law Tina Edström's family became our family in Sweden, and treated us as one of their own, taking us berry and mushroom picking and introducing us to everyone they thought would be helpful. Warmest thanks to Gunnar and Berit Edström, to Maria Edström and Andreas Löfgren and their boys, to Cecilia Edström and her family, and to Anna Sanders, who was our guide and boon companion in Östersund. Thanks to Karin Mellin and her family for a lovely fika and dinner in Östersund.

Thanks to Anders Lindqvist, who cooked for us night after night at his home in Vännäs, and introduced us to *surströmming*, fermented Baltic herring. (A special thanks for the *surströmming*, Anders.) Håkan Särnåker was a fabulous host in Alingsås and provided our orientation to the excellent convention of the inexpensive Swedish lunch. Thanks to Christine Boyd and Svante Larsson for the bed, the reindeer blood crêpes and a tour of the traditional baking house, and to Walter and Irmelli Lindh for a lovely afternoon in Sangis. Jan-Age Riseth and Randi Nymo, thank you for the roof over our heads, the excellent company and the introductions in Narvik.

A special thanks must go to the chefs and artisans who spent time with us, cooked for us and shared their ideas with us. Susanne Jonsson, Vegard Stormo, Martin Jönsson and Laila Spik, thanks for everything. Thanks to Magnus Nilsson and Johan Agrell for spending time with us at Fäviken, and especially for telling us about *Pinguicula vulgaris*, a story that didn't make it into this cookbook and will have to wait for the next. Similarly, thanks to the Skärvången Dairy and to Hans Nooitgedagt at Skabram for the tours of their premises, the beautiful cheese, and the discussions about coffee cheese and *långfil*.

At home in Canada, thanks to the Parks Canada Yukon Field Unit, particularly Christine Hedgecock, Carmen Wong, Kate Alexander and Michael Prochazka

In the alpine, fall colours flare for a brief moment before the snow falls.

for adventures and research assistance. A big thanks must go to the gang who took on the task of recipe testing and reporting back, honestly and in detail, about their experience: Fia Jampolsky, Jen Jones, Sophia Brown Marnik, Elise Maltin, Brigitte Parker and Janet Patterson.

Thanks to the dear usual suspects I can call in at the last minute for a glass of wine or another hand in the kitchen: Priscilla Clarkin, Michele Emslie, Guiniveve Lalena, Sophia Brown Marnik, Meshell Melvin, Carolyn Moore, Laurel Parry and Michelle Rabeau. Thanks to Suzanne de la Barre for great conversations and thoughtful help on Sweden, and thanks to Lynn Cairns for scouring the flea markets for just the right plates and dishes. Warm thanks to my lifelong pal in writing and cooking Anne DesBrisay, for her pursuit of excellence, and to Anita Stewart for her dedication to the cause of great Canadian food.

Thanks to Laurel Parry and my sister Anne Louise Genest, for reading, inspiration and constant encouragement. To the MacKenzies, for loving good food. To my brother Paul, for responding with enthusiasm to every culinary proposition, however outlandish. To Barbara Jessup, for chilling the glasses. To André Genest and Tina Edström for the test kitchen on Lantau. To John Genest, for timely phone calls, and my mother, Janet Genest, for coming to Whitehorse at least once a year and knowing what to say.

To Team Book: photographer Cathie Archbould, who's been my hard-working, wonderful collaborator every step of the way and who always goes one step further to get the shot, thank you. Thanks to stylist Tara Kolla-Hale, who knows how to make everything beautiful. Thanks (a third time!) to illustrator Laurel Parry for her magic pen.

A special thanks to the team at Harbour Publishing: editor Anna Comfort O'Keeffe, who always believes the writer can do it, and sends chocolate rations; copy editor Nicola Goshulak, who asks the right questions; and publicist Heather Lohnes, who is cheerful and brilliant. Thank you Diane Robertson for the beautiful page design, and the late nights.

It may not be a good strategy to leave the biggest one until almost last, but I only do it because there's too much to be said. You know who you are, Hector MacKenzie. The best travelling companion, sous-chef, roadie, troubleshooter, taster, reader, wine opener, tagine wielder, pasta maker and friend.

Thanks finally to the boreal forest, to the indigenous people who know it so well and to everyone who loves it.

Michele Genest

Whitehorse, March 2014

CHAPTER ONE

Spring

Sometime in mid-February we notice the
evening sky is much lighter now. We're
moving from the cold and dark into the cold
and bright. Sunglasses come out for the
first time in months. The snow is older, with
layers that tell the story of freeze and thaw.
By mid-March we're gaining light by minutes
each day. Fathers take their daughters ice
fishing. The cod season starts in the Lofoten
Islands. In Sápmi the reindeer move to the
calving grounds before the snow gets too
soft. Trappers shut down their traplines; the
ice on the creeks is not so trustworthy for
travel anymore. Late-March walkers risk
post-holing in snow up to their thighs if they
stray from the path. Dawson does Thaw di
Gras. Finns flock to the Spring Market in
Rovaniemi. Bikers take to the highway in
early training runs. Skiers go out in the early
morning and don't come back until their
cheeks are burnished. The parking lot in
the White Pass is full every weekend with
sledders and backcountry skiers and on
Marsh Lake the swans and waders are back
in their quacking, whistling thousands. Tiny
buds appear on the cottonwood trees. You
can smell earth. It's time to go muskratting.
Time to fish for grayling and whitefish.
Time to look for crocuses on the clay cliffs.
Peel off a layer. Listen to the ice melt.

*Purple crocus, one of the first signs
of spring after the snow melts.*

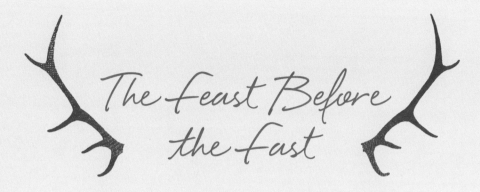

The Feast Before the Fast

Note: You may not want to try all three kinds of pancakes at the same meal. However, my girlfriends and I did and enjoyed the exercise of compare and contrast, so familiar from high school history exam questions, but way more fun.

MENU FOR EIGHT

Finnish Pancakes **11**

Homemade Cranberry Juice **11**

Blini with Walnut-Mushroom Filling **12**

Smoked Salmon Roe **241**

Quinoa and Beet Ukrainian Pancakes **14**

Rhubarb and Blood Orange Jam **206**

Spring Cleaning

Ah, February! How we rejoice in the returning light, the shedding of heavy winter layers, the gentle warmth of the sun on an afternoon ski. But then, eeek! How we despond when the sun, grown bold, reveals the streaks on the window, the grime of dust and woodsmoke on every surface, and most alarming, our own shaggy hair and unkempt clothing. After months of winter hibernation we find ourselves Not Ready for Spring, and the urge to scour the interiors of our houses and persons takes hold. We purchase cleaning supplies and start looking up cleanses online. Let the renewal begin!

The fun and feasting has its roots in pagan rituals, both those that celebrate spring, fertility and the beginning of new life and those that honour the dead.

But wait. The fridge is full of butter, milk and eggs. The cupboard bulges with booze. Clearly, before we cleanse, we must party. And thus, around the world, begin the great spring rituals: *Carnaval* in South America, *Apokries* in Greece, Shrovetide in Britain, *Maslenitsa* in Russia, *Fettisdagen* in Sweden, Yukon Sourdough Rendezvous in Whitehorse, Thaw di Gras in Dawson, celebrations that usher out the winter, welcome in the spring, and use up the last of the meat and dairy.

In the Christian calendar this week of masks and lanterns, of bonfires and mock brawls, is the last party before the six austere weeks of Lent, but the fun and feasting has its roots in pagan rituals, both those that celebrate spring, fertility and the beginning of new life and those that honour the dead. The food of choice during this week, and especially on the last day before the fast, is often some version of the pancake.

Before the fast, pancakes (or blini, or crêpes or *tiganites*) help ease the transition away from meat (*Carnaval* and *Apokries* mean "goodbye to" or "away from" meat; *Maslenitsa* means "butter week"); they also empty the fridge of prohibited items. (In Greece the last day of Apokries is called *Kathara Deftera* or "Clean Monday.") There's some suggestion that the eating of pancakes is linked to the foods buried with the dead—grain, honey. Blini were eaten in pre-Christian Russia on feast days honouring the god Volos, whose domain was domestic animals and fertility.

In the Jewish tradition, the eating of blintzes, cheese and sour cream accompanies the holiday of Shavuot in June, which celebrates both the handing down of the Torah and the June harvest of grain. Pancakes surely originated with an agricultural people: they require flour, which requires grain, which requires staying in one place and growing a crop. But nomadic peoples of the north, once introduced to the pancake (or bannock, which is

Each spring, trumpeter and tundra swans congregate on open water in the Yukon to rest up and feed on nutrient-rich plants before continuing the journey to their nesting grounds.

essentially a fat, eggless pancake) quickly adopted it as a staple. In the Yukon bannock is essential to every First Nations feast. The Sámi people make a pancake with reindeer blood, a special food for pregnant women. You can buy reindeer blood in the supermarkets in Sweden. Our friends Christine Boyd and Svante Larsson made us blood pancakes one night in their house on the Kalix River; to my unaccustomed palate the flavour (not the texture) was closest to Yorkshire pudding and gravy.

Now let us follow the pancake trail up from the Middle East, through Greece and the Slavic countries into Finland, Russia and Ukraine, there to experiment with the variety of pancakes concocted by our fellow northerners with liberal doses of eggs, milk, butter and grains. The beet pancakes might seem odd, but they are delicious: sweet and grainy. The Finnish version is similar to French crêpes, and brings back fond memories of Kanga Sauna restaurant in Thunder Bay, Ontario. And the blini made with yeast, yogourt and buckwheat flour, well, honestly, who could resist? Those spring purgers who, like me,

have laid in vast stores of millet, buckwheat, quinoa and other grains in anticipation of the annual 10-day dietary cleanse, only to be left with a glut once the cleanse is over, will be glad to find a use for them at last.

The mushroom and walnut accompaniment to the blini, overleaf, is the result of another spring cleaning, this one by my friend David Neufeld, a historian who was briefly the archivist at the University of Saskatchewan in his graduate student days. One recent February he cleaned out his basement and came across a file box of corporate and government-issued food pamphlets deaccessioned by the university's archives 30 years before, which he had carted from home to home until he landed in the Yukon, in the vague belief that someday they would come in handy. Well, they did! He gave them to me, and this mushroom and walnut recipe was suggested by one of them, a pamphlet of "Authentic Canadian Mushroom Recipes" called *Mushrooms At Home*, published by Mushrooms Canada; no publication date; cost: $1.00. Thank you, David.

Finnish Pancakes

2 eggs, beaten

1 tsp (5 mL) vanilla

1 tsp (5 mL) salt

2 Tbsp (30 mL) sugar

1½ cups (350 mL) sifted flour

2 cups (475 mL) milk

1 Tbsp (15 mL) melted butter, plus extra butter for the pan

Yogourt or crème fraîche, for serving

Birch syrup, for serving

Berries, for serving

1. Beat together eggs, vanilla, salt and sugar. Add flour in three additions, alternating with milk. Stir in melted butter. At this point, you can let the batter rest for a few hours, refrigerated, or make your pancakes right away.

2. Heat a cast iron frying pan over medium heat until drops of water fly off when you flick them onto the surface. Melt a small pat of butter in the middle and brush it evenly over the entire surface. Pour a scant ladleful of batter into the middle of the pan, and quickly tilt the pan from side to side so that the batter spreads almost to the edges (keep an oven mitt handy for the hot handle). Wait for the bubbles to show on the surface (about a minute), then flip the pancake and cook for another minute. Tip onto a plate and keep warm in the oven, or deliver to your eager customers right away.

3. Serve with dollops of yogourt or crème fraîche, birch syrup and your favourite berries (now's the time to raid the freezer).

Makes about 16 × 6-inch (15-cm) pancakes.

Homemade Cranberry Juice

1 cup (250 mL) wild lowbush cranberries (lingonberries) or substitute cultivated whole cranberries

4 cups (1 L) cold water

Birch or maple syrup to taste

1. Blend cranberries and half the water in a blender or food processor. For a thinner juice, pour through a sieve, pressing solids with the back of a spoon. If you don't mind small particles in your juice, skip this step. (Think of it as orange juice with pulp.)

2. Pour juice into a clean glass jar. Add remaining water, close lid and shake well. Add syrup 1 tablespoon (15 mL) at a time until the juice is sweet enough to your taste. Store in the refrigerator, where the juice will keep for several days.

Makes about 4 cups (1 L).

Blini with Walnut-Mushroom Filling

This recipe comes from Lyn Fabio, who stood at the stove on Thanksgiving in 2013 and churned out blini after blini for the dinner guests. We ate the pancakes hot off the griddle with smoked coho roe and dollops of crème fraîche. Lyn taught me the trick of filling a nozzle-topped squeeze bottle with batter and squeezing small rounds onto the frying pan or griddle; it's much easier to control the size and thickness of blini with this method.

   This recipe makes a considerable number of blini. Lyn says she doesn't halve the recipe but simply refrigerates leftover batter and uses it for breakfast or lunch until it's gone.

BLINI

3 cups (710 mL) milk, divided

2 tsp (10 mL) dry active yeast

1 tsp (5 mL) sugar

1 cup (250 mL) all-purpose flour, divided

1 cup (250 mL) buckwheat flour

½ tsp (2.5 mL) salt

2 Tbsp (30 mL) melted butter

4 eggs, separated

TOPPINGS

Mushroom, Walnuts and Cream filling, recipe on next page

Smoked Salmon Roe for filling, instructions on page 241

Pickled Spruce Tips for garnish, recipe on page 226

Crème fraîche for garnish

Finely chopped red onion for garnish

1. Heat 1 cup (250 mL) milk until lukewarm, or 115F (45C). Pour into a large mixing bowl, stir in yeast, sugar and ½ cup (125 mL) all-purpose flour and let stand until bubbly, about 10 minutes.

2. In a separate bowl, combine remaining ½ cup (125 mL) all-purpose flour, buckwheat flour and salt.

MUSHROOM, WALNUTS AND CREAM

½ cup (125 mL) each dried morel and shaggy mane mushrooms (or substitute dried chanterelles, shiitake or porcini)

1 cup (250 mL) white wine

3 Tbsp (45 mL) butter

1 medium onion, chopped

2 cups (475 mL) cremini or field mushrooms, cleaned and quartered

2 cloves garlic, minced

½ cup (125 mL) walnut pieces

½ cup (125 mL) 35 percent cream

Salt and pepper to taste

1. Soak morel and shaggy mane mushrooms in white wine until softened, about 15 minutes.

2. Once mushrooms are rehydrated, remove them from the wine, squeezing out any excess moisture, and pat dry. Strain the wine through a fine sieve into a pot and boil vigorously until reduced to 2 tablespoons (30 mL).

3. In the meantime, melt butter in a cast iron pan over medium heat. Once butter foams, add chopped onions and sauté until translucent, reducing heat if necessary so it doesn't brown. Add the morels and shaggy manes, stir so they're coated in butter, then add cremini mushrooms and garlic.

4. Cook until mushrooms begin to brown, 5 to 7 minutes, then add walnuts, cream and reduced wine. Stir and cook another 5 to 7 minutes until the mixture is thick but not solid. Remove from heat and serve at once.

Makes about 3 cups (710 mL) filling, enough for 120 canapé-sized blini.

---

3. Pour remaining 2 cups (475 mL) milk into the yeast mixture and gradually whisk in dry ingredients until batter is smooth and thick.

4. Whisk in melted butter. Cover bowl with plastic wrap. Leave at room temperature until batter is doubled in size, about 2 to 3 hours. At this stage you can refrigerate the batter overnight. Bring to room temperature before proceeding to the next step.

5. When you are ready to cook the blini, stir down batter, which will be quite frothy. Beat egg yolks and whisk into batter. In a separate bowl, beat egg whites until stiff. Gently fold egg whites into batter.

6. For canapé-sized blini, pour batter through a funnel into a nozzle-topped squeeze-bottle and squeeze onto a hot, lightly greased cast iron griddle, making rounds of about 1½ inches (3.8 cm) in diameter. Cook for about 2 minutes, until bottom is well browned and surface is covered in bubbles. Flip and cook 1 minute more. Keep warm in a 200F (95C) oven.

   For breakfast-sized blini, spoon batter onto griddle in 3-inch (7.5-cm) rounds and cook for an extra minute on the second side.

7. To serve, arrange blini and mushroom filling on a warmed platter and pass separate bowls of crème fraîche, smoked coho roe, finely chopped red onion and pickled spruce tips. Guests can alternate between the mushroom and smoked roe, spooning each one onto a blini and eating in one bite.

Makes about 60 × 3-inch (7.5-cm) blini, or 120 × 1½-inch (3.8-cm) blini.

Quinoa and Beet Ukrainian Pancakes

Adapted from Marion Trutter's Culinaria Russia.

⅔ cup (160 mL) quinoa

1⅓ cups (330 mL) chicken or vegetable stock

3 medium-sized beets (1 lb/455 gr)

½ cup (125 mL) all-purpose flour

1¼ cup (300 mL) quark or ricotta cheese

½ cup (125 mL) yogourt

1 egg, beaten

1 Tbsp (15 mL) sugar

½ tsp (2.5 mL) kosher salt

1 tsp (5 mL) lemon juice

1 tsp (5 mL) coarsely ground black pepper

Butter and oil for frying

¾ cup (180 mL) sour cream or crème fraîche, for garnish

Chopped fresh dill, for garnish

1. Rinse the quinoa under cold, running water. Bring quinoa and stock to a boil, then reduce heat, cover and simmer for 15 minutes. Fluff with a fork, transfer to a bowl and let cool to room temperature.

2. In the meantime, cook the beets (scrubbed but not peeled) for about 30 minutes, until partially cooked but not soft. Immerse in cold water, and when they're cool enough to handle, peel and grate finely.

3. When quinoa has cooled to room temperature, add the beets, flour, quark or ricotta, yogourt, egg, sugar, salt, lemon juice and pepper.

4. Heat a heavy frying pan over medium heat until drops of water fly off when you flick them onto the surface, then add about 1 teaspoon (5 mL) each of butter and oil. Drop spoonfuls of batter into the pan and flatten them with the back of the spoon until they're about 3 inches (7.5 cm) in diameter. Cook for 2 to 3 minutes on each side, then keep warm in the oven. Replenish the oil and butter as necessary.

5. Serve hot with a dollop of crème fraîche (or sour cream) and chopped dill on each pancake. These are really good warmed up the next day, or toasted and spread with butter and Rhubarb and Blood Orange Jam (page 206).

Makes about 15 × 3-inch (7. 5-cm) pancakes.

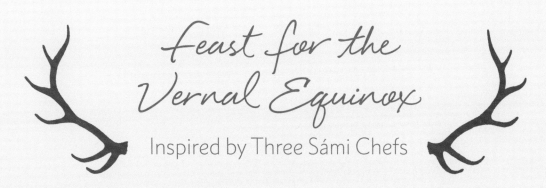

Feast for the Vernal Equinox

Inspired by Three Sámi Chefs

Sometime in mid-March, cooks across the north take stock of the freezer situation. Though the first wild greens are at least eight weeks away the prospect of replenishment draws closer, and we can release those moose ribs we've been hanging onto, liberate that whole sockeye salmon or unzip that jealously guarded bag of blueberries. The vernal equinox is a perfect time for a feast that celebrates the winter that's passing and the coming renewal of spring.

MENU FOR EIGHT

Parmesan Crisps **21**

Warm Apple Juice with a Splash of Calvados **21**

Halloumi, Alaskan Spot Prawn and Tomato Skewers **22**

Gravad of Beef or Moose with Pickled Radish and
Morel Mayonnaise **22**

Morel-Crusted Bison Short Ribs **24**

Yukon Herb Jelly **207**

Saffron Potato Soufflés **26**

Endive, Daikon and Kohlrabi Salad
with Walnuts and Cranberries **27**

Blueberry and White Chocolate Mousse Parfait
with Haskap Liqueur **28**

From Gällivare to Narvik,
on the Trail of Three Sámi Chefs

After leaving Gällivare in northern Sweden the train to Narvik rolls through a landscape of tundra lakes and wind-blown trees. You gaze out the window, looking for reindeer, until the waste rock and detritus from the iron mines outside Kiruna appear, and you barely have time to absorb the change before you pull into Kiruna's red brick station. From Kiruna the train climbs up into the snowy mountains at Abisko National Park, pulling cars of iron ore destined for the seaport and a few late-season hikers destined for Kebnekaise, Sweden's highest mountain. You know you've crossed the border when the colour of the holiday cottages scattered among the rocks changes. There's not so much Falu red paint anymore, and more white and green and blue. You have arrived in Norway. Right on cue, there is a fjord

hundreds of metres below. The train clings to a granite wall for a few kilometres, then plunges down through tunnels to Narvik and the sea.

Hector and I rode the line between Gällivare and Narvik four times in September 2012, on the trail of three Sámi chefs: Martin Jönsson, Vegard Stormo, and Laila Spik. Jönsson and Stormo are remarkable chefs who share a love of local food, Sámi tradition and contemporary cuisine; both are winners of prestigious Sápmi Awards bestowed annually by Slow Food Sápmi. Laila Spik, reindeer herder, elder, cultural ambassador and herbalist, is one of the best-known Sámi women in international culinary and traditional medicine circles.

In August of 2012, fresh from winning his 2012 Sápmi Award, Martin Jönsson was hired by the Quality Hotel Grand Royal in downtown Narvik to steer Linken, the hotel's showcase rooftop restaurant, towards a cuisine focused on local food. Martin's twist at Linken is "fun dining," a play on fine dining designed to loosen things up by introducing whimsy and surprise, while sticking to the seriousness of good local ingredients and refined technique.

Narvik is a busy industrial seaport: from here thousands of tons of iron ore from Gällivare and Kiruna move out into the world on ships. But the city is also a skiing town and a university town. This makes for an

Sámi Elder Laila Spik prepares reindeer meat in the kitchen of her home in Muorjevare.

A clifftop view of the main lodge at Tinja Fjellgård.

interesting clientele at Linken, where boisterous business types gather at the bar and tables of serious diners focus on the food.

Martin has to be one of the nicest guys in the food industry, with a calm, gentle manner and an understated sense of humour. When I visited his kitchen, a vat of reindeer and chanterelle stock bubbled on the stove. One chef stood at the grill sautéing several pounds of chanterelles, while another one took a baking tray of long, skinny bread sticks from the oven and returned to his task of cutting a sheet cake of compressed cod, potato and dill into perfect cubes.

The bread sticks would show up at dinner that night, with one end planted in a sawed-off piece of birch trunk, the other end supporting the cube of cod cake, now breaded and deep-fried: a tall tree in a tiny landscape of hors d'ouevres. This was just one of the whimsical interludes between courses in a prix fixe dinner that included smoked reindeer wrapped around a celeriac purée, halibut with melon salsa and frozen lemon, and sautéed

quail in red wine reduction. The pre-cheese course was Parmesan ice cream, and lingonberry sorbet with spruce foam preceded the main dessert of goat cheese parfait with cloudberry sorbet and white chocolate snow. We looked at our fellow patrons, especially the guys at the bar, and hoped they knew how good this food was.

Next day Martin drove Hector and me across the fjord into the mountains to meet Vegard Stormo, Martin's friend and colleague, a fellow hunter and fisher, and head chef at Tinja Fjellgård, the Stormo family's lodge on a piece of property tucked underneath a cliff. Martin wore a beautiful green wool Sámi jacket, and brought a supply of delicacies such as reindeer-nose terrine, reindeer loin and reindeer broth. We were going to have a Sámi picnic on the land.

Vegard's father, Odd Stormo, greeted us when we arrived at the Tinja Fjellgård. It was Odd's vision to create a lodge on the property where his family had homesteaded since the mid 1800s, and he showed us around the woods, the fire pit and the traditional *lavvu*

The traditional, grass-roofed storage house at Tinja. Odd Stormo's family first homesteaded on the property in the mid-1800s.

Lingonberry leaves, roasting over the fire before being made into tea.

tent frame with the pride of a person who has built something he loves. He pointed across to the hills in the west, where his grandmother lived as a teenager, and where his grandfather walked at night to see her after the farm work was done.

Martin lit a fire and laid out reindeer skins on the benches by the fire pit. Vegard was in the middle of a lunch service, so we roamed the property picking lingonberries and flowers. Martin was in his element; he's a country boy from a small town in the woods near Gällivare, and the wilderness is home. He heated the reindeer and chanterelle broth on the fire, sautéed the Yukon morel mushrooms we had brought, cut thin slices from the terrine, cooked the steak and invited us to dig in.

We sat by the fire nibbling our starters. After a while Vegard, free at last, brought out a steaming pot of reindeer stew. The other kitchen staff joined us and we ate stew from wooden bowls and chatted and stared at the flames. Vegard roasted lingonberry leaves in a frying pan and made tea. "When you cook the leaves like this it's more of a black tea," he said.

Soon Martin had to say goodbye and head back to Narvik. Hector and I checked into our room at the lodge: clean, bare wooden floors, slanted ceilings and a window that looked out over the mountains to the south. Vegard suggested we go for a walk to build up our

appetite, because, yes, we were going to dine at five, on a multi-course prix fixe meal with wine pairings. Oh, it was a good thing we'd become dining marathoners! We climbed the cliff behind the lodge and lay in the tundra, looking across the sea towards the Lofoten Islands and snoozing in the sun.

Vegard seated us in a room named for his grandmother, Berit, just off the main dining room; there was a portrait of her on the wall. She looked serious and slightly apprehensive. The pale wooden table was decorated with a candle and a jar of mountain ash berries and several different sizes of wine glasses. There were only two other diners that night in the main room, oafish sorts who yelled when they wanted something, which made us burn on Vegard's behalf but he was unfazed.

Instead of the usual sparkling wine, the first courses were accompanied by birch beer, made by Vegard and brewmeister Shea-Arne Engevik from young birch leaves. It was as dry and light as champagne. And then the procession of dishes began: smoked, cured reindeer; *lutefisk* served with slivers of whey cheese, salted pork and puréed green peas; Arctic char, roasted over the fire on one side, served with its skin and roasted beetroot, apple sauce and smoked trout roe; smoked king crab and pork risotto served in a tiny casserole that billowed with smoke when you lifted the lid.

The traditional Sámi lavvu at Tinja Fjellgård, stripped of its covering for winter. In summer, guests can sleep inside.

Cooking pot with view, at Tinja Fjellgård, where the advice before a meal is to build up an appetitie.

The moon rose over the ridge in the direction where Berit used to live, as Vegard told us stories about her. To get to school she rowed across the fjord and then walked three hours. There was one pair of shoes and five kids, so each kid went to school one day a week.

Vegard left and came back with hare tenderloin served with Victoria plum and lichen, duck liver and reindeer rillettes blended with cream and sprinkled with a muesli of seeds, tiny potato chips and celeriac purée. For dessert, cloudberry and rosemary preserve, rhubarb chutney, arctic raspberry—my notes get wavery at this point. We talked to Vegard about his cuisine. He said he wanted above all to serve excellent food from ingredients harvested nearby; it was very simple. A century and a half ago Odd's ancestors gave up the uncertainty of reindeer herding for the uncertainty of farming life; both traditions meet in Vegard's sure hand.

We arrived back in Gällivare in the darkness to six inches of wet snow, and our suitcases acted like snow plows as we wheeled them from the railway station to the hostel. The next day we drove the deserted highway from Gällivare through a quiet scene of spruce, snow and grey sky to Laila Spik's house in the tiny hamlet of Muorjevare.

We had found Laila in a roundabout way, through Chef Susanne Jonsson, a culinary genie we met in Umeå who worked many miracles for us in Sweden. Susanne said we must look up her cousin, the reindeer herder Arild Skaltjie, when in Gällivare; his reindeer *gravad* was to die for. I called Arild to set up a meeting and a charming woman answered the phone; Arild was away but she would be happy for us to visit the house and sample his meat, and she could tell us all about reindeer herding. At the end of the conversation she gave her name: Laila Spik.

Not only is Laila a cookbook author (*How to Cook a Reindeer*), herbalist and specialist in wild foods who counts the King of Sweden among her fans, she is a friend of Whitehorse herbalist Beverley Gray. Laila had visited Whitehorse in the summer of 2010, and I just missed meeting her. Now, I was sorry to miss Arild but thrilled to connect with Laila.

Laila ushered us into the family home, and we gathered around the dining table tucked into the cozy lower level of her house. Laila's daughter Sunna Skaltjie made tea. We found common ground quickly. Laila is a reindeer herder from a family of reindeer herders. Hector asked if she might know a reindeer herder who had moved to Inverness, whom Hector used to visit when he was a young man at school. Laila did know him.

This led to a discussion about reindeer herding, and her father's knowledge of plants and animals, and Laila's

The bartenders at Linken specialize in boreal cocktails like Cloudberry Sky.

long apprenticeship with her father on the land. He taught her to start by learning one plant well, to learn every part of it: the roots, the stem, the leaves and the flower, to know it and remember it.

Laila pulled her plant books down from a shelf and piled them on the table. She and Hector pored over them, discussing the flowers they knew, their habitat and distribution and how the taxonomy had changed, while I took notes, as the conversation roamed across continents and through history.

"Nature decides how much the yield will be." When you live off the land, you eat the whole animal or fish including head and eyes.

Because she knew my interest was in the food uses of wild plants, Laila focused there, but she could easily have switched to their medicinal properties. Her knowledge is vast. Here are some of the seeds of wisdom she let fall: "Nature decides how much the yield will be." When you live off the land, you eat the whole animal or fish including head and eyes. "This is the food you eat because you must." You boil fish bones, dry them and grind them into flour. Moss berries and fish liver are a delicacy. Pick the

sorrel leaves before the cuckoo sings. Season rhubarb soup with blueberry flower and dried licorice flower. Make soup with lamb's quarters. Eat the seeds of bistort in the fall, like nuts, or mix them into bread; add the seeds of roseroot kings crown to bread, for crunch, and dried yarrow flowers for flavour. And "Birch! You could talk about birch all day."

Laila cooked three different kinds of reindeer for us: the classic *suovas*, or smoked gravad of inner thigh, smoked gravad fillet, and smoked fillet. As Susanne had promised, the gravad was to die for. All of it was. We ate roasted potatoes and flatbread, scooped cloudberry preserves out of a gallon jar and spooned fermented sorrel leaves onto the meat. Sunna showed us pictures of the last moose she'd shot. I asked if she had field-dressed it too. She laughed and said, "That's my brother's job." After dinner Sunna took us upstairs to show us what she was working on: a series of traditional bags made from reindeer skin and trimmed with felt. The aura of industry, care and attention to detail was remarkable in the house, as though the lessons learned on the land were being lived every day.

There were a few occasions during our travels when all that we had been learning suddenly gelled. Our visit with Laila and Sunna was such an occasion. Laila's knowledge of plants and animals, grounded in the traditional knowledge of her people and acquired over years of study and experience on the land, is also the bedrock of the fierce experimentation at Fäviken, or Martin Jönsson's fun dining and his moose-nose terrine, or Vegard Stormo's authentic cuisine on his family's land at Tinja Fjellgård. Chefs who don't have that knowledge aspire to it, those who do enshrine it.

On our last night in Gällivare I received an email from a friend who works for a charity in Whitehorse. She asked if I would offer a dinner for eight with wine pairings as a silent auction item. Inspired by the experiences of the last few days, I said yes. I composed the menu on the train from Gällivare to Narvik on our way to the Lofoten Islands. Here it is, a feast for the vernal equinox, inspired by three Sámi chefs.

A sleepover in a wall tent is a great way to reconnect with the land in early spring.

Parmesan Crisps

FOR JOSÉ JANSSEN

When I worked at the Chocolate Claim in Whitehorse we served *fougasse*, an oniony, cheesy bun that required lots of grated cheese to be sprinkled over top. When the trays came out of the oven, junior cooks and dishwashers swarmed to gobble up stray bits of melted cheese from the parchment paper. Sometimes the baker would accidentally sprinkle way more cheese than necessary over the fougasse, just for us. Until one day our eagle-eyed boss, José Janssen, caught him in the act. That was the end of that particular accident. Occasionally there were other, similar accidents José chose not to see, in the interests of keeping her kitchen happy; she ruled the roost with generosity and humour. This old favourite is dedicated to José and wise bosses everywhere.

1 cup (250 mL) grated Parmigiano Reggiano

1. Preheat oven to 400F (205C). Line two baking sheets with parchment paper.

2. Pile grated cheese in loose, tablespoon-sized (15 mL) heaps on the parchment paper about one inch (2.5 cm) apart. Lightly press down on each pile.

3. Bake for 3 to 5 minutes, until cheese is crisp and golden. Cool on trays on a rack and loosen with a spatula when it's time to serve.

Makes about two dozen crisps.

Warm Apple Juice with a Splash of Calvados

4 cups (1 L) homemade or organic apple juice or cider

¼ cup (60 mL) Calvados (apple brandy)

1. Warm apple juice in a medium saucepan over medium-low heat, without bringing it to the boil.

2. Remove from heat and stir in Calvados. For an elegant, hostess-y touch, pour into a warmed teapot. Serve in tea cups accompanied by a Parmesan Crisp perched on the saucer.

Makes eight ½-cup (125-mL) servings, with extra for top-ups.

Halloumi, Alaskan Spot Prawn and Tomato Skewers

3 Tbsp (45 mL) fireweed honey, divided

2 Tbsp (30 mL) lime juice, divided

36 spot prawns, peeled

12 oz (340 gr) halloumi, sliced into 9 thick slices

2 Tbsp (30 mL) olive oil

36 grape tomatoes

18 wooden skewers

1. In small bowl, combine 2 tablespoons (30 mL) honey and 1 tablespoon (15 mL) lime juice. Pour over prawns, toss and marinate for 30 minutes.

2. While the prawns are marinating, prepare the halloumi: heat the oil in a cast iron frying pan over medium heat until it shimmers and add the cheese slices. Sauté for 3 minutes on each side, then remove and drain on paper towel. When cool, cut each halloumi slice into four squares.

3. Drain prawns and pat dry, discarding marinade. On each skewer, thread a prawn, a piece of halloumi and a tomato, and repeat once. Mix the remaining tablespoon (15 mL) lime juice with the remaining tablespoon (15 mL) honey and brush each skewer with the mixture.

4. In the oven: Place the rack 6 inches (15 cm) below the broiler, and preheat at high for 5 minutes. Place skewers on baking tray (no parchment paper, it burns at high heat). Broil for 2 minutes, remove from oven, turn kebabs over, coat with glaze once more and broil another 2 minutes.

   On the barbecue: preheat at high for 5 minutes and brush grill with oil. Place kebabs on grill and reduce heat to medium. Grill on one side for 2 minutes, turn with tongs, add another coating of glaze and grill another 2 minutes, or until prawns are no longer translucent.

5. Remove from heat, let stand for a couple of minutes and serve.

Makes 18 skewers, or 9 appetizers.

Gravad of Beef or Moose with Pickled Radish and Morel Mayonnaise

It's a good idea to start small with this recipe, until you know you're going to like it, because sirloin is an expensive cut. The curing mixture will make enough for two 1-pound (455-gr) steaks or one 2-pound (910-gr) steak about 1 inch (2.5 cm) thick.

I asked Susanne Jonsson what would make this dish really Swedish, and she said, "Berries or pickled mushrooms, but mushrooms are already in the sauce, so…Actually, you could pickle radishes really quick, then it will be instantly Swedish!" So that's what I did.

1 lb (455 gr) sirloin steak, about 1 inch (2.5 cm) thick*

1 Tbsp (15 mL) juniper berries

3 Tbsp (45 mL) coarse sea salt

2 tsp (10 mL) coarsely ground black pepper

3 Tbsp (45 mL) brown sugar (light or dark)

1. Rinse sirloin with cold water and pat dry with paper towel. With a sharp knife, trim away any fat, gristle or silver skin.

2. Crush juniper berries in a mortar and pestle until they resemble coarsely ground pepper. Mix with salt, pepper and sugar. Spread half the curing mixture on a dinner plate.

3. Press the meat into the curing mixture, making sure each side and the ends are thoroughly coated. Add more of the curing mixture as needed. Wrap sirloin tightly in plastic wrap and wrap again in a second piece.

*If you're using game, it's best to freeze the meat first in case there are parasites present: the rule of thumb for a piece of meat less than 6 inches (15 cm) thick is to freeze for 20 days at 5F (-15C); 12 days at -10F (-23C); or 6 days at -20F (-39C).

4. Place the wrapped sirloin in a flat, rimmed glass or ceramic baking dish; don't use metal. Find a smaller dish that will fit inside the first. (A 9-inch/22.5-cm square dish on the bottom and an 8-inch/20-cm square dish on top work well.) Place the second dish on top of the sirloin and fill with 2 to 3 pounds (1 to 1.5 kg) of weight, such as a few cans or a bag of rice or sugar.

5. Refrigerate, weights and all, for 48 to 72 hours. As time passes the salt will extract liquid from the meat and it will become increasingly firm to the touch.

6. Remove sirloin from its plastic wrapping; it's not necessary to rinse unless you want to remove the pepper and juniper berries, but I find they add interest to the flavour. With a sharp knife slice a thin piece from one end of the steak for a tester. The meat should have a silky texture like cold-smoked salmon, a rich brown colour with a tinge of pink, and a similar appearance to prosciutto. The flavour is hard to describe: deep, like rich gravy, sweet and peppery, with an occasional hit of juniper. The combination of texture and taste is dynamite.

7. To serve, slice on the diagonal with the knife held almost flat so that you end up with thin, lacy slices. Arrange on a platter with thin slices of toasted sourdough rye bread and small bowls of Pickled Radish (recipe right), chopped fresh radish leaves, Morel Mushroom Mayonnaise (page 232) and Lowbush Cranberry and Rosehip Jam (page 219). Encourage guests to mix and match flavours.

Makes about 12 × 1-oz (340-gr) servings of gravad.

PICKLED RADISH

Whenever you can, save radish leaves for salad, garnish or salsa verde. They have a bright, peppery flavour similar to that of arugula. When I lived in Greece we used to make a simple salad of chopped radish leaves and quartered radishes, dressed with red wine vinegar and green olive oil.

To prepare radish greens: remove wilted or damaged leaves. Wash and dry thoroughly. Store wrapped in a tea towel in a plastic bag. Chop finely as a garnish for gravad or tear into a salad of mixed greens.

1 cup (250 mL) thinly sliced radishes, about 6 large radishes
¼ cup (60mL) apple cider vinegar
¼ cup (60mL) cold water
2 Tbsp (30 mL) white sugar
2 tsp (10 mL) coarse sea salt

1. Top and tail radishes, reserving the leaves. Wash radishes thoroughly and dry with a paper towel. Slice as thinly as possible and transfer to a bowl.

2. In a separate bowl whisk vinegar, water, sugar and salt together until sugar and salt are dissolved. Pour over radishes, refrigerate for 30 minutes and serve. Radishes are best eaten right away or on the same day, before they lose their crispness. Tip: the vinegar mixture turns a lovely pale pink and is great in salad dressings.

Makes 1 cup (250 mL) radishes.

Morel-Crusted Bison Short Ribs

Adapted from Bon Appétit, *February 2002*

2 oz (60 gr) dried morel mushrooms

2 cups (475 mL) boiling water

2 tsp (10 mL) dried yarrow leaves and blossoms (or substitute dried thyme)

1 tsp (5 mL) dried pineapple weed (or substitute chamomile)

1 tsp (5 mL) dried rosemary

1 tsp (5 mL) coarse sea salt

1 tsp (5 mL) ground black pepper

8 meaty moose or bison short ribs: about 3–4 lbs (1.4–1.8 kg)

2 Tbsp (30 mL) olive oil

1 large onion, chopped

1 medium carrot, peeled and chopped

3 large garlic cloves, minced

2 cups (475 mL) dry white wine

2 cups (475 mL) Beef, Bison or Moose Stock, (page 173), or organic beef broth

1 bay leaf

1 tsp (5 mL) crushed juniper berries

2 Tbsp (30 mL) butter at room temperature

2 cups (475 mL) fresh panko or coarse bread crumbs*

¼ cup (60 mL) Dijon mustard

1. Rinse morels briefly under running water, then place in a small bowl. Pour boiling water over and soak for about 15 minutes. Drain, reserving water, and squeeze dry. Set aside.

2. Preheat oven to 325F (160C). Mix yarrow leaves and blossoms, pineapple weed, rosemary, salt and pepper in a small bowl and divide in half. Rub half the mixture over short ribs, pressing firmly. Heat oil in a deep, heavy ovenproof casserole over medium heat. In batches, brown ribs on all sides, transferring to a large bowl as each batch is complete.

3. Pour off all but 2 tbsp (30 mL) fat from casserole. Add onion and carrot and sauté until they begin to soften, about 5 minutes. Add garlic and sauté another 2 minutes. Add wine, scraping up any browned bits from bottom of pot. Add stock, bay leaf, juniper berries, reserved morels and mushroom water (leaving any sediment behind).

4. Return ribs to pot, meat side down, and bring to boil. Cover pot tightly; transfer to oven and bake until ribs are tender, about 2 hours and 15 minutes. Remove from oven. (Short ribs can be prepared ahead to this point: remove ribs from pot, place on a parchment-lined baking sheet and cool on rack for 30 minutes. Refrigerate ribs uncovered until cold, then cover and keep chilled. Reheat in braising liquid over medium-low heat for 25 minutes before proceeding with next step.)

Bison ribs in their braise.

5. Preheat oven to 450F (230C). Transfer ribs to a large roasting pan, bone side down. Remove ½ cup (125 mL) mushroom mixture from pot and finely chop. Place in medium bowl. Add butter and remaining herbs and blend with a fork. Mix in bread crumbs.

6. Spread 1 teaspoon (5 mL) mustard onto the top surface of each rib, followed by the bread crumb mixture, pressing with the back of the spoon, or your hands, to adhere. Bake until topping is crisp and golden, about 10 minutes.

7. In the meantime, prepare the sauce. Strain sauce, reserving morels and vegetables. Spoon off any fat from the top and discard. Over medium-high heat, reduce sauce, stirring frequently, until it has thickened into a satiny gravy of about 2 cups (475 mL). Taste and add salt and pepper as needed.

8. To serve, place each rib on a small pool of sauce on warmed plates, and drizzle more sauce over top. Accompany with reserved morels and vegetables, individual Saffron Potato Soufflés (next page) and Yukon Herb Jelly (page 207). Pour remaining sauce into a gravy boat and pass at the table.

Makes eight servings.

Saffron Potato Soufflés

You don't need to worry about these soufflés collapsing; the potato provides lots of structure. They set in the oven, rather than rise, and the top gets crispy while the inside stays light and fluffy.

12 medium-sized Yukon Gold potatoes, peeled and rinsed

4 Tbsp (60 mL) butter

2 generous pinches of saffron threads

6 Tbsp (90 mL) 35 percent cream

Salt and pepper to taste

2 egg yolks at room temperature

3 egg whites at room temperature

1. Heat oven to 350F (180C). Grease a 12-cup muffin tin generously with butter. Quarter potatoes and cover with water in a 12-cup (3-L) saucepan. Cover saucepan and bring to the boil over high heat. Reduce heat to medium-low and simmer until fork-tender, about 15 minutes.

2. Melt butter over medium-low heat and add saffron, crumbling it between the fingers. Pass potatoes through a food mill or ricer, if available, or mash with a potato masher followed by a fork. With the fork, beat in melted butter and saffron, followed by cream. Add salt and pepper.

3. Beat in egg yolks one at a time. In a separate bowl, with clean beaters beat egg whites until stiff. Fold whites into the potato mixture with a spatula, one third at a time.

4. Spoon mixture into muffin cups in a rough heap, filling the cups without pressing down heavily on the mixture. Bake in the middle of the oven for 25 to 30 minutes, or until the tops are just beginning to brown. Keep warm, loosely covered with foil, while the ribs and sauce are finishing. When you're ready to serve run a knife around each one, lifting slightly underneath, and remove soufflés from muffin cups. Transfer to dinner plates and serve at once. Can be reheated, wrapped in foil, for 15 minutes at 350F (180C), but they're best right away. Tip: call the soufflés "potato muffins" and serve them at brunch.

Makes 12 individual soufflés.

Endive, Daikon and Kohlrabi Salad with Walnuts and Cranberries

This salad is a great palate-cleanser after a rich entrée.

¼ cup (60 mL) toasted walnut halves

3 Belgian endives

1 medium-sized kohlrabi

3-inch (7.5-cm) length of daikon radish

¼ cup (60 mL) wild lowbush cranberries (lingonberries), thawed if frozen (or substitute dried cranberries)

HIGH-BUSH CRANBERRY VINAIGRETTE

2 Tbsp (30 mL) Highbush Cranberry Vinegar (page 225)

6 Tbsp (90 mL) extra-virgin olive oil or Spruce Tip Oil (page 230)

½ tsp (2.5 mL) coarse sea salt

1. Toast walnuts in a 350F (180C) oven for 5 to 7 minutes.

2. Separate endives into leaves; wash and dry. Peel kohlrabi, slice thinly and then cut slices into matchsticks. Peel daikon and slice as thinly as possible into rounds; use a mandolin if you have one.

3. In a small bowl, whisk together vinegar, oil and salt. Taste and adjust seasonings if desired.

4. Arrange 3 or 4 endive leaves on each plate in a fan shape. Arrange daikon slices in an over-lapping semicircle halfway down the length of the endives, and make a small pile of kohlrabi matchsticks at the base. Sprinkle cranberries in a row between kohlrabi and daikon and finish with a few walnuts here and there. Drizzle vinaigrette down the lengths of the endives. There. Now you have a streaky vernal equinox sunrise.

Makes eight servings.

Blueberry and White Chocolate Mousse Parfait with Haskap Liqueur

The Haskap (*Lonicera caerulea*) is an old varietal with a new northern history, a hardy plant that can withstand winter temperatures of -53C, yielding a delicious, elongated berry the same dusky blue colour as a wild blueberry, with a unique flavour the Haskap Canada Association describes as somewhere between a blueberry, raspberry and blackcurrant. Though the Haskap looks like a cousin to the blueberry, it's actually a member of the honeysuckle family, and grows in the wild in the circumpolar north (though, apparently, not in Alaska or Norway), in northern, northeastern and eastern Asia and eastern Europe. Haskap is the ancient Ainu name for the berry, and in Canada has been adopted to differentiate Haskaps from other edible wild blue honeysuckles. The Haskap berry is higher in antioxidants than blackcurrants, cranberries and wild blueberries and packed with vitamin C, making it a candidate for super-food status. Watch for it on healthy living blogs and on restaurant menus.

The Haskap is currently being grown in most Canadian provinces and in the Yukon. John Lenart is experimenting with four varieties of Haskap in partnership with the University of Saskatchewan at his Klondike Valley Nursery & Market Garden; some of those he can't sell but others he can. You can find them at the Farmers' Market in Dawson. Several farmers in the Whitehorse area grow Haskaps and sell plants at the Fireweed Community Market. One of those growers recently partnered with the Yukon Brewing Company, which produced a Haskap liqueur in the fall of 2013 with a limited run of 750 half-litre bottles. They were snapped up. Look for the next edition in the fall of 2014. Until Haskap berries are more generally available in markets, the best thing is to find out if there's a U-pick near you, or plant a few bushes in your backyard (you'll need two different varieties for pollination), wait a couple of years and then harvest the bounty.

BLUEBERRY COMPOTE

4 cups (1 L) fresh or frozen wild blueberries (or substitute Haskaps)

2 Tbsp (30 mL) birch syrup

2 Tbsp (30 mL) lemon juice

1–2 Tbsp (15–30 mL) brown sugar (optional)

2 tsp (10 mL) Haskap liqueur (or substitute cassis)

WHITE CHOCOLATE MOUSSE

White chocolate has a lower melting point than other chocolates and scorches or seizes more easily. The cream helps to mitigate that tendency. As always, be careful not to let condensation drip into the chocolate. Wipe the bottom of the double boiler with a towel before you transfer the melted chocolate to a bowl.

6 oz (180 gr) white chocolate

2 cups (475 mL) plus 2 Tbsp (30 mL) 35 percent cream, divided

TOPPING

2 Tbsp (30 mL) wild blueberries, thawed if frozen

1½ Tbsp (22 mL) Haskap liqueur (or substitute cassis)

1. Combine blueberries, syrup and lemon juice in a medium saucepan. Bring to a boil over high heat and cook, stirring frequently, for 5 minutes, reducing the blueberries by half. The boiling will become quite intense, and you will want to turn down the heat; do so if you must, but only near the end, and only to medium-high. The rapid evaporation reduces the liquid in the blueberries so that you don't need to thicken the compote with cornstarch.

2. Remove blueberries from the heat. Dip in a taster spoon, let cool, and check for both sweetness and bite; you need that lemony bite in order to offset the sweetness of the white chocolate mousse. If necessary, add 1 tablespoon (15 mL) sugar, taste, and add the second tablespoon only if needed. Stir in the Haskap liqueur. Cool to room temperature and refrigerate.

3. Chop the white chocolate finely and combine with 2 tablespoons (30 mL) cream in the top of a double boiler. Turn heat to medium-low and melt chocolate, stirring frequently with a spatula. When melted, transfer to a medium bowl and stir with a spatula to cool to room temperature. Don't refrigerate; it will get too stiff.

4. Whip remaining 2 cups (475 mL) cream until stiff, beating ½ cup (125 mL) of cream vigorously into the chocolate in order to prevent it from clumping, then folding the remainder in, about ½ cup (125 mL) at a time, keeping as much air as possible in the mixture. Refrigerate for two hours to set.

5. To build parfaits: spoon 2 to 3 tablespoons (30 to 45 mL) of mousse into 8 wine or martini glasses, mason jars or pretty glass bowls, followed by a layer of blueberry compote and ending with a second layer of mousse. Don't worry about smoothing out the layers: it will look gorgeous no matter what you do. Finish with a few blueberries and drizzle about ½ teaspoon (2.5 mL) of Haskap liqueur over top.

Makes eight servings.

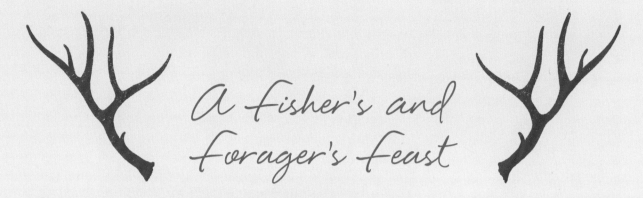

A Fisher's and Forager's Feast

MENU FOR EIGHT

Toasted Sunflower Seed Soup **33**

Dandelion and Chèvre Bruschetta **34**

Grilled Dandelion Crowns **35**

Cucumber, Mint and Rhubarb Salad **35**

Grilled Whitefish with Spruce Tip Gremolata **36**

Roasted New Potatoes **37**

Rhubarb Pavlova with Birch Syrup Ice Cream **38**

A Feast in Whitefish Season

Paul Sparling is a biology field technician and a fisherman, and to hear him talk about fish is to hear a grand and epic story about spawning and movement and oxygen and ice. Paul fishes for whitefish under the ice at the Yukon end of Atlin Lake, a long, deep and cold lake that straddles the BC–Yukon border. He fishes with a net, and the way he gets the net in place is with a jigger, basically a board with a hinged tooth at one end.

 Everything goes boom: the sound of spring.

Paul augers a hole in the ice and ties one end of a long rope to the end of the jigger. The jigger noses along underneath the ice, drawing the rope behind it. The jigger is pushed by the water and pulled by the tooth, which flattens as the board moves and then springs up and hooks into the under-surface of the ice when it stops, pulling the board forward again. The jigger is painted orange so you can see it (sometimes) under the ice. When the jigger has drawn the full length of the rope, about 150 feet, under the ice, Paul augers the second hole where the jigger has stopped. Now there are two holes connected by a line. The net is in a box at one hole; Paul ties it to the rope, goes to the other end and pulls, and the weighted net snakes along under the ice, opening as it goes. Paul anchors the rope with a pole on the ice, leaves it overnight, and comes back in the morning to pull it in.

Paul's been netting whitefish for 20 years and selling them in the Yukon (he's not allowed to sell outside the territory) under his business name, Great Northern Fish Company, largely through private orders until the spring of 2013, when the newly formed Potluck Food Co-op in Whitehorse started up and provided him with a venue to reach more people. "That was really positive," he said. "That's a great crowd of people who really appreciate what kind of food it is. Local protein. And it tastes good, and it's sustainable."

His average yield is about 600 to 700 fish annually. The season is short: pretty much early April into May. Sometimes the ice farther out on the lake is still strong enough into mid-May, but because it weakens and melts first near the shore where the Lubbock River and High Creek come into the lake, there's no safe way to get to the thicker ice. Paul used to have a season in December, but the ice hasn't been forming early enough for the past 10 years.

According to the Environment Yukon website, there are four species of whitefish in the Yukon: lake whitefish (also known as humpback or humpies for the slight hump behind the head), which inhabit most lakes in the Yukon; broad whitefish, which tend to hang out in larger bodies of water like Teslin Lake or the Yukon River; the mysterious pygmy, about which little is known except for its habitat (Squanga Lake and the Alsek drainage); and

Some of the many stages of the dandelion harvest: picking, sorting, cleaning…

After winter hibernation, brown, black and grizzly bears feed on the tender shoots of new dandelions.

round whitefish, also widely distributed in Yukon lakes. The fish that Paul catches are lake whitefish, *Coregonus clupeaformis*, probably the most widespread fish throughout North America, and they vary hugely in quality.

In the Mackenzie Delta, lake whitefish are so mushy "they're really only good for dog food," says Paul. "[People] eat broad whitefish there." On the other hand, "The whitefish from Lake Winnipeg were very highly prized by the Jewish community of New York. They sold them down there for years and years, and still do." But Atlin Lake whitefish are the best, "so far above anything I've seen anywhere. They just don't compare." The healthy whitefish have a bluish opalescence and a firm, almost rubbery texture when he fillets them. There are unhealthy whitefish among the population, which is entirely normal, and those ones tend to look dull, flat and pasty. Needless to say, they don't make the cut. "If I see something that doesn't look right, I don't want to sell it."

Here is the magic that happens at the Yukon end of Atlin Lake in April: the melt begins in the river and creeks, and the flow, especially the surface flow, brings nutrients and oxygen down to the lake, where at the same time the water is warming up. In these conditions small organisms explode into life. "Everything goes

boom," says Paul. And the whitefish in nutrient-poor Atlin Lake "just wait and wait for that to happen, and then they go in and just gorge themselves." Everything goes boom: the sound of spring.

Paul and his family eat whitefish twice a week year-round; in season they probably eat it three or four times a week. (By the time the season is over, the family "isn't that interested in whitefish anymore.") Paul has a few tips for the best way to treat whitefish. Number one is, don't overcook it. "Don't be afraid to cook it when there's still a bit of frost inside. In fact, try to do that. It's way better than letting it thaw. It's almost like you're cooking it fresh." Paul's favourite method is to fry the fish in butter with crushed garlic and pepper. He thinks onions overwhelm the flavour of the fish—"all you taste is onion"—but admits that's his particular prejudice, and he really loves whitefish cooked in coconut.

Paul and his family came to my house for a greens and fish feast in late spring; I wanted to run my recipe by him. He thought it was pretty good. And he liked the dishes that accompanied the fish. So did the family—the dandelion greens bruschetta was a particular favourite. So, you spring fishers and early foragers, here's a spring feast that has won the stamp of approval from the maestro.

Toasted Sunflower Seed Soup

1 head garlic

2 Tbsp (30 mL)
olive oil, divided

2 cups (475 mL) plus
1 Tbsp (15 mL)
sunflower seeds, divided

1 Tbsp (15 mL) butter

1 tsp (5 mL) crushed
chili pepper

1½ cups (350 mL)
onion, chopped

4 cups (1 L) organic
chicken stock

1 cup (250 mL)
35 percent cream

Coarse sea salt and
freshly ground pepper
to taste

1. Preheat oven to 350F (180C). Slice the top off the head of garlic to expose the flesh, oil the outer skin and drizzle 1 tablespoon (15 mL) olive oil over top. Spread sunflower seeds on a parchment-lined baking sheet and place garlic at one end. Toast seeds for 7 to 10 minutes and transfer to a bowl. Return garlic to oven and roast for another 30 to 40 minutes, until soft.

2. Heat remaining tablespoon (15 mL) oil and the butter in a medium saucepan over medium heat. Add crushed chili pepper and sauté for 2 minutes. Add onion and sauté until translucent, 5 to 7 minutes.

3. Squeeze roasted garlic from the papery skin right into the pot. Add sunflower seeds, reserving one tablespoon (15 mL). Add stock, bring to the boil over high heat and reduce to medium-low. Simmer for 5 minutes.

4. Remove soup from heat and purée with an immersion blender or in small batches in food processor or blender until smooth. Press soup through a sieve.

5. Transfer soup to a clean saucepan, add cream and heat through. Add salt and pepper to taste. Serve with a sprinkle of seeds over top.

Makes eight ½-cup (125-mL) servings.

Dandelion and Chèvre Bruschetta

1 lb (455 gr) dandelion leaves

⅓ cup (80 mL) pine nuts

4 cloves garlic

1 Tbsp (15 mL) olive oil

1 baguette, sliced into 24 thin slices

1 Tbsp (15 mL) Spruce Tip Oil, recipes on page 230 (or substitute olive oil)

4½ oz (125 gr) chèvre

1 Tbsp (15 mL) fireweed honey (or substitute other wildflower honey)

Clean the root end of each plant with a knife, removing all the black or brown until the base shows white. Cut the leaves off about 1 inch (2.5 cm) above the crown, leaving the crown intact. Put crowns to soak in cold water and reserve to make Grilled Dandelion Crowns (previous page).

1. Wash leaves several times, lifting them out into a strainer and emptying the water from the bowl each time; continue until there's no residue of dirt left in the bottom of the bowl. Shake leaves dry, chop coarsely and reserve. (If you've bought dandelion leaves from the market, they're usually detached from the crown and fairly clean, needing just a rinse and a shake dry.)

2. Toast pine nuts in a dry cast iron pan over medium-low heat until golden. Peel garlic and slice thinly lengthwise. Heat olive oil in the same pan over low to medium-low heat; sauté garlic slices until they are crisp and just beginning to brown, from 5 to 6 minutes. Remove from heat and drain on paper towel.

3. In the same oil, sauté dandelion greens until wilted, about 5 minutes.

4. Toast baguette slices in the oven under the broiler, about 1 minute per side. Brush one side with Spruce Tip Oil.

5. Spread with chèvre. Pile dandelion greens over chèvre. Arrange 3 to 4 garlic slices on top. Sprinkle with pine nuts and drizzle with honey. Serve at once.

Makes 24 bruschetta.

DANDELIONS

As we hear more and more, dandelions are one of the great wild plants, beloved in Europe and Asia, finally catching on in North America. Roots, crowns, greens, buds and flowers are packed with nutrition and they're delicious. Roots are best harvested in spring and fall, crowns and greens before the plant flowers, and flowers as soon as they, well, flower. Young greens don't need blanching; older greens might, as the bitter flavour (so loved in so many cultures) becomes more pronounced.

To pick dandelion greens, choose your spot: avoid roadsides, cutlines, lawns or parks that might have been sprayed. Ask for permission to pick on private property. Grasp the leaves where they meet in a crown near the root, pull slightly and cut just underneath the crown, keeping the plant in one piece. Sometimes several plants are packed tightly together; then you'll need to dig with your fingers to discover where each crown emerges from the root. Sometimes you can free a number of plants with one cut.

A word about dandelion greens: once cooked, the leaves collapse against the stems and the texture of the stems is like al dente spaghetti. In Greece we loved this; we doused the stringy greens with olive oil and lemon and twirled them around our forks. But for bruschetta it's best to chop the greens either before or after they're cooked.

Grilled Dandelion Crowns

I used to throw dandelion crowns away. Then I read John McPhee's classic *New Yorker* account of a fall foraging expedition with Euell Gibbons in the Appalachian Mountains and along the Susquehanna River, when for the first few days they ate only what they could gather from the wild. Dandelion crowns were a frequent menu item, and Gibbons and McPhee considered them a delicacy. Dandelion crowns require a lot of cleaning and sorting, which adds to their appeal when they are finally cooked and on the table: you've worked for that treat. I find them reminiscent of artichoke hearts, but more subtle. Sometimes there are a few tightly curled buds in the crowns; this adds another dimension of flavour. I should add that Hector is underwhelmed. Fair enough. Try them in small batches. Or start with spinach crowns, a Japanese favourite. When you buy spinach, don't throw away the crowns; steam them briefly and toss in a miso vinaigrette. But whether dandelion or spinach, be sure that crowns are free of dirt, or you'll lose fans quickly.

30–40 dandelion crowns	Salt and pepper
Olive oil	Lemon, quartered

1. Trim dandelion crowns and wash them well several times. Pat dry in a tea towel.
2. Toss with olive oil and sprinkle with salt and pepper. Grill on the barbecue on a piece of foil or in a grilling basket over medium heat until wilted, about 7 minutes. Serve warm or at room temperature with a squeeze of lemon over top.

Makes eight servings of three to four crowns each.

Cucumber, Mint and Rhubarb Salad

Adapted from Paula Wolfert's The Slow Mediterranean Kitchen

4 young rhubarb stalks

1 medium English cucumber, halved lengthwise

1 Tbsp (15 mL) coarse sea salt

1 head butter lettuce

1 handful fresh mint, washed, dried and roughly chopped

3 Tbsp (45 mL) freshly squeezed lemon juice

3 Tbsp (45 mL) olive oil

15 grape tomatoes, cut in half (optional)

1. Using a mandolin or sharp knife, cut the rhubarb on the diagonal into very thin slices. Repeat with both halves of the cucumber.
2. Toss the rhubarb and cucumber with the salt and let stand for 10 minutes. Rinse and drain.
3. Wash and pat dry lettuce. In a salad bowl, toss the rhubarb and cucumber with the mint. Add lettuce and toss gently. Whisk together lemon juice and olive oil for a simple vinaigrette. Toss salad with vinaigrette, adding tomatoes at the end if desired.

Makes eight servings.

Grilled Whitefish with Spruce Tip Gremolata

In the marinade, substitute dill or fennel for yarrow leaves and fresh thyme or basil for pasture sage leaves.

1 cup (250 mL) white wine

1 Tbsp (15 mL) lime juice

2 Tbsp (30 mL) honey

2 Tbsp (30 mL) each chopped fresh yarrow leaves and pasture sage leaves

1 Tbsp (15 mL) safflower or other neutral oil

Freshly ground black pepper

3 lbs (1.4 kg) whitefish fillets, skinned and boned

¼ cup (60 mL) butter, melted

1. Combine wine, lime juice, honey and herbs in a small saucepan over medium heat. Bring to the boil, stirring to dissolve honey, and simmer until reduced by half.

2. Strain into a bowl and whisk in oil and pepper. Cool to room temperature.

3. Arrange whitefish fillets in a shallow baking dish. Pour cooled marinade over top, lifting fillets to allow marinade to penetrate. Refrigerate for two hours, turning every 40 minutes or so.

4. About thirty minutes before you're ready to barbecue, remove whitefish from marinade and pat dry. Discard marinade.

5. Lay fillets on a sheet of thick foil. Brush each side with thin coats of melted butter, allowing butter to cool and harden before applying the next coat.

6. Preheat barbecue on high with a closed lid for 10 minutes. Keeping heat at high and the barbecue lid open, cook whitefish on foil, without turning, just until flesh is no longer translucent, about 5 minutes. Whitefish fillets cook fast, and the fillets will continue to cook after they're removed from heat.

7. Remove from heat and transfer fillets to a warm platter. Sprinkle with Spruce Tip Gremolata (recipe next page), bring to the table and serve family style, with more gremolata on the table.

Makes eight generous servings.

SPRUCE TIP GREMOLATA

4 Tbsp (60 mL) fresh spruce tips, finely chopped (or substitute thawed frozen spruce tips)

2 Tbsp (30 mL) finely grated lemon zest

1 clove garlic, grated

1 tsp (5 mL) Spruce Tip Oil (page 230) or olive oil

1. Combine ingredients in a small bowl and use right away, or store tightly covered in the refrigerator. The flavours are best the first day.

Makes 6 Tbsp (90 mL).

Roasted New Potatoes

With all those sharp, bright spring flavours, we need the warm contrast of a simple roasted potato.

2 lbs (910 gr) new Yukon Gold potatoes

1 tsp (5 mL) coarse sea salt

1 Tbsp (15 mL) olive oil

1. Wash potatoes and trim away any blemishes. Pat dry in a tea towel and transfer to a medium-sized bowl.

2. Toss with olive oil and salt. Roast at 400F (205C) for 25 to 30 minutes, until fork tender. Serve at once.

Makes eight servings.

Rhubarb Pavlova with Birch Syrup Ice Cream

Well. Apparently both New Zealand and Australia take credit for the creation of this dish, named for the Russian ballerina Anna Pavlova, who leapt and floated onstage the same way our hearts do when spring has really arrived. Soon this year's harvest of Uncle Berwyn's Yukon Birch Syrup will be in stores, and the rhubarb's poking up in the garden. Birch syrup ice cream steps in for the usual custard in this happy, airy concoction. At our spring feast Lizzie Sparling and Tara Kolla-Hale had a good time constructing each serving of this four-part dish in a slightly different way. If there's a junior chef in the house, enlist their help when it's time to put it all together. All of the components can be made ahead and assembled just before serving. If you want to prepare the whipped cream in advance, see the instructions for stabilizing whipped cream in the sidebar on page 133.

RHUBARB COMPOTE

3 cups (710 mL) fresh or frozen rhubarb, cut into 1-inch (2.5-cm) pieces

½ cup (125 mL) granulated sugar

½ cup (125 mL) water; or ¼ cup (60 mL) if rhubarb is frozen

Zest and juice of 2 oranges

1 Tbsp (15 mL) pomegranate or cranberry juice

2 Tbsp (30 mL) frozen wild lowbush cranberries (lingonberries) or substitute cultivated cranberries

1. Combine all ingredients in a wide saucepan and cook over medium-low heat until the rhubarb is cooked but still holds its shape. Remove the rhubarb with a slotted spoon to a shallow dish.

2. Reduce the liquid left in the pot until it's thick and syrupy. Pour over the rhubarb. Cool to room temperature and refrigerate.

Makes about 2½ cups (600 mL).

BIRCH SYRUP ICE CREAM

3 egg yolks

1½ cups (350 mL) 35 percent cream

1½ cups (350 mL) 10 percent cream

1 × 3-inch (7.5-cm) strips lemon zest

⅓ cup (80 mL) birch syrup

2 Tbsp (30 mL) lemon juice

¼ tsp (1 mL) salt

1. Whisk the yolks in a medium heatproof bowl until light in colour and thickened slightly, about 2 minutes.

2. In a medium saucepan, bring cream and lemon zest to the boil over medium heat. Remove from heat and gradually pour about ½ cup (125 mL) into the yolks, whisking constantly.

3. Add yolk mixture to the saucepan with the remaining cream mixture over medium-low heat. Cook, stirring constantly, until the custard is thick and coats the back of a spoon, about 3 minutes.

4. Remove the custard from heat and stir in the birch syrup, lemon juice and salt. Pour the custard through a sieve into a medium bowl. Cool to room temperature, stirring occasionally, and refrigerate until thoroughly chilled, about 3 hours.

5. Freeze in an ice cream maker according to the manufacturer's instructions, then decant into a bowl with a lid and freeze for another 2 hours.

   Or, if you don't have a machine, pour ice cream into a shallow dish and place in freezer. Remove from freezer after 30 minutes and whisk to incorporate air. Do this five times, for a total of 2 hours 30 minutes, then transfer to a bowl with a lid and return to freezer.

6. Twenty minutes before serving, remove ice cream from freezer to soften.

Makes about 3½ cups (830 mL).

MERINGUE

Meringues can be made the day before you plan to serve and stored in a tin with a tight lid.

4 egg whites at room temperature

¼ tsp (1 mL) cream of tartar

2 cups (475 mL) loosely packed brown sugar

¼ tsp (1 mL) vanilla

1. Preheat oven to 250F (120C). Line two baking trays with parchment paper.

2. Beat egg whites and cream of tartar until the whites hold stiff peaks.

3. Still beating, add sugar 1 tablespoon (15 mL) at a time. Add the vanilla at the end.

4. Shape the meringue into 12 circles 3 to 4 inches (7.5 to 10 cm) in diameter. Bake for 1 hour, until firm to the touch. Turn off the oven and leave the meringues inside for another 30 minutes. Cool on a rack until ready to serve.

Makes 12 meringues.

ASSEMBLY

1 cup (250 mL) 35 percent cream

Edible flowers, for decoration

1. When ready to assemble, whip cream until soft peaks form.

2. Gather the ice cream, whipped cream, meringues, compote and flowers and start building. Mix it up: meringue on the bottom, compote over top, ice cream and whipped cream on either side. Or, ice cream, compote and whipped cream under a meringue hat. There are many possible variations.

Makes 12 individual Pavlovas.

CHAPTER TWO

Summer

After a few years in the north you learn:
summer starts in mid-May. The farmers'
markets open in Whitehorse, in Dawson,
in Mayo. At the beginning of June, we
stop sleeping. They close the schools two
weeks later; the kids can't sit still. Bears
have come out of the trees to mow the
dandelions in roadside ditches. The time
has come to earmark the reindeer calves.
The kayaks are on the river before the
ice is gone; they're playing in the waves at
the intake already. The ravens leave town
and the seagulls move in. In a backyard on
Wheeler Street someone says "Summer
came to Whitehorse today," and it's true,
the city has turned green. On the Pelly River
they're already harvesting vegetables. Tiny
flowers bloom in alpine meadows: mountain
avens, moss campion, purple mountain
saxifrage. The spruce tips come into season
and then the wild roses; the blueberry and
the kinnikinnick are in flower. The creeks
bring perfume down from the hills into
the valleys. RVs clog the highways, and
silvertops in pastels move through town
in waves. Hikers on the Kungsleden from
Abisko to Kebnekaise crunch a piece of
knäckebröd and consult their maps. There's
dancing on the riverbank by the cultural
centre and it's festival season in Finland.
We're eating flowers; we're eating leaves;
we're devouring summer before it's gone.

*The perfume coming down from the hills
in creeks is a sweet sign of summer in the north.*

The Summer Solstice Feast

By late June in the Yukon the Labrador tea and the wild rose are blooming, the pasture sage is ready to be picked, the sockeye are running and rhubarb flourishes in backyards and alleyways. This solstice feast relies on both local and neighbouring seasonal fare; potatoes and cucumbers don't appear in the north until mid-August. Buckwheat doesn't grow here either, but it's a sturdy grain with a long pedigree of cultivation in colder climates. It also goes very well with salmon. Finally, the pine nuts in the stuffing are a nod to Yukon horticulturalist John Lenart, who is growing a pine nut–producing Siberian pine at his farm on the Klondike River near Dawson. It is conceivable that one day we will be eating home-grown pine nuts in the north; so let's call pine nuts an indigenous food-in-waiting, and use them where we can.

MENU FOR EIGHT

Salmon Caviar and Chèvre on Rice Crackers **46**

Solstice- or Vodka-Cured Lake Trout Gravlax **47**

Leaf and Flower Salad with Wild Rose Vinaigrette **48**

Cucumber Marinated in Apple Cider Vinegar and Honey **48**

Grilled Sockeye Salmon Stuffed
with Buckwheat, Berries, Mushrooms and Herbs **49**

Juniper Aioli **50**

New Potatoes Tossed in Wild Onion Pesto **51**

Wild Cranberry Biscotti **52**

Birch Syrup Panna Cotta with Rhubarb Compote **53**

BONUS

Solstice-Infused Raspberry Ice Cream **54**

Penne with Smoked Salmon, Tomato, Rosehips and Solstice **55**

A Swedish/Canadian Solstice Party

In the north the summer solstice is a time of bonfires, dances, festivals and staying up all night to watch the sky change. In southern Yukon the sun sinks briefly between two and four in the morning; in that brief half-light a person could change shape or disappear into a different life. Farther north the sun barely dips below the horizon. The townspeople in Dawson climb the Midnight Dome behind town for a 360-degree view of the Yukon River valley and the surrounding hills to watch the sun set and then rise again, two inches to the east on the skyline. This is the time of year visitors are most vulnerable to the spell of the Yukon, and residents feel most intensely alive. Across the territory we revel in the clear, pastel light that signals summer's high point.

Midsummer is a serious affair in Sweden and in Scandinavia.

I have two favourite solstice memories. One is playing cards all night by the fire on a canoe trip with my sister Anne Louise and her beau Tony in the summer of 1994. I had just arrived in the Yukon and was terrified by the possibility of bears. We were camped in a clearing beside the cabin where Tony had homesteaded in the 1970s. The Stewart River flowed beside us, pearly grey under the pale sky, and the air was spiced with the smell of water and spruce trees. As we sipped tea and played hand after hand of Hearts, I kept glancing over my shoulder into the shadowy forest, until Tony said, "You know, it's very unlikely that a bear will come charging into camp and eat you, my dear." Then, as he dealt out another hand, he described bear behaviour in such a clear and calm manner that the nation of bears rumbled out of the realm of nightmare into the realm of light, where creatures are knowable, with habits we can learn. This was a great gift, and meant I could sleep that night. Well, not sleep, because who can sleep in all that light? But rest in the absence of low-grade terror.

My other favourite solstice memory is not a Yukon but an Ontario memory: the memory of a celebration at our family cottage a week after my dad died, nearly 25 years ago. My brother André and his wife, Tina, who is Swedish, organized a Swedish solstice feast with pickled herring, boiled potatoes, raw onions, aquavit, gravlax, baby lettuce salad and lots of dill in everything.

Midsummer is a serious affair in Sweden and in Scandinavia. In Sweden they erect giant leafy crosses in fields and town squares and dance around them, holding hands and singing ancient songs, and the feasting carries on all night. Tina, who is affectionately known in our family as The Viking, thought we needed a Midsummer feast that year and gave us gentle instructions on the rituals we were to observe.

My job was to pick wildflowers for the garlands we would wear around our heads. In the meadow near the sailing club I found grasses and wildflowers that I'd never

In a season when the spell of the Yukon is strong, the sun sets on a lake near Beaver Creek in the western Yukon.

paid attention to before, whose names I didn't know, and picked them until I had an armful of sweet-smelling colour.

The whole family sat on the porch surrounded by flowers and grasses and wove wreaths, inexpertly—they were all lopsided and droopy—and took turns wearing them, passing the garlands from head to head until they arrived on the heads of my three brothers. In my opinion there's nothing lovelier than men wearing crowns of flowers and smiling with that sweet openness that comes with

grief, or great happiness, which sometimes fill the same space. The paradox of summer solstice is similar to that moment of grief and great happiness: our delight in the concentration of light coincides with sadness that from here on the light diminishes.

In recent years, our local distillery, Yukon Spirits, has provided us with some consolation, concocting a spirit entitled Solstice Botanical Vodka, a grain alcohol flavoured with a combination of Yukon herbs and fruits, similar to the Scandinavian aquavit (*snaps*, or *nubbe*, in Swedish), which is the beverage of choice for Midsummer

Waking up like the rest of the north is this fox pup, yawning after a nap in the sun.

celebrations. The Scandinavian version is usually fla-voured with licorice-y herbs such as caraway, dill, anise or fennel, whereas in our local vodka the whole boreal summer is represented. Each of the infused botanical ingredients ripens at a different time, from June (sage) and July (raspberries), well into late August and early September (rosehips).

Like aquavit, Solstice by itself is a powerful drink, best enjoyed in small doses, calibrated in tiny glasses. (When I was travelling through Scandinavia in the fall of 2012 I became obsessed with tiny snaps glasses and collected them in second-hand shops from Umeå to Rovaniemi.) For the faint of heart, I'd suggest starting the meal with snaps and continuing with a light white wine or lager. At the end of this section, you'll find a couple of recipes that work well with Yukon Spirits' Solstice, and are worth trying with your local version of aquavit, snaps or nubbe. The solstice feast here is not entirely faithful to the Swed-ish tradition, lacking as it does the pickled herring, for which I haven't acquired a taste. In its place, a Solstice- or Vodka-Cured Lake Trout Gravlax offers a northern Canadian salute to our Scandinavian neighbours.

Salmon Caviar and Chèvre on Rice Crackers

In sockeye salmon season, it's sometimes possible to procure fresh roe, and then it's time to make caviar, a time-consuming but highly rewarding task. It's a good idea to process the roe a couple of days before you want to serve. Follow the instructions on page 241; for this solstice feast for eight, the quantities of caviar should satisfy. Rice crackers are not traditional Midsummer fare, but the crunchy, slightly chewy texture is a fine complement to the chèvre and roe. If you're feeling ambitious, try your hand at homemade Rice Crackers, page 237; otherwise the plain, store-bought version is just fine.

32 rice crackers

5 oz (140 gr) fresh chèvre

5¼ oz (150 gr) Salmon Roe, instructions on page 241

2 Tbsp (30 mL) wild onion, chives or green onion, chopped

1. On the day of the feast, spread chèvre thinly on rice crackers, add a dollop of salmon roe, and top with chopped onion. Instruct feasters to eat in one bite.

Makes 32 canapés.

Solstice- or Vodka-Cured Lake Trout Gravlax

Start making the gravlax two to three days before you want to serve; it needs at least 24 hours to cure. Note: opinions are mixed about whether or not to cure the fish under a weight, said to result in a firmer texture. I haven't found it necessary. However, if in the process of removing pin bones from the fillet one has also removed small chunks of flesh, weighting the fish under a baking pan with a couple of cans on top can be useful in compacting the flesh. It is recommended that fish be frozen at -4F (-20C) for 24 hours before you make gravlax, in case there are any parasites present. Before starting, defrost the fish in the refrigerator.

1 fillet of fresh lake trout, skin on, about 1½ lbs (680 gr)

3 Tbsp (45 mL) white sugar

2 Tbsp (30 mL) coarse salt

2 Tbsp (30 mL) Solstice Botanical Vodka, aquavit or vodka

A handful of fresh pasture sage (*Artemisia frigida*), or substitute the fresh herb of your choice; dill is traditional in Scandinavia

1. Lay the fillet skin side down on a large piece of plastic wrap on a baking tray. Remove pin bones with kitchen tweezers or clean needle-nose pliers. Find the pin bones by running your finger down the fish's middle, from head to stomach. The pin bones end at the stomach.

2. Combine sugar, salt and spirit and spread evenly over the fish, making sure the flesh is entirely covered. Lay the herbs thickly over top.

3. Wrap a sheet of plastic tightly over the fish, lay another piece of plastic over top, and wrap tightly again. Refrigerate on the baking tray for 24 to 48 hours, turning the fish every few hours to ensure even curing. The salt will draw moisture from the flesh, creating a brine in which the fish cures.

4. Taste-test after 24 hours. If the flesh is firm and the flavour is sweet–salty enough for your liking, rinse, pat dry and wrap in fresh plastic until you're ready to serve. Otherwise, leave for another 24 hours, still turning periodically. Then rinse, pat dry and store. The fish will keep in the refrigerator for up to 10 days.

5. To serve, slice thinly with a sharp knife held at a close angle to the fish. Arrange slices on a platter accompanied by a basket of Rye Flatbread (page 239) and a bowl of crème fraîche.

Makes 24 × 1-oz (30-gr) servings. Makes one filet; will keep in the refrigerator for up to 10 days.

Leaf and Flower Salad with Wild Rose Vinaigrette

8 cups (2 L) mixed wild and cultivated young greens— spinach, kale, fireweed shoots, arugula, lettuces

2 cups (475 mL) mixed wild and cultivated edible flower petals—wild rose, fireweed, nasturtiums, violas, begonias

1. Wash and dry greens and flowers and arrange on a platter or in a pretty bowl. Just before serving, toss with Wild Rose Vinaigrette.

Makes eight servings.

WILD ROSE VINAIGRETTE

2 Tbsp (30 mL) rose petal jelly

2 Tbsp (30 mL) white wine vinegar

6 Tbsp (90 mL) sunflower or canola oil

2 tsp (10 mL) rosewater

1. Whisk jelly and vinegar together. If necessary, heat jelly for 15 seconds in microwave to soften.

2. Whisk in oil and rosewater. Let sit at room temperature until ready to serve.

Makes just over ½ cup (125 mL).

Cucumber Marinated in Apple Cider Vinegar and Honey

2 English cucumbers

¼ cup (60 mL) apple cider vinegar

¼ cup (60 mL) honey

1 tsp (5 mL) coarse salt

¼ cup (60 mL) finely chopped fresh dill

1. Slice cucumber super-thin; use a mandolin if you have one. The thinner the slices the better. Transfer slices to a bowl.

2. Whisk together the vinegar, honey and salt, pour over the cucumber, add chopped dill and toss thoroughly.

3. Refrigerate for several hours before serving, to allow flavours to combine.

Makes eight servings.

Grilled Sockeye Salmon Stuffed with Buckwheat, Berries, Mushrooms and Herbs

Make the stuffing ahead of time and refrigerate until you're ready to cook the salmon. There are several small steps.

1 whole wild sockeye salmon, 3–4 lbs (1.4–1.8 kg)

½ cup (125 mL) pine nuts

1 oz (30 gr) dried morel mushrooms

2 Tbsp (30 mL) butter, divided

1 clove garlic, minced

1 cup (250 mL) buckwheat groats

1 Tbsp (15 mL) fresh or dried Labrador tea, chopped finely

2 Tbsp (30 mL) fresh or dried pasture sage (substitute the fresh herbs in season in your area), chopped finely

3 green onions, chopped finely

½ cup (125 mL) frozen wild lowbush cranberries (lingonberries), thawed (or substitute cultivated cranberries)

Salt and pepper to taste

A bit of melted butter, some birch or maple syrup or a splash of white wine (optional)

Juniper Aioli for serving, recipe on next page (optional)

continued on next page

The challenge with buckwheat groats is they tend to get mushy. Toasting the grains first then cooking them like a risotto works well to keep them firm; so does taking them off the heat while they're still al dente. In this recipe the groats will cook twice so al dente is definitely the way to go.

Grilled Sockeye Salmon continued

1. Rinse the salmon inside and out and pat dry.

2. Toast pine nuts in a cast iron pan over medium-low heat for 5 to 7 minutes, stirring occasionally. Watch closely near the end: they brown quickly. Remove from heat and set aside.

3. Rinse morels under running water, then soak in 2 cups (475 mL) warm water until softened, about 15 minutes. Drain, reserving liquid, pat dry and chop into smallish pieces. Strain reserved liquid through a fine sieve, leaving dirt and debris behind. Set aside.

4. Sauté morels in 1 tablespoon (15 mL) butter over medium heat for 2 minutes, add garlic, cook for another 2 to 3 minutes, remove from heat and set aside.

5. Toast buckwheat over medium-low heat in a dry cast iron frying pan until the groats start to brown, about 7 minutes. Add remaining tablespoon (15 mL) of butter and ½ cup (125 mL) of the reserved mushroom water, and cook, stirring occasionally, adding water until all of it is absorbed. Test for doneness after about 10 minutes, and continue testing until buckwheat is cooked but still firm to bite. Remove from heat and cool to room temperature.

6. Combine buckwheat with morels, pine nuts, herbs and green onion and mix thoroughly. Add cranberries last. Taste and season with salt and pepper; if the mixture is dry, add a bit of melted butter, some birch or maple syrup or a splash of white wine.

7. Stuff the salmon and wrap in buttered foil. Grill on a barbecue set at medium flame for about 20 minutes per inch (2.5 cm) of thickness. A 4-pound (1.8-kg) stuffed salmon should take about 40 minutes, but start checking at 35, and remember the fish will keep cooking off the heat. If you're cooking over an open fire, set the grill about 6 inches (15 cm) above the coals, and have someone on fire duty to keep the supply of fresh coals coming.

8. Remove the fish from the heat and let sit for 10 to 15 minutes, still wrapped in foil. To serve, spoon the stuffing into a bowl. Peel the skin from the upper side of the salmon, run your knife down the centre lengthwise, cut serving-sized pieces crosswise and ease them off the bone and onto plates or a waiting platter. (If you manage to keep the pieces of skin large and fairly intact, you can grill them separately until crisp, a fine treat.) When one side is complete, grasp the tail and lift the bone from the fish (save for stock). Watch out for rib bones as you serve the remainder of the salmon. Serve with the bowl of stuffing and the Juniper Aioli.

Makes 8 to 12 servings.

Juniper Aioli

It's important to have all ingredients at room temperature before starting. For more notes on using raw eggs, see Mayonnaise, page 231.

2 egg yolks at room temperature

1 tsp (5 mL) apple cider vinegar

½ tsp (2.5 mL) Dijon mustard

½ cup (125 mL) canola oil

¼ cup (60 mL) olive oil

1 tsp (5 mL) juniper berries, toasted and ground

1 clove garlic, minced

Salt to taste

1. Beat egg yolks, vinegar and mustard until yolks thicken somewhat.

2. Combine canola and olive oil and whisk into egg mixture, about a tablespoonful at a time. I know, this is heresy; we should be adding the oil drop by fearful drop. But I've done this many times, as advised by James Peterson in his cookbook *Sauces*, and it works, as long as you whisk well after each addition of oil. The aioli will thicken slowly as you whisk. Trust.

3. Add juniper berries, garlic and salt to taste. Refrigerate overnight.

Makes about ¾ cup (180 mL).

New Potatoes Tossed in Wild Onion Pesto

WILD ONION AND PUMPKIN SEED PESTO

1 cup (250 mL) chopped green or wild onions

1 clove garlic

¼ cup (60 mL) pumpkin seeds, lightly toasted

¼ cup (60 mL) canola oil

1 tsp (5 mL) apple cider vinegar

1 Tbsp (15 mL) hot water (optional)

¼ cup (60 mL) crumbled feta cheese

Salt and pepper to taste

1. Combine onions, garlic and pumpkin seeds in food processor and whizz to a rough paste.

2. Pour oil through the spout as machine is running. Add vinegar and, if necessary, hot water to loosen the pesto.

3. Pour into bowl and stir in crumbled feta. Add salt and pepper to taste. Refrigerate overnight.

Makes about ¾ cup (180 mL).

POTATOES

Roast potatoes while salmon is cooking.

2 lbs (910 gr) new potatoes

Olive oil

Sea salt to taste

1. Preheat oven to 375F (190C) and line baking sheets with parchment paper.

2. Wash potatoes, pat dry and cut each one in half. Toss with olive oil, sprinkle with sea salt to taste and spread out, skin side down.

3. Bake until surfaces are slightly browned and insides are soft, about 30 to 35 minutes.

4. Toss with Wild Onion and Pumpkin Seed Pesto and keep warm until you're ready to serve.

Makes eight servings.

Wild Cranberry Biscotti

A good item to make the day before. With thanks to Teppo Tauriainen, Swedish Ambassador to Canada from September 2010 to July 2014, an enthusiastic cook and berry picker; we met in the summer of 2011, when he and other diplomats stopped in Whitehorse on their annual tour of northern Canada. Mr. Tauriainen provided the recipe for Birch Syrup Panna Cotta with Rhubarb Compote (next page) and suggested cranberry biscotti might be a nice addition to a Swedish-Canadian feast.

3 eggs

1 tsp (5 mL) almond extract

¾ cup (180 mL) dried wild lowbush cranberries (lingonberries) or substitute cultivated dried cranberries

2 cups (475 mL) all-purpose flour, divided

½ cup (125 mL) white sugar

1 tsp (5 mL) baking powder

Pinch of salt

1. Preheat oven to 300F (150C) and line a baking sheet with parchment paper.
2. Beat eggs and almond extract together.
3. Toss cranberries with 1 tablespoon (15 mL) of the flour and set aside.
4. Combine remaining flour with dry ingredients. Add egg mixture, stirring with a wooden spoon until a dough forms. Add cranberries at the end.
5. With floured hands, divide dough in half. On a lightly floured counter, shape each half into a log about 10 inches (25 cm) long and 2 inches (5 cm) wide. Place the logs on the baking sheet, leaving about 3 inches (7.5 cm) between them to make room for spreading.
6. Bake for 35 to 40 minutes, until firm to the touch.
7. Remove from the oven and cool for 10 to 15 minutes on a rack.
8. With a serrated knife, cut each log on the diagonal into ¾-inch (2-cm) slices.
9. Arrange slices on parchment-lined sheet. Bake at 300F (150C) for 10 to 12 minutes, turn over, and bake for another 10 to 12 minutes.
10. Remove from the oven, cool on a rack, and when thoroughly cool, store in a cookie tin.

Makes about 40 biscotti.

Agar powder or flakes are a good substitute for gelatin, but there are some key differences between them. Agar is not the best choice for stabilizing or setting liquids that won't be cooked, because it must be dissolved in liquid first and then brought to the boil. It sets as the ingredients cool down. The common recommendation is to use one teaspoon (5 mL) of agar powder or one tablespoon (15 mL) of agar flakes to thicken one cup (250 mL) of liquid. However, for this recipe I had better results using ½ teaspoon (2.5 mL) of powder per cup (250 mL) of liquid; the full amount produced a panna cotta that was too stiff. (Similarly, in later tests I found 1 Tbsp (15 mL) of agar flakes to be too much; try using 2 tsp (10 mL) flakes per cup of liquid.) Agar gels more firmly than gelatin, so don't expect the same results if substituting agar for gelatin.

Birch Syrup Panna Cotta with Rhubarb Compote

The original recipe calls for gelatin as a thickening agent, but with agar powder the dessert is also suitable for those who avoid pork products.

2 tsp (10 mL) agar powder (see sidebar above)

2 cups plus 3 Tbsp (520 mL) 35 percent cream, divided

¼ cup (60 mL) sugar

1 Tbsp (15 mL) birch syrup

1 vanilla bean

2 cups plus 3 Tbsp (520 mL) 2 percent Greek yogourt or 3 percent regular yogourt

1. Stir agar powder into ½ cup (125 mL) of the 35 percent cream.
2. Bring remaining cream to the boil with sugar and birch syrup. Split the vanilla bean and scrape seeds into the cream.
3. Add agar mixture, stir vigorously and simmer for 2 minutes.
4. Remove from heat, whisk in the yogourt, strain into a large measuring cup and working quickly, pour into 10 ramekins, clear glass bowls or ½-cup (125-mL) mason jars.
5. The panna cotta will set as it cools. When thoroughly cool, cover and refrigerate. Just before serving, spoon Rhubarb Compote over top, garnish with mint and an edible flower, and serve with Wild Cranberry Biscotti (previous page) on the side.

Makes ten ½-cup (125-mL) ramekins.

RHUBARB COMPOTE

4 cups (950 mL) chopped fresh rhubarb

1 cup (250 mL) white wine

¼ cup (60 mL) wild lowbush cranberries (lingonberries) or substitute cultivated cranberries

½ cup (125 mL) sugar

2 Tbsp (30 mL) birch syrup

1. Combine all ingredients in a medium saucepan, bring to the boil, reduce heat and simmer until rhubarb is tender but still holds its shape, about 8 to 10 minutes.
2. Pour through a strainer, transfer cooked rhubarb to a bowl and return the strained liquid to the pot.
3. Simmer liquid until reduced to a thick syrup. Remove from heat and pour syrup over rhubarb. Cool rhubarb compote to room temperature, then cover and refrigerate.

Makes about 1½ cups (350 mL).

Two Solstice-Inspired Summer Dishes

The addition of Solstice Botanical Vodka (produced by Yukon Spirits distillery) to raspberry ice cream intensifies the sour notes present in the wild raspberries and buttermilk, but you'll be hard-pressed to discern the taste of the drink. This is not true of the penne dish, inspired by the favourite 1990s combination of vodka, penne and smoked salmon. Wild sage and rosehip purée turn the creaky classic into something new and uniquely northern; both sage and rosehip highlight the bracing flavours present in Solstice, whose slight astringency is counterbalanced by cream and sweet, ripe tomato. Remember, you don't want to cook the smoked salmon and lose the silky texture. Pile it on top of the pasta just before adding the final dose of sauce. If you have leftover Solstice- or Vodka-Cured Lake Trout Gravlax (page 46), try substituting it for the smoked salmon.

Solstice-Infused Raspberry Ice Cream

If you use frozen raspberries, slightly thawed, you won't have to wait as long for the mixture to chill in the fridge before freezing. Note that because alcohol doesn't freeze, the ice cream takes longer to set than usual. Plan on making it the day before you want to serve.

2 cups (475 mL) wild raspberries, fresh or frozen

1 cup (250 mL) buttermilk

1 cup (250 mL) whipping cream

⅔ cup (160 mL) sugar

3 Tbsp (45 mL) Solstice Botanical Vodka, aquavit or vodka

1. Purée raspberries with buttermilk in a food processor and press through a sieve to remove seeds.

2. Add whipping cream and sugar and whisk until the sugar is dissolved. Add Solstice, whisk again, and pour mixture into a shallow dish.

3. Chill in fridge until mixture is quite cold, then put in freezer.

4. If you have an ice cream maker, follow the manufacturer's instructions.

    If you don't have an ice cream maker, take the mixture from the freezer after 30 minutes and whisk vigorously to incorporate air into the ice cream and assist in even freezing. Do this five times (for a total of 2 hours and 30 minutes), then leave to freeze fully for 6 to 8 hours.

Makes about 3 cups (710 mL).

Penne with Smoked Salmon, Tomato, Rosehips and Solstice

A peaceful evening in high summer.

3 Tbsp (45 mL) unsalted butter

1 cup (250 mL) finely chopped onion

1 medium clove garlic, minced

1 tsp (5 mL) pasture sage, crumbled

3 plum tomatoes, chopped

1 Tbsp (15 mL) rosehip purée

¼ cup (60 mL) Solstice Botanical Vodka, aquavit or vodka

½ cup (125 mL) 35 percent cream

8 oz (225 gr) penne

4 oz (110 gr) smoked salmon cut into bite-sized pieces

3 Tbsp (45 mL) parsley, minced

1. Melt butter over medium heat in a 9-inch (22.5-cm) cast iron frying pan. When it's bubbling add onion and garlic, turn heat to medium-low and sauté until the onion is translucent, about 5 to 7 minutes, then add sage.

2. Add the chopped plum tomatoes and simmer for about 5 minutes. Add the rosehip purée, stir, cook for a minute and then add the spirits.

3. Cook for about two minutes, or until the smell of alcohol subsides, and stir in the cream. Cook for a further three minutes and remove from heat.

4. While preparing the sauce, boil water in a large pot, add penne, and cook until al dente. Drain pasta and return to pot.

5. To serve, stir all but ½ cup (125 mL) of the sauce into the drained pasta, spoon into two bowls, arrange half the smoked salmon on top of each (you don't want to cook the salmon, just warm it), pour over the remaining sauce and sprinkle with chopped parsley. Serve with a green salad, set up the deck chairs and bask.

Makes two servings.

ROSEHIP PURÉE

1 cup (250 mL) fresh or frozen rosehips

1 cup (250 mL) water

1. Bring rosehips and water to the boil, lower heat to simmer and cook, covered, until rosehips are soft, about 20 minutes. Press through a strainer.

2. Use as you would tomato paste. Will keep in the fridge for up to two weeks.

Makes ½ cup (125 mL).

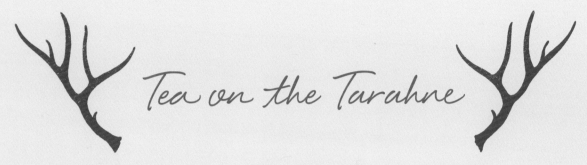

Tea on the Tarahne

MENU FOR 12

Savouries

Potted Smoked Salmon with Toast Fingers **59**

Roasted Strawberry Bruschetta **59**

Summer Greens and Walnuts in Rose and
Saffron Pastry **60**

Tomato and Chèvre Canapés **61**

Sweets

Cream Puffs, Whipped Cream and Cloudberry Jam **62**

Rose Petal Meringues **64**

Classic Sugar Cookies with Candied Spruce Tips **64**

A Northern Tea Party

Icame late to the enjoyment of tea parties; in my youth I was a tomboy and eschewed dresses, skipping ropes and tiny tea sets. As a teenager I discovered the early 20th century British authors: Virginia Woolf, Aldous Huxley, E.M. Forster, writers who exploited the tea table to illustrate the chafing of youth against the restrictions of the old order, or the shifting balance of power between the classes. Oh, how my rebellious 15-year-old self ate this up!

The scene is resplendent with linen and lace, top hats and white shirts, bright tablecloths and china, flowers and scrubbed, shining faces

Then, in July 2011, I attended for the first time a tea party on the *Tarahne*, a restored, early 20th century sternwheeler in Atlin, BC, the bite-sized northern town that Yukoners have voted "The Best Yukon Community That's Not in the Yukon." Tea on the *Tarahne* is an annual fundraiser for the Atlin Historical Society, and it is so popular that there are two sittings, one at noon, the other at 2:30 in the afternoon, and both sell out.

Atlinites come in from their off-the-grid homesteads, from their tiny colourful houses, from their cabins scattered along the clear bright creeks that empty into Atlin Lake. They dress in turn-of-the-century clothes or the closest approximation they can find and crowd

Delightful delicacies and no crooked pinkies are the order of the day at the annual tea on the Tarahne *in Atlin, BC.*

up the stairs and onto the upper deck of the *Tarahne*, which sailed upon Atlin Lake moving goods and people from 1916 until the mid-1930s, and is now beached in a cradle on shore.

The scene is resplendent with linen and lace, top hats and white shirts, bright tablecloths and china, flowers and scrubbed, shining faces. Courteous little girls in summer dresses dart to and fro with plates of goodies, saying things like "Would you care for a crab bite?" (My

Retired from active service in the 1930s and carefully restored by the Atlin Historical Society, the Tarahne lies beached and cradled on the shore of Atlin Lake.

inner tomboy is awed by their poise.) The ladies who serve tea stop to chat; old-timers greet each other with slaps on the back and conversations leap across tables. Ladies and gents and latter-day tomboys, there is nothing to fear at this tea party. It's a hoot. Not stuffy! No crooked pinkies! Lots of jokes and stories!

Part of the fun was getting ready at our host's cabin on Lina Creek. We took sponge baths from an enamel basin, shivered into our finery in a wall tent, piled into

dusty pickups in our long dresses and top hats and then bumped along Warm Bay Road to town, charmed by ourselves and by the treat to come. We delight in contrasts, and there is no contrast more delightful than the rough-hewn and the elegant side by side.

One day I might work up the nerve to tackle the Commissioner's Tea in Dawson. In the meantime, here are some summer delicacies suitable for the at-home northern tea table.

Potted Smoked Salmon with Toast Fingers

8 oz (225 gr) hot-smoked wild salmon—home-smoked, flaky salmon works best

1 Tbsp (15 mL) chopped fresh chives, green onions or wild onions

1 tsp (5 mL) grated lemon zest

½ tsp (2.5 mL) freshly ground black pepper

½ cup (125 mL) unsalted butter

1 Tbsp (15 mL) lemon juice

9 thin slices sourdough brown bread

1. Flake the salmon into a bowl, add chives, lemon zest and ground pepper and mix lightly with a fork. Pack the salmon into four ½-cup (125-mL) ramekins.

2. Melt the butter over low heat until the water has evaporated (you'll know because the butter will have stopped bubbling and hissing), the sediment on top turns pale brown, the specks on the bottom are a darker brown, and the butter develops a nutty aroma.

3. Remove from heat and let cool to room temperature before whisking in the lemon juice.

4. Pour the butter and lemon juice over the potted salmon to cover. Refrigerate.

5. Remove from fridge at least 30 minutes before serving; the butter is best when softened slightly. Serve with unbuttered toast fingers or triangles; cut bread first into the desired shape and, at the last minute, cook under the broiler for 1 to 2 minutes per side, until golden.

Makes 12 servings.

The browned butter and lemon juice mixture is essentially the classic Beurre Noisette. For a true Beurre Noisette, you would use the clarified butter only, leaving the solids behind, but in my opinion, there's so much flavour in those solids it's a shame to waste them.

Roasted Strawberry Bruschetta

There are many ways to roast a strawberry. I've found that the trick to getting the right caramelized, sweet-and-tart effect is to cut the strawberries in quarters and roast them quickly at high heat, almost but not quite letting the birch syrup burn.

1 lb (455 gr) cultivated strawberries

2 Tbsp (30 mL) balsamic vinegar

2 Tbsp (30 mL) birch syrup

Kosher salt

Half a baguette

Olive oil

1. Preheat oven to 450F (230C) and line a baking sheet with parchment paper.

2. Wash, hull and quarter strawberries. Combine balsamic vinegar and birch syrup, pour over strawberries and toss gently. Spread berries out on baking sheet and sprinkle with salt.

3. Roast for 10 to 15 minutes, or until the syrup and vinegar mixture is bubbling and the berries are slightly browned on top and caramelized around the edges. They should stick to the paper slightly.

4. Cut the baguette into ¼-inch (0.6-cm) slices and spread out on a baking sheet. Broil until toasted, about 1 minute. Turn the toasts over, brush with olive oil and broil for 1 minute.

5. Place 3 or 4 strawberry quarters on each slice of baguette. Arrange on a platter garnished with flowers and serve.

Makes about 24 pieces.

Summer Greens and Walnuts in Rose and Saffron Pastry

Adapted from Renaissance cook Cristoforo di Messisbugo's Torta d'Herbe recipe in *Festive Feasts Cookbook* by Michelle Berriedale-Johnson. For the filling, use cultivated greens such as spinach, chard and arugula, or a combination of wild greens in season such as young dandelion leaves and fireweed tips, or plantain, chickweed and lamb's quarters. Choose a mixture of greens that wilt easily (spinach, arugula, lamb's quarters) and sturdier types (kale, plantain).

PASTRY

¼ cup (60 mL) sugar	1 egg yolk
1 Tbsp (15 mL) dried wild rose petals	3 Tbsp (45 mL) rosewater
10 saffron threads (about ¼ tsp/1 mL)	1 Tbsp (15 mL) cold water (if needed)
1½ cups (350 mL) all-purpose flour	1 egg, beaten, for glazing the pastry
½ cup (125 mL) cold butter	

1. Combine sugar and rose petals in the bowl of a food processor and whizz until the rose petals are the size of coarsely ground pepper. Add the saffron, pulse, add the flour to the bowl and pulse once or twice.

2. Cut the butter into small pieces, add to the bowl and pulse until the butter is the size of dried peas.

3. Beat the egg yolk with the rosewater, add to the bowl in two additions and pulse briefly after each one. Pinch the pastry between your fingers to test if it clumps together and will roll out nicely. If not, add the tablespoon of cold water and pulse.

4. Turn out the pastry onto a piece of waxed paper, press lightly into a ball, wrap and chill for 30 minutes.

FILLING

2 Tbsp (30 mL) extra-virgin olive oil	6 dried Mission figs, finely chopped
2 lbs (910 gr) mixed greens	½ tsp (2.5 mL) cinnamon
2 Tbsp (30 mL) finely chopped dried apricot	1 tsp (5 mL) freshly ground nutmeg
2 Tbsp (30 mL) sultanas or currants	Salt and pepper to taste
½ cup (125 mL) walnut halves	1 egg, beaten
	2 Tbsp (30 mL) bread crumbs

1. Heat 2 Tbsp (30 mL) olive oil in a cast iron frying pan over medium heat. Add any tougher greens first, followed by the more tender, and sauté until wilted but still bright green. Remove from heat and let cool. Squeeze greens to remove as much liquid as possible, then chop roughly and place in a bowl.

2. Mix in walnuts, dried fruit, spices, salt and pepper, and adjust seasonings if desired. Add egg, mixing well.

3. Bring pastry out of fridge, cut in half and form each half into a rough ball. Now, you have a choice: to make one big pie or tartlets of various sizes. For a pie, use a 9-inch (22.5-cm) pie plate. For tartlets, more elegant and therefore more suitable for a tea, use 3-inch (7.5-cm) or 1½-inch (3.8-cm) tartlet moulds and be prepared to roll and cut, roll and cut.

4. Roll out the first ball of dough until ⅛ inch (0.13 cm) thick. Drape lightly over the pie plate or cut into the right size for your tart moulds and press the dough gently into the plate or mould.

5. Sprinkle the bottom of the pie or tartlets with bread crumbs. Spoon in filling. For 3-inch (7.5-cm) shells use 2 tablespoons (30 mL) filling; for 1½-inch (3.8-cm) shells use 1½ teaspoons (7.5 mL) filling.

6. Roll out remaining dough to ⅛-inch (0.13-cm) thickness. Drape over top of the pie. Clean up edges, crimp bottom and top layers together, and cut two vents to allow steam to escape. Brush with beaten egg. For tartlets, cut pastry into circles, brush with beaten egg and set on top of filling at a jaunty angle. Don't worry about joining the tops and bottoms together.

7. Bake 9-inch (22.5-cm) pie for 45 minutes at 350F (180C) or until pastry is golden brown; bake 3-inch (7.5-cm) tartlets for 30 minutes and 1½-inch (3.8-cm) tartlets for 25 minutes. Serve warm or at room temperature.

Makes 1 × 9-inch (22.5-cm) pie, about 18 × 3-inch (7.5-cm) tartlets or 48 × 1½-inch (3.8-cm) tartlets.

Tomato and Chèvre Canapés

A note on puff pastry: if you make your own, bravo! But if not, there are good frozen products in the supermarket; be sure to choose one made with butter. It is best to thaw frozen puff pastry overnight in the refrigerator, so plan ahead.

1 lb (455 gr) all-butter puff pastry, defrosted

3 medium tomatoes

3 Tbsp (45 mL) feta cheese, crumbled

2 cloves garlic, minced

½ tsp (2.5 mL) ground black pepper

¼ tsp (1 mL) salt

2 Tbsp (30 mL) olive oil

8 oz (225 gr) chèvre, sliced into ¼-inch-thick rounds

¼ cup (60 mL) green onion, finely chopped

Olive oil, for drizzling

1. Preheat the oven to 400F (205C) and line two baking sheets with parchment paper.

2. Working with one sheet of pastry at a time, cut the pastry into 2-inch (5-cm) squares. Place squares on baking sheets and chill while preparing the topping.

3. Quarter and thinly slice the tomatoes, saving the juices. Combine tomato, juices, feta, garlic, pepper, salt and olive oil and toss gently to combine.

4. Spoon the tomato mixture onto the pastry.

5. Place a slice of chèvre on each square, sprinkle with green onion and bake 18 to 20 minutes, until the pastry is deep golden.

6. Serve with a drizzle of olive oil over top.

Makes about 50 pieces.

Cream Puffs, Whipped Cream and Cloudberry Jam

There has to be at least one creamy, fruity item on the tea table. The contrast of crispy cream puff, chunky jam or compote and smooth whipped cream is unbelievably good. Warning: rogue whipped cream will escape onto fingers and chins. Call in the napkins.

The success of cream puffs depends on a crisp exterior and a light, dry interior; the best way to achieve this is to start baking at a high temperature, which poufs up the puff, continue at a lower temperature to finish the baking, and, when the cream puffs are done, turn off the oven, open the door slightly and let them cool completely before removing from the oven.

CHOUX PASTRY

Choux pastry sounds intimidating but it's actually one of the easier pastries to make and opens up a world of possibilities, both sweet and savoury.

½ cup (125 mL) all-purpose flour

½ tsp (2.5 mL) granulated white sugar

¼ tsp (1 mL) salt

½ cup (125 mL) water

¼ cup (60 mL) unsalted butter, cut into pieces

2 eggs at room temperature (very important)

FILLING

½ cup (125 mL) Cloudberry Jam, recipe on page 215 (or substitute Quick Apricot Compote, recipe on next page)

2 cups (475 mL) Whipped Cream, recipe on next page

1. Preheat oven to 400F (205C) and line a baking sheet with parchment paper.

2. Combine dry ingredients in small bowl.

3. Heat water and butter over medium-high heat, stirring constantly so that butter melts quickly, bring to the boil and add the dry ingredients in one fell swoop. Reduce heat to medium, and working quickly, stir until the dough is one smooth ball that pulls away from the sides of the pan. There will be a film of butter and dough on the bottom of the pan.

4. Remove from heat, stir dough once or twice to release steam, transfer to a bowl and let cool for 2 minutes.

5. Using a wooden spoon, beat in the eggs one at a time, mixing well after each addition. The dough is ready for the next egg when it is no longer lumpy and does not look shiny. The final dough should be stiff enough that a small piece holds its shape when it's picked up with a spoon.

6. Using two dessert spoons or a pastry bag, make 12 2½-inch (6.5-cm) mounds of dough on the parchment paper, spacing them 2 inches (5 cm) apart. For smaller puffs, use two teaspoons or a smaller nozzle to make 24 1½-inch (3.8-cm) mounds on two baking sheets, spacing them 1 inch (2.5 cm) apart.

7. Bake for 10 minutes at 400F (205C); turn down heat to 350F (180C) and bake for another 25 minutes.

8. Test to make sure the exteriors of the puffs are hard, then turn off oven, open door and let cool completely.

9. To fill, cut cream puffs in half. They should be hollow and quite dry inside, however there may be damp filaments of dough joining the floor to the ceiling—if this is the case just remove them.

10. Just before you're ready to serve, fill the puffs with whipped cream and Cloudberry Jam at a ratio of 3 parts cream to 1 part jam.

Makes one dozen cream puffs or two dozen miniature cream puffs.

Members of the Taku River Tlingit First Nation paddle Atlin Lake in a traditional long canoe.

QUICK APRICOT COMPOTE

If you aren't lucky enough to have a jar of Cloudberry Jam in the cupboard, this quick and delicious compote is a great substitute.

1 cup (250 mL) dried apricots, chopped into small pieces

1 cup (250 mL) water

⅓ cup (80 mL) sugar

3 Tbsp (45 mL) lemon juice

1 Tbsp (15 mL) Labrador tea, chopped finely (or substitute 1 inch/2.5 cm of vanilla bean, split and scraped)

1 tsp (5 mL) cloudberry liqueur (optional)

1. Combine all ingredients except liqueur in a small saucepan and bring to the boil. Reduce heat and cook for 15 minutes, stirring occasionally. Stir in liqueur, if using. Let cool to room temperature.

2. If the compote hasn't thickened quite enough, transfer to a food processor and pulse a few times, making sure you leave some chunks of fruit for texture.

Makes 1 cup (250 mL).

WHIPPED CREAM

In hot weather, or when preparing cream puffs more than a few hours ahead of tea time, you may wish to stabilize the whipped cream—see sidebar on page 133.

1 cup (250 mL) 35 percent cream

1 Tbsp (15 mL) birch or maple syrup

1. Combine cream and syrup and whip until stiff peaks form. If the weather is hot and/or humid, chill bowl and beaters for 15 minutes before whipping cream.

Makes about 2 cups (475 mL).

Rose Petal Meringues

1 cup (250 mL) sugar

¼ cup (60 mL) dried rose petals

4 egg whites at room temperature

¼ tsp (1 mL) cream of tartar

1 tsp (5 mL) rosewater

1. Preheat the oven to 225F (105C). Line four baking trays with parchment paper.

2. Whizz sugar and rose petals in a food processor until rose petals are the size of ground pepper. Set aside. Beat the egg whites on medium-low speed just until slightly thickened and frothy. Add cream of tartar and rosewater, increase speed to medium-high, and beat until the egg whites thicken and start to take on a uniform colour. Now slowly add the sugar mixture, still beating, until the egg whites stand up in stiff peaks.

3. Make 1-inch (2.5-cm) meringues by dropping the meringue from a teaspoon onto the parchment paper. Or use a pastry bag and a notched nozzle.

4. Bake for 45 minutes or up to an hour if your meringues are larger than 1 inch (2.5 cm) in diameter. The bottoms should be pale brown and the tops just off-white. Turn off the heat, open the oven door and leave the meringues in the cooling oven for 20 minutes. Remove and cool on racks away from drafts. Store in a covered tin.

Makes about 6 dozen 1-inch (2.5-cm) meringues.

Classic Sugar Cookies with Candied Spruce Tips

2¾ cups (650 mL) all-purpose flour

1 tsp (5 mL) baking soda

½ tsp (2.5 mL) baking powder

1 cup (250 mL) butter, softened

1½ cups (350 mL) white sugar

1 egg

1 tsp (5 mL) Spruce Tip Liqueur or aquavit, recipe on page 158 (or substitute vanilla or almond extract)

¾ cup (180 mL) coarsely chopped Candied Spruce Tips, recipe on page 209 (or substitute candied lemon or orange peel)

1. Preheat oven to 375F (190C).

2. In a small bowl, stir together flour, baking soda and baking powder. Set aside.

3. In a large bowl, cream the butter and sugar until smooth. Beat in egg and liqueur. Gradually blend in the dry ingredients, then stir in spruce tips.

4. Roll rounded teaspoons of dough into balls, and place on ungreased baking trays.

5. Bake 8 to 10 minutes, or until golden. Let stand on cookie sheet 2 minutes before removing to cool on wire racks.

Makes about four dozen 2-inch (5-cm) cookies.

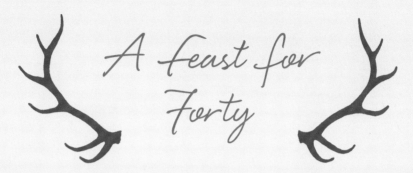

A feast for Forty

MENU

A Gathering of Elders

The antique White Pass & Yukon Route train travelling from Carcross, Yukon to Bennett, BC, hugs the shore of Bennett Lake as it travels deep into the mountains of the coastal range. The old wooden coaches rock gently from side to side, and the interpreter tells gold rush-era stories over a loudspeaker that crackles and hisses, her voice intermittently audible above the clackety-clack of iron wheels on narrow-gauge rails. Passengers crowd to the windows on the right side and snap pictures of glacial blue water and mountains that rise straight up from the lake.

When the train pulls into Bennett the world opens up into a clearing of light and space. An isthmus connects the sites of the station and the historic town, and the water sparkles on either side. As soon as you step from the train you notice the air, clean and dry and scented with pine and sub-alpine fir, and you convince yourself that way at the back of your throat you can taste the faint tang of the sea, brought in from the coast through the mountain passes.

The red station house is a stone's throw from the shore where, more than 100 years ago, stampeders built the boats that would take them, they hoped, the 1,000 kilometres from the headwaters of the Yukon River to the goldfields at Dawson. Today, Bennett is part of the Chilkoot Trail national historic site, and the last stop for hikers who have walked the Chilkoot Trail from Dyea, Alaska. When the horn toots they come scrambling down the sandy paths to catch the train that will take them back to Carcross, the last stage of their adventure.

For Cathie Archbould and me, in the summer of 2013, arrival at Bennett was the beginning of a two-day adventure. We had been invited to the annual gathering for Elders from the Carcross/Tagish First Nation, hosted by Parks Canada at Bennett each summer; I was a volunteer cook, Cathie the photographer. It was first day of August and 27 degrees, the lake was riffled glass, the mountains receded down the long line of the lake in waves of shadow and light, and we were in heaven.

Carcross/Tagish First Nation Elder Mrs. Edna Helm trotted down the path from her cabin to meet us, pushing a yellow wheelbarrow. Edna was our host for the next few days, and this was our first glimpse of her no-nonsense, get-it-done style. We loaded our supplies and bumped back along the path to the Helm cabin, the only inhabited dwelling in what used to be a thriving town of hotels stores, and saloons.

Today, there is a church, a shoreline littered with rusting artifacts, the Parks Canada shelter and campground, and the Helms' homestead. Tourists often mistake their trapping cabin for a national historic site, and sometimes Edna has to put a "No Trespassing" sign on the outhouse. This is the Helm family's traditional territory; here they

A rusted Great Majestic wood stove is one of many artifacts scattered throughout the former Gold Rush town of Bennett, BC.

Guests and hosts at the annual Elders Gathering at Benett, BC, congregate on the steps of the Parks Canada shelter. Edna Helm and Esau Schaefer, in the front row, flank the White Pass & Yukon Route train conductor.

have fished and trapped since long before the gold rush. Although they have a house in Carcross, Bennett is where their hearts reside.

Edna's husband, Walter, and their daughter, Nancy, arrived by boat from Carcross, with the family dogs. Walter had brought a green garbage bag full of rhubarb and a cabbage the size of a giant's head from his garden. He offered it to us and we broke off creamy chunks and crunched them like apples.

It was time to get to work, in a holiday kind of way. Parks Canada field officer Christine Hedgecock supervised the packing away of the food coolers into the bathhouse, a small shack with an old cast iron bathtub in the back, sheltered by spruce trees and the coolest place on the property. Christine is an adopted member of the Helm family and was officially adopted into the Ishkìtàn (Frog) Clan. The gathering is primarily Christine's

responsibility, and it was her job to shepherd the rest of us into some semblance of order.

The Helm family has played a central role in the Elders Gathering since the early 2000s. They cast nets in Bennett Lake for the lake trout and whitefish that are the centerpiece of the luncheon, along with Edna's bannock. Parks Canada brings in a cooler of sockeye salmon for backup and commissions a large, celebratory cake.

Timing is tight on the day of the gathering. The Elders arrive on the 11:20 a.m. train, walk nearly a kilometre to the Parks Canada shelter, have lunch, and walk back in time for the 12:35 p.m. return train to Carcross. (One year, Edna's wheelbarrow was pressed into service as Elder transport.)

The next day the serious work started. We set up a potato peeling, washing, and chopping station on the steps of Edna's bathhouse. Parks Canada field officer Stephanie Ryan and promotion officer Lily Gontard

Sockeye salmon, floured and ready for the frying pan. Parks Canada brings in a backup cooler of salmon for the occasion.

peeled and chopped like seasoned camp cooks. Nancy brought out a folding camp stove and balanced it on the roof of a small cupboard beside the bathhouse while I rigged up a shelter against the wind with a piece of plywood and set the potatoes to boil. Walter sat on a bench under a spruce tree a few metres away and told stories to Cathie and Christine. His voice rose and fell over the roar of the stove; I heard "lynx" and "jerry can" and "overflow," and Cathie's voice asking animated questions.

When you're cooking outdoors in unfamiliar surroundings everything takes longer, and potato salad for 40 becomes an epic. I got to know the system at Edna's: which barrel to get the water from, how the pump worked, where to dump the potato water (into the garden under the window), whether it was okay to enter the cabin and bug Edna for a spoon or a pot. Of course it was okay. Edna sat at the table by the window, beading a piece of moose hide that would become moccasins or mittens.

Being with the Helms was like being at a summer cottage: relaxed and homey.

In the late afternoon Walter, Edna and Nancy took the boat out and set the fishnets in a small cove across the bay. Some of us walked down to the shore to watch them. Walter drove slowly in reverse while Edna held the net open from the top and she and Nancy guided it into the water, hand over hand, an ancient and beautiful sight.

We workers set up our colony of tents in a campsite just above the Parks Canada shelter, where the gathering would be held the next day. That evening we dined on pork medallions in a cream sauce. We sat in camp chairs, balancing our plates in our laps, and admiring the excellent manners of the family dogs.

Edna held the net open from the top and she and Nancy guided it into the water, hand over hand, an ancient and beautiful sight.

After dinner I was in the bathhouse sorting food when Cathie appeared, looking anxious. "I think you're in trouble," she said. "You used Edna's bannock pan to make supper." Oh, great way to anger the Elder. But Edna just laughed. "If I saw what pan you were going to take I would've stopped you," she said. We re-seasoned the pan with vegetable oil over the burner on the picnic table, and Edna declared it fit for use.

We workers retired to our campsite and settled in. From the tent door I could see all the way down the lake to the vanishing point. I woke up in the middle of the night and looked out: the sky was clear, and the hillside across the water a sharp outline against the blue. I imagined the sleeping hikers and Parks employees and Helm family members and dogs, breathing under the same deep sky, and went comfortably back to sleep.

Cathie and I got up at six; she started the coffee while I got the hot water going and set up the cooking station. The Parks Canada gals arrived, rubbing sleepy eyes as we put coffee mugs into their outstretched hands. Edna came out of the cabin with a plateful of bannock, "so you can keep up your strength!"

At 8:30, Walter said, "If we're going to go and get that net, it's now or never." He and Nancy took off in the boat accompanied by Cathie and her camera. Fifteen minutes later, they were back. Cathie came up from the dock. "So?" we said. "Two small lake trout and a sucker," she replied. "Skunked!" said Edna.

Plan B was called into action: Parks Canada's backup sockeye salmon. It was nine o'clock and we had a lot of pan frying to do. Stephanie and Nancy set up cooking stations of two burners and two frying pans each on either side of the table. Cathie shifted from photographer to cook, and she and I dipped endless salmon pieces in Edna's flour mixture.

We burnt the first pieces. "Elders don't like burnt fish," Christine said. We turned down the heat. Christine came back to inspect. "Better," she said. More Parks Canada workers arrived from Lindeman; so did a couple of Alaska park rangers. Everyone pitched in.

Then we heard the toot of the train. "All hands to the shelter," cried Christine. Parks Canada rangers with radios ran to greet the train. There were fifteen Elders, along with special guests from the Alaska National Park Service, and Esau Schaefer, a Vuntut Gwitchin First Nation Elder and Parks Canada First Nation liaison officer from Old Crow, who had never been to Bennett.

The Elders descended in a clump and took their places at picnic tables underneath a tarp extending from the roof of the shelter. Their caretakers and younger relatives swarmed in for their plates, which Lily and I were filling as fast as we could with bannock, fish, potato salad and coleslaw. Word came back—don't stint on the fish! We loaded the plates with three pieces instead of two. We could afford to: we had fish for 40.

Elder Winnie Atlin said a prayer in Tlingit, thanking the Creator for the day and the food. Esau Schaefer stood up and thanked the Helm family and Carcross/Tagish First Nation for hosting in this beautiful place. He said he came from a beautiful place too, and he hoped some of the people here would come up and see him sometime to keep this connection strong. Christine Hedgecock introduced Cathie and me. That's when we realized that we too were honoured guests.

Wheelbarrows are the favoured means of transporting goods at Bennett, and have occasionally been used to carry an Elder too.

And then it was time for cake. Lily and I carried it out so everyone could see the inscription, "We are pleased to see you," written in Tlingit: *Yak'é ixhwsatìní* and "It is good to see you" in Tagish: *Dahts'eneh'įh sùkùsen.* Everyone had cake, including hikers, the White Pass & Yukon Route conductor, White Pass passenger agents, Alaskan rangers, families, the Elders and us.

It was 12:15. Inside the shelter we worked furiously to fill and wrap plates for those who couldn't make it to the gathering. Elders came in and said, "Thank you for the great food." Outside, the whole group posed for a picture and 20 cameras whirred and clicked.

Suddenly, it was time to go. "I've saved the whitefish and the trout for our supper tonight," Edna whispered. I hated to tell her that Cathie and I also had to get on the train. When I did, her face fell. "It's going to be so quiet here when all you girls are gone." We would have loved to stay and visit with Edna under the evening sky. Next time we will.

Just before we left, Edna called us into the cabin. "This is for you," she said, and put a small container in each of our hands. It was her homemade salve, made with the pitch of the sub-alpine fir. Now when I open the tiny box, I smell the sweet air at Bennett and remember the wind blowing down the passes from the sea.

Pan-Fried Salmon

Estimate a 4-ounce (110-gr) serving of salmon per person, and if you're feeding fewer than 40, reduce the amount of fish and coating accordingly. A 1½-pound (680-gr) fillet will feed 6 people comfortably.

12 to 14 wild salmon fillets, skin on, about 1½ lbs (680 gr) each

4 cups (950 mL) flour

1 Tbsp (15 mL) freshly ground black pepper

2 tsp (10 mL) coarse salt

2 tsp (10 mL) baking powder

1 cup (250 mL) canola oil, for frying

1 cup (250 mL) butter, for frying

1. Cut raw salmon into portions: slice fillet lengthwise down the middle, following the line naturally present in the fish, then slice each piece crosswise into 3 or 4 pieces, depending on the size of the fillet.

2. Combine dry ingredients in a medium bowl. Melt 1 tablespoon (15 mL) each oil and butter in as many large frying pans as you can muster—we had four.

3. Dredge pieces of salmon in flour mixture. Separate the thinner tail pieces from the rest—these will cook in less time. At Edna's we cooked the thick and thin pieces in separate frying pans.

4. Fry salmon pieces for about 3 minutes per side for the thick pieces, 2 minutes for the thin, turning once. Add butter and oil to the pan as needed, scraping out the bits of browned flour that accumulate.

5. Keep cooked salmon warm in covered containers lined with paper towel until ready to serve.

Makes 40 servings.

Edna Helm's Best Bannock

Edna Helm makes the best bannock I've ever tasted. Christine says the secret is, "she doesn't rush it and she doesn't squash it." Edna says the secret is cooking with a cast iron frying pan on a cast iron stove. The cast iron stove might be hard for most of us to replicate, but the frying pan is within our control. Eschew the non-stick pan! Edna's measurements are approximate. I've tried to quantify them more precisely, but there is a certain amount of magic in making a great bannock. Good luck.

5 cups (1.2 L) flour

½ cup (125 mL) sugar

2 Tbsp (30 mL) baking powder

½ tsp (2.5 mL) salt

3–4 cups (710 mL–1 L) water

½ cup (125 mL) solid vegetable shortening, for frying

1. Combine dry ingredients.

2. Gradually add water, stirring constantly, just until the mixture is thoroughly moistened and not too lumpy, with a texture similar to biscuit dough.

3. Over medium heat, melt enough shortening in a cast iron pan to reach ¼ inch (0.6 cm) in depth.

4. For 3-inch (7.5-cm) bannock, drop about ¼ cup (60 mL) bannock dough into the hot fat from a serving spoon; for 2-inch (5-cm) bannock, drop about 2 tablespoons (30 mL) of dough. Fry bannock for 4 to 5 minutes on each side, or until golden brown. Dry on paper towels and keep warm in a 200F (95C) oven until ready to serve.

Makes 30 × 3-inch (7.5-cm) or 40 × 2-inch (5-cm) pieces of bannock.

Picnic Potato Salad

Every now and then it falls to one of us to cook large quantities of food for our community. This recipe will please all, including children and older folks.

10 lbs (4.5 kg) Yukon Gold potatoes

1 tsp (5 mL) sea salt

½ cup (125 mL) olive oil

2 Tbsp (30 mL) apple cider vinegar

10–12 green onions, finely chopped

8 stalks celery, finely chopped

DRESSING

1½–2 cups (350–475 mL) good quality mayonnaise

¼ cup (60 mL) Dijon mustard

¼ cup (60 mL) apple cider vinegar

Sea salt and freshly ground pepper to taste

1. Peel potatoes, rinse and cut into ½-inch (1.25-cm) dice. Bring a large saucepan of water to the boil, add salt and potatoes and bring to the boil again. Reduce heat and simmer for about 10 minutes, or until potatoes are cooked but still firm.

2. Drain potatoes thoroughly and transfer into a large bowl. Whisk together the oil and 2 tablespoons (30 mL) vinegar, pour over the potatoes and gently toss. Refrigerate for several hours or overnight.

3. About two hours before you're ready to serve, sprinkle onions (both whites and greens) and celery over the potatoes. For dressing, whisk together the mayonnaise, Dijon mustard and ¼ cup (60 mL) vinegar, pour over the potatoes and gently toss. Add salt and pepper to taste.

4. Refrigerate until ready to serve. Just before serving, taste again and adjust salt, pepper and vinegar if necessary.

Makes about 26 cups (6 L), enough for 40 × ⅔ cup (160 mL) servings.

Classic Coleslaw

2 medium-sized, tight green cabbages, about 4 lbs (1.8 kg) total

1 lb (455 gr) carrots

10–12 green onions

6 stalks celery

1 bunch parsley, either curly or flat-leafed

DRESSING

½ cup (125 mL) olive or canola oil

⅓ cup (80 mL) apple cider vinegar

2 Tbsp (30 mL) lemon juice

1 cup (250 mL) good quality mayonnaise

1 cup (250 mL) sour cream or crème fraîche

Salt and pepper to taste

1. Cut cabbage into quarters and slice as thinly as possible into a large bowl. If you have a mandolin, even better.

2. Grate carrots into the bowl. Chop onions finely. Cut celery stalks on the diagonal into very thin slices—again, a mandolin is great for this job. Add onions and celery to the bowl.

3. Separate parsley leaves from the stems (save the stems for stock) and chop finely, then add to the bowl. Toss salad, cover and refrigerate until ready to dress and serve.

4. Whisk dressing ingredients together and refrigerate; 15 minutes before serving, pour over coleslaw and toss thoroughly. Add salt and pepper as necessary.

Makes about 35 cups (8.3 L), enough for 40 × ¾ cup (180 mL) servings.

Chocolate Cranberry Brownies

This recipe assumes you've still got some lowbush cranberries in the freezer in early August; if not, substitute dried cranberries or fresh wild raspberries or even blueberries, if they're ready. The important thing is the tang of the berries to offset the rich, deep chocolate flavour.

4 oz (110 g) unsweetened chocolate

½ cup (125 mL) butter

4 eggs at room temperature

1½ cups (350 mL) sugar

1 tsp (5 mL) vanilla

1 cup (250 mL) flour

¼ cup (60 mL) cocoa

1 cup (250 mL) wild lowbush cranberries (lingonberries) or substitute cultivated cranberries

1. Preheat the oven to 350F (180C) and grease a 9- × 13-inch (22.5- × 32-cm) baking dish.

2. Melt chocolate and butter together in a double boiler over boiling water. Stir to combine and cool to room temperature.

3. Beat eggs until light and foamy. Still beating, add sugar gradually until mixture is thick and creamy. Beat in vanilla.

4. In a separate bowl, whisk together flour and cocoa.

5. With a spoon, mix the cooled chocolate into the eggs and sugar, just until combined, then fold in flour with a few strokes—it's important not to over-mix.

6. Pour into baking dish and smooth into place with the back of a spoon or a spatula. Sprinkle berries evenly over top, pressing lightly into the batter.

7. Bake for about 25 minutes, until a tester inserted in the centre comes out with a few moist crumbs attached. Cool to room temperature before icing with ganache.

Makes about 42 brownies (each 1 × 1½ inches/ 2.5 × 3.8 cm).

GANACHE

5 oz (140 g) dark chocolate, at least 70 percent cocoa

1 cup (250 mL) 35 percent cream

3 Tbsp (45 mL) butter

1. Break chocolate in small pieces into a bowl.

2. Bring cream and butter to a boil over medium-high heat and pour over chocolate.

3. Place a plate over the bowl and wait for 5 minutes for the chocolate to melt.

4. Beat thoroughly until smooth and creamy. Cool to room temperature and then refrigerate to a spreadable consistency.

Makes about 2 cups (475 mL), enough to generously ice one pan of brownies with some left over.

Melted ganache is an excellent topping for Birch Syrup Ice Cream (page 38). Or, make truffles: bring ganache to room temperature, beat in 2 teaspoons (10 mL) of Spruce Tip Jelly (page 208), chill until firm and roll into truffles.

Birch Syrup Pecan Squares

Birch syrup plays a minor role in quantity but a major role in flavour in these traditional pecan squares. The squares were a special favourite with the Elders at the gathering. (Hint, hint, grandchildren!)

BASE

¾ cup (180 mL) butter, softened

½ cup (125 mL) sugar

1 egg

2 cups (475 mL) flour

½ tsp (2.5 mL) salt

1 tsp (5 mL) baking powder

TOPPING

¾ cup (180 mL) butter

1 cup (250 mL) brown sugar

2 Tbsp (30 mL) birch syrup (or substitute golden corn syrup)

2 cups (475 mL) chopped pecans

1. Preheat the oven to 350F (180C) and grease a 9- × 13-inch (22.5- × 32-cm) baking dish.

2. For the base: beat butter and sugar together until light, add egg and beat until fluffy.

3. Sift together dry ingredients and beat into the butter mixture.

4. Press into baking dish and bake for 10 minutes, or until base just begins to colour. Remove from heat, leaving the oven on, and let cool for 10 minutes before covering with topping.

5. For the topping: melt butter and sugar together over medium heat, stirring to combine. Stir in birch syrup, then stir in pecans.

6. Spoon onto the cooled base and spread evenly. Bake for 15 minutes, or until entire top is bubbling.

7. Remove and cool on a rack. Cut into squares when thoroughly cool.

Makes about 42 squares (each 1 × 1½ inches/2.5 × 3.8 cm).

Get out of Dodge Farewell Feast

MENU FOR SIX

Fingerling Potatoes with Spruce Tip Mayonnaise **79**

Spinach and White Peach Salad **79**

Smoked, Braised, Barbecued Moose Ribs **80**

Rubbed, Grilled Halibut **82**

Raspberry-Lemon Pudding Cakes **83**

Raspberry-Lemon Tart **84**

BONUS

Leftover Raspberry-Rhubarb Jam **85**

Time to Hit the Road, Gang

The Yukon is remarkable for an affliction that overtakes long-term residents at an alarming rate: a condition commonly known as "needing to get out of Dodge." Once struck, the sufferer assembles the family, farms out the pets, rents out the home and embarks on a lengthy adventure: a year counting hippopotami on the Zambezi; a trek, with donkey, through Peru; a sojourn in an apartment in downtown Montreal.

The Yukon is remarkable for an affliction that overtakes long-term residents at an alarming rate: a condition commonly known as "needing to get out of Dodge."

There is a happy side effect: before they go, these pilgrims purge their households of unwanted goods such as popcorn makers, hair dryers, and that overstuffed armchair found in the free store at the dump, thereby adding much-needed consumer durables to the local inventory and providing garage sale tourists with a lively schedule on a Saturday morning.

Sometimes, if we are lucky, they also purge their freezers. Such was the case in the summer of 2013, when the Moore–Campbell family of Whitehorse prepared for a year-long stay in Northern Ireland by divesting their freezer of a quantity of moose. Some of it came to me.

One afternoon before they left I called their house, hoping to trade some sockeye salmon for a bit of moose.

Carolyn Moore said, "We just happen to have a plateful of ribs defrosting in the fridge and you are welcome to them." Mere hours later, she dropped off six pounds of ribs and eight pounds of frozen sausage. "There's more where that came from," she said.

Six pounds of defrosted moose ribs is a lot of material to deal with at one time. My husband made a batch of Moose Ribs Braised in Espresso Stout, which took care of half the bounty. But four chunks of ribs remained. I called Gordon Campbell, chief cook for the Moore–Campbell team, and asked for his advice.

I should mention that Gordon was from 1997 to 2002 proprietor of Blackstone Café in downtown Whitehorse, where he ruled the kitchen with a cheerful hand, dispensing grilled chicken and avocado sandwiches in the hundreds to the starving masses. I was a cook in his kitchen.

I was not an easy employee, challenging his ideas and questioning his methods at every turn, gripped by the conviction that I knew best. But our friendship survived, and now I'm a frequent guest at his home, where Gordon is the kind of host who calmly produces acres of delicious halibut ceviche, barbecued moose burgers and roasted sockeye salmon while the chaos of children, guests, dogs, a guinea pig and a bearded dragon rages around him. (On these occasions Carolyn's role is to keep calm and carry on dispensing the festive cup.)

Chaos raged on the Saturday I called for advice; the

*The long and lonely Dempster Highway from the North Klondike Highway near Dawson to Inuvik,
Northwest Territories is famous for its beauty and its ability to puncture tires.*

family was packing. I could hear the rip of packing tape and the shouted exchange of clothes-sorting instructions in the background. Cheerful as ever, Gordon described the dish he was making at that very moment: moose ribs rubbed with spices, smoked, braised in the oven, then finished on the barbecue—slathered with a sauce made from the reduced braising liquid. He was at step one: making the rub. I decided this was the recipe for me. He warned me: it was going to take two days.

For the next several hours I pestered him with phone calls: What are you putting in the rub, how long are you smoking the ribs, what are you braising them in and for how long and, finally, do you let the ribs sit for a while to firm up before barbecuing?

Because I still harbour traces of the conviction that I know best, I didn't *exactly* follow Gordon's suggestions, except for the long, long cooking time. These were short

ribs, and as he said, they need long cooking to thoroughly break down the tough bits. "Once, I braised them for eight hours, and they were absolutely fabulous. The only thing I didn't like was they became detached from the bone, which is okay for me but not for my kids. They like to eat ribs with their hands." When cooking ribs, he said, "it's important to consider your audience."

For my rub, I roasted cumin in a frying pan on the stove; this resulted in nostalgia for the old Blackstone Café days, when downtown Whitehorse was suffused with the aroma of roasting cumin seeds at seven in the morning, and I would walk to work through the sleepy back alleys, following the smell to the Blackstone door, happy in the knowledge that Gordon was busy making cumin-lime mayonnaise and work was underway.

Dry rubs are a great way to prepare large or irregular cuts of meat like moose short ribs for the barbecue or oven; you don't have to turn the meat constantly as you

Gordon and Rufus Campbell watch closely over moose ribs grilling on the barbecue. The dish takes two days to prepare.

For smoking his ribs, Gordon used a simple smoker, essentially an aluminum box with an electric element in the bottom and a frying pan full of wood chips set on the element. With this model, in ideal conditions (outside temperature of at least 10C, no wind), the interior temperature reaches a maximum of about 75C, or 165F, not hot enough to cook the meat unless you leave it in for several hours. Three hours is enough to give the meat a nice, smoky flavour and the meat will still be quite pink. The oven-braising afterwards ensures that food safety requirements are satisfied.

I used a Bradley smoker with the oven temperature set at 140F (60C) and smoked the ribs for three hours, then braised them for one and a half hours in a 320F (160C) oven the first day. The next day I braised them for another three hours. Neither Gordon nor I had time to finish the dish in one day, but these ribs are more flavourful if done over two days. This is definitely a dish for a weekend feast.

After braising, the next step was to remove the ribs from the pot, strain out the vegetables, skim the fat from the braising liquid, reduce the liquid to a thick sauce and then slather it onto the ribs before finishing them for 10 minutes on a hot grill. The result was a tender, dark, smoky, sweet-and-salty rib in a beautiful, complex sauce.

For those who don't have access to a smoker, try increasing the amount of smoked paprika in the rub, or adding a teaspoon or so of liquid smoke to the braising liquid. With this option, I'd leave the rubbed ribs wrapped in plastic in the fridge overnight, and braise for about five hours.

A couple of days after this rib extravaganza, Carolyn revealed that she didn't really enjoy moose ribs, there was just too much meat and fat. So I felt honour-bound to create a halibut rub, just for her. I feel sure that Gordon will tweak it. Because like me, and perhaps rightly, Gordon is utterly convinced that he knows best.

would in a marinade, and the rub penetrates the meat more effectively than a marinade would. (Marinades are best for flatter, thinner cuts.)

In researching dry rubs I learned that the salt draws moisture out of the meat, and some of the salt (not all) dissolves in the moisture. The dissolved salt is drawn back into the meat by osmosis, bringing the spices with it. The reason you wrap the rubbed meat in plastic and let it sit from one hour to overnight is to enable this dissolving–absorbing process. The salt tenderizes the meat, and melts the interior and exterior fat as the meat cooks. Then, on the barbecue or in the smoker, the sugar in the rub caramelizes on the surface of the meat, adding both colour and flavour.

Fingerling Potatoes with Spruce Tip Mayonnaise

If the children are already eating ribs with their hands, why not fingerling potatoes with their fingers?

1 lb (455 gr) fingerling potatoes

1 tsp (5 mL) coarse salt

1–2 Tbsp (15–30 mL) olive oil

Spruce Tip Mayonnaise,
recipe on page 232

1. Wash and dry potatoes. Cut away any blemishes and toss potatoes in coarse salt and olive oil.

2. Spread potatoes in a grilling basket and cook them on a barbecue over medium heat, tossing and stirring frequently until done, about 30 minutes. Keep warm while ribs and halibut are grilling.

3. Serve with a bowl of Spruce Tip Mayonnaise for dipping.

Makes four to six servings.

Spinach and White Peach Salad

In late July white peaches from the Okanagan start showing up in the Yukon. I discovered white peaches through my husband, who grew up on the European variety and has a fierce nostalgia for these savoury-sweet beauties.

8 cups (2 L) baby spinach leaves, rinsed and dried

2 ripe white peaches, sliced

3 green onions, finely chopped

¼ cup (60 mL) sunflower seeds, toasted

¼ cup (60 mL) feta cheese, crumbled (optional)

SUMMERY VINAIGRETTE:

2 Tbsp fireweed flower syrup (or substitute white grape juice)

2 Tbsp white wine vinegar

6 Tbsp olive oil

Salt and pepper to taste

1. Combine salad ingredients in a large bowl.

2. Whisk together vinaigrette ingredients and toss with salad.

Makes six to eight servings.

Smoked, Braised, Barbecued Moose Ribs

THE RUB

1 Tbsp (15 mL) kosher salt

1 Tbsp (15 mL) brown sugar

1 Tbsp (15 mL) toasted cumin seeds

1 Tbsp (15 mL) coriander seeds

1 Tbsp (15 mL) onion powder

1 Tbsp (15 mL) garlic powder

1 Tbsp (15 mL) dried spruce tips

1 tsp (5 mL) smoked mild paprika

1 tsp (5 mL) dried orange peel

1 tsp (5 mL) each white and black pepper

3 lbs (1.4 kg) moose short ribs

1. Combine dry ingredients.
2. Rinse the ribs briefly under cold running water and thoroughly pat dry.
3. Coat the ribs on all sides with the rub, pressing the mixture into the meat, then wrap tightly in plastic and refrigerate, from 1 hour to overnight.
4. Hot-smoke for 3 to 4 hours at 140F (60C). While the ribs smoke, prepare the braising liquid.

THE BRAISING LIQUID

1 Tbsp (15 mL) each oil and butter

1 stalk celery, chopped

1 medium onion, chopped

1 medium carrot, chopped

2 cloves garlic, chopped

1 inch (2.5 cm) fresh ginger, peeled and chopped

1 tsp (5 mL) juniper berries, crushed

2 Tbsp (30 mL) tomato paste

3 cups (710 mL) strong bison or moose stock

2 cups (475 mL) red wine

½ cup (125 mL) birch syrup

1 Tbsp (15 mL) soy sauce

1. Preheat the oven to 325F (160C).
2. Heat oil and butter in a 6-quart (6-L) ovenproof dish; add vegetables and sauté until soft over medium-low heat.
3. Add garlic, ginger and juniper berries and sauté another few minutes.
4. Stir in the tomato paste; cook for two minutes, then add remaining ingredients.
5. Bring to the boil over medium-low heat, and add smoked moose ribs.
6. Place in oven and cook for 3 to 4 hours.
7. Remove ribs from the pot and let sit at room temperature while you finish the sauce.

THE SAUCE

1. Strain the braising liquid and remove the fat that's floating on top. (If you haven't yet invested in a fat strainer, think about it. It will save you much time and headache.)

2. Return the sauce to the heat in a wide saucepan and simmer until reduced to a thick, spreadable consistency.

3. Coat the ribs with the sauce and grill on a preheated barbecue for about 10 minutes, or until ribs are slightly charred and aromatic.

Makes four to six servings.

From left to right: The palette of spices. Sauce and ribs, ready to be put together. Rufus, Ewan and Claire Campbell tuck into their favourite summer meal.

The Klondike River flows from the Oglivie Mountains to Dawson, where it joins the Yukon River.

Rubbed, Grilled Halibut

1 tsp (5 mL) fennel seed

1 Tbsp (15 mL) dried spruce tips

1 tsp (5 mL) black peppercorns

1 tsp (5 mL) juniper berries

1 Tbsp (15 mL) brown sugar

1 tsp (5 mL) kosher salt

1 lb (455 gr) halibut steaks or fillets

1. Crush the fennel seed, spruce tips, peppercorns and juniper berries in a mortar and pestle, then combine with the remaining dry ingredients.

2. Rinse and pat dry the halibut, then coat with rub, pressing it in with your hands.

3. Wrap tightly in plastic and refrigerate for 1 or 2 hours.

4. Preheat barbecue. Oil the grill, then add halibut and grill for about 3 to 4 minutes on each side, depending on thickness. A 1-inch (2.5-cm) piece takes about 5 minutes on each side. The fish is ready when it's opaque all the way through. Halibut is easy to overcook, so if in doubt, remove it early. It will continue to cook for a minute or two off the heat.

Makes four servings.

Raspberry-Lemon Pudding Cakes

Who does not love the miracle of cake on top and pudding underneath? This childhood favourite will find an appreciative audience with the adults too.

2 large eggs, separated

½ cup (125 mL) granulated sugar

3 Tbsp (45 mL) flour

2 Tbsp (30 mL) melted butter

Grated zest of 1 lemon

3 Tbsp (45 mL) fresh lemon juice

1 cup (250 mL) milk

Pinch of cream of tartar

2 cups (475 mL) wild raspberries, divided*

½ cup (125 mL) 35 percent cream

*If you're using frozen berries, defrost in a strainer and save the juice for Leftover Raspberry-Rhubarb Jam (page 85).

1. Preheat oven to 350F (180C) and place a rack in the centre of the oven. Set eight ½-cup (125-mL) ramekins in a 9- × 13-inch (22.5- × 32-cm) baking pan.

2. Whisk egg yolks and granulated sugar until thick and creamy. Whisk in flour, butter, lemon zest and juice, and the milk until blended.

3. In another bowl, beat egg whites and cream of tartar until whites hold stiff peaks when beater is lifted. Stir a quarter of whites into yolk mixture until blended, then gently fold in remaining whites. Fold in half of the raspberries.

4. Spoon batter into ramekins. Pour enough boiling water into baking pan to come halfway up sides of ramekins.

5. Bake for 30 to 35 minutes, or until cake layers are set and tops are golden. Start checking after 25 minutes.

6. Remove ramekins from water, place on a rack and let cool to room temperature, about 35 minutes. The cakes can be refrigerated overnight, tightly covered, but are best served at room temperature.

7. When ready to serve, whip cream and pile each ramekin with a few berries and a dollop of whipped cream.

Makes eight cakes.

Raspberry-Lemon Tart

For this recipe you'll need a 9-inch (22.5-cm) tart pan with a removable base. If you're using an ordinary pie or quiche pan, the filling will be deeper, so add a few minutes to the cooking time. Make the tart shell first and work on the filling after.

CRUST

1 cup (250 mL) flour

⅓ cup (80 mL) icing sugar

Pinch of salt

½ cup (125 mL) cold unsalted butter, cut into small pieces

1. Place flour, sugar and salt in the bowl of a food processor and pulse to combine. Add butter and process until the pastry clumps together in the bowl. Note that this takes a minute; you may be tempted to add water but don't. If you don't have a food processor, work the butter into the flour with your fingertips and knead it briefly before transferring it to the pan.

2. Transfer pastry to the tart pan and press evenly onto the bottom and up the sides of the pan.

3. Prick bottom of pastry with a fork and place in the freezer for 30 minutes. (The freezing will help to reduce shrinkage during baking.)

4. Fifteen minutes before baking, preheat oven to 375F (190C) and place a rack in the centre of the oven. Place pastry in the oven directly from the freezer and bake for 20 minutes, or until the edges are just beginning to colour. Remove from oven and let cool to room temperature.

This shell, if fully baked, works well for cooked fillings such as chocolate or lemon custard. In this case, bake for 30 to 35 minutes in total and cool to room temperature before filling. Don't bake pastry any more than one day ahead or the flavour will deteriorate.

FILLING

For a recipe that uses up the juiced lemon rinds, see Leftover Raspberry-Rhubarb Jam, next page.

2 medium lemons

3 egg yolks

½ cup (125 mL) sugar

¾ cup (180 mL) 35 percent cream

1½ cups (350 mL) wild raspberries

1. Preheat the oven to 300F (150C) and place a rack in the centre.

2. Grate the zest of both lemons and reserve. Juice the lemons. Ideally there will be 4 tablespoons (60 mL) of juice, for a tart lemony flavour.

3. Beat egg yolks, sugar and lemon juice until thick and creamy. Whisk in the zest and cream.

4. Scatter the berries over the bottom of the crust and pour the filling over top. Bake for 35 to 40 minutes, or until the filling is set in the centre.

5. Remove from the oven, transfer the tart to a rack and cool to room temperature.

6. Cut into wedges and serve as is, or accompany with vanilla ice cream and raspberry coulis or whipped cream sweetened with a dash of birch or maple syrup. But it really doesn't need any of those extras; this tart is complete and delicious on its own.

Makies 8 to 10 servings.

Leftover Raspberry-Rhubarb Jam

Use the following amounts as general guidelines only, and adjust according to what you have on hand. This recipe is based on what I had in the fridge after a session of recipe testing. If you don't have homemade pectin, don't worry about it; the lemon adds tons of gelling power, and you can always just cook the jam a bit longer. For more tips on making jam, see Jam and Jelly-Making Tips, page 202.

½ cup (125 mL) frozen raspberries, thawed and strained

4 cups (1 L) chopped frozen rhubarb, thawed and strained

2½ cups (600 mL) sugar, divided

Leftover rinds of 2 lemons, finely chopped

3 cups (710 mL) juice from thawed fruits

1 cup (250 mL) Homemade Pectin, recipe on page 202 (optional)

1. Combine raspberries, rhubarb, 2 cups (475 mL) sugar and lemon rinds in a saucepan, bring to the boil over medium heat and cook, stirring frequently but gently (so as not to break up the rhubarb too much) for 20 minutes.

2. Combine fruit juices and remaining sugar in a separate saucepan and bring to the boil. Reduce heat to medium-high, cooking the mixture rapidly down to 1 cup (250 mL).

3. Add reduced juice to the fruit mixture, along with pectin if using. Stir to combine and continue to cook until the jam has reached the gelling stage.

4. Pour into sterilized 1-cup (250-mL) jars using a funnel; clean tops of jars with a hot, damp cloth, and seal. Process in a hot-water bath for 10 minutes, adding 2 minutes for every 1,000 metres above sea level.

Makes five or six 1-cup (250-mL) jars

Fall

Fall in the Boreal: colours dug from the earth
fill the market stalls with purple, orange,
yellow and gold; the same colours ignite
the forest and burn in the alpine and on the
tundra. Woodsmoke perfumes the air with
resin; people are lighting their stoves again.
Rigel pulses in the western sky; we haven't
seen a star since May. The auroras return
and the swans depart, writing their message
on the sky: *fall, fall, fall*. The blackcurrants
ripen in the garden on the Vindelälven. Our
knees are stained red with lingonberry juice.
The rivers and lakes are a deeper blue. Kalix
löjrom comes into season, and the Baltic
Herring Fair fills Helsinki's Market Square.
Moose battle in the meadows; bears fatten
on berries; spawned salmon fertilize the
shore. Lichens crunch underfoot. We hunt
and gather, dig and harvest, preserve and
store. The most urban inhabitant becomes a
child of nature now; all she has to do is look
up. Breathe in. Pick a berry. Cook a beet.

*Fall on the Dempster Highway.
Hikers and road warriors make pilgramages
north to see the transformation.*

Early Fall Houseboat Tour on Lewes River

MENU FOR EIGHT

Prohibition Cocktail: The Bee's Knees **92**

Modernist Celery and Olives **92**

Wild Berry and Gewürztraminer Soup **94**

Honey-Mead Glazed Carrots **95**

Green Salad with Nectarines
and Spruce Tip Oil Vinaigrette **95**

Dall Sheep Steaks with Sage Butter **96**

Turnip Gratin **97**

Honey Cake with Crème Fraîche **98**

A Feast for the Riverboat Era

Iregret that I never got to ride a riverboat downriver to Dawson or take a holiday cruise in a keelboat on Tagish Lake from Carcross to Ben-My-Chree. The era of paddlewheeler travel ended in the early 1950s, when an all-weather road from Whitehorse was pushed through to Mayo and then to Dawson. The decommissioned boats slowly disappeared from the landscape: sold outside the territory, ransacked for wood or sunk. By the mid-1970s, all that remained were five boats in dry dock: the *Casca*, the *Whitehorse* and SS *Klondike II* in Whitehorse, SS *Keno* in Dawson and SS *Tutshi* in Carcross.

The White Pass & Yukon Route Railroad donated SS *Klondike II* to the federal government, and in 1966 a crew of 12 inched the sternwheeler along Front Street to its current location at the south end of town over a period of three weeks, with the help of wooden rollers and eight tonnes of Palmolive Princess soap.

The *Casca* and the *Whitehorse* remained in the shipyards and became a playground for local kids and an occasional shelter for young travellers. On June 21, 1974 my husband, Hector, age 28, was across the river on the Long Lake Road when he crested the hill in his van and saw smoke rising from the boats' chimneys in the old shipyards. He thought someone had fired up the boilers. He stopped the van, and as he watched, the decks burst into flames. People came running. Firemen appeared with hoses. The air roared and crackled and in fifteen minutes it was so hot, even across the river, that Hector was afraid the windows would pop out of the van, and he drove on.

The *Whitehorse Star* tells us that down in the shipyards, a large crowd gathered to watch the fire. Old-timers wept. The boats burned to the ground in two hours. A White Pass & Yukon Route employee said, "The Yukon just lost a bit of its soul." In the *Whitehorse Star* photograph of the burning ships, Hector's van is just visible up in the right-hand corner.

The Yukon government bought the *Tutshi* in 1971 and was just finishing a massive restoration of the boat in 1990 when it too burnt to the ground. Today only SS *Klondike II* and SS *Keno* remain. But we can take heart: both boats are Parks Canada national historic sites open for guided or self-guided interpretive tours from May to September every year.

My favourite compartment in SS *Klondike* is the long galley, lit by a series of tiny windows up near the ceiling. The shelves are packed with white and green restaurant crockery and vintage cans and packages; there's an old coal-fired stove, enamel coffee pots and saucepans, no sink and not much counter space. From here, the galley crew of mess boy, pantry man, second cook and chief cook produced seven-course meals for the crew and Stewart River- or Dawson-bound passengers.

It was the chief steward's job to compose the menu. Fred Walsh was chief steward in 1929, 1936 and 1942 and clearly enjoyed that aspect of his work. There's an aura of fun pervading one of his 1942 menus: desserts such as Bonanza Plum Pudding with Hard Rock Sauce, Sourdough Blueberry Pie and Cheechako Apple Pie, followed by Nuggets of Cheese (and Christie's Crackers!).

Peter Heebink's houseboat chugs along the Yukon River (above), while SS Klondike II *(right) is in permanent dry dock at the south end of Whitehorse*

Mr. Walsh appears to have wanted his passengers to know where their food came from: his menu features Dawson City Tomatoes, Yukon Radishes, Marsh Lake Whitefish, Boiled Brisket of Pelly River Beef, Stuffed Haunch of Carmacks Veal and Roast Loin of Stewart River Moose with Jelly. Meals started with a Prohibition Cocktail, a nod to those concoctions invented when booze was illicit and just plain bad, and the mixer had to work hard to disguise the flavour of bathtub gin or rotgut rye.

SS *Klondike II*, like its predecessor the *Klondike I*, was intended primarily as a freight vessel to haul silver ore from the Mayo and Keno mines; passengers were a lucrative sideline. But SS *Tutshi* was built by the British Yukon Navigation Company at Carcross in 1917 expressly as an excursion boat for the thriving tourist trade. The *Tutshi*'s menus from 1936 are written in a more sober tone than the *Klondike*'s, but the fare is familiar: Radishes and

Tomatoes with Queen Olives, Lake Whitefish, Grilled Loin of Moose, Haunch of Mountain Sheep... But if the menus were not so lively, the waiters were: throughout the summer of 1952 two of them played the piano on the freight deck for dances, and tourists swung and twirled on a canvas floor laid over the boards.

The paddlewheeler era has ended, but the thrill of evening cruises on lakes and rivers has not. Peter Heebink lives on the shores of Marsh Lake, about 40 kilometres south of Whitehorse, and though he owns a canoe and a kayak, their capacity for guests is small, and Peter likes to entertain. So he built a houseboat, essentially a plywood box on a pair of pontoons with an engine in the stern and a deck out front.

The paddlewheeler era has ended, but the thrill of evening cruises on lakes and rivers has not.

When the ice is off the lake the houseboat goes in, and all summer long and into the fall he takes small parties of friends on tours of the stretch of Yukon River between Marsh Lake and the dam, the stretch known as the Lewes River. There are moments of excitement, such as when too many passengers crowd the front deck and a surge of lake washes over the boards, causing shrieks and a restrained rush to the stern. But Peter strives to keep these moments to a minimum, and generally the boat glides along the river in a sedate manner, the plates stay on the table and the diners behave.

In the golden early fall of 2013 one of Peter's guests was his fellow Marsh Laker Katherine Alexander, who keeps bees on her porch and entertained the other passengers with tales from her apiary. Katherine has named her queen bees after her grandmothers: Margot, who kept bees herself during the Second World War in the town of Turriff in Aberdeenshire; and Delphine, a French Canadian who married a Scot and moved to Los Angeles after the First World War to become a silent film actress. Delphine and her husband were extras in several films, and though their careers did not progress Delphine kept her spirit and, as Katherine says, "wore stiletto heels until she fell off them at age 88 and broke her hip." Against

Fireweed syrup and soda water make a refreshing alternative when a break from Prohibition Cocktails is indicated.

all odds Delphine the queen bee survived a cold spring; Katherine discovered she was still alive when she introduced new queens into the hive and they kept dying. Delphine was doing them in.

Delphine and her workers and drones come from New Zealand via Alberta; they collect pollen from fireweed flowers and the honey they produce is fireweed honey, light and fragrant. For our autumn feast, Katherine provided a jar of honey and a growler of mead, and the spirit of queens Margot and Delphine infused the menu. The Prohibition cocktail that starts this dinner off is The Bee's Knees, made with gin, honey and lemon, and brings to mind images of Delphine dancing the Charleston in her stilettos in Prohibition-era Los Angeles, tourists twirling on the freight deck of SS *Tutshi*, and SS *Klondike* Chief Steward Fred Walsh smiling in his office as he composed his menu in 1942.

Houseboat dinner guests enjoy the evening sun on the Yukon River. The guest in the life jacket was the captain's right-hand man.

Prohibition Cocktail: The Bee's Knees

1 Tbsp (15 mL) honey
1 Tbsp (15 mL) hot water
1 tsp (5 mL) lemon juice
1½ oz (40 mL) gin

1. Make honey syrup by combining honey and hot water. Whisk until honey is dissolved and allow to cool.

2. Shake honey syrup and remaining ingredients over cracked ice and strain into a cocktail glass. Garnish with a thin slice of lemon.

Makes one cocktail.

Modernist Celery and Olives

Assemble the following on a large platter for a contemporary take on an old-fashioned paddlewheeler appetizer.

GRILLED CELERY

½ tsp (2.5 mL) coarse sea salt
½ tsp (2.5 mL) crushed juniper berries
1 bunch celery, washed and trimmed
2 Tbsp (30 mL) olive oil

1. Heat barbecue to medium. Combine salt and juniper berries. Brush both sides of celery stalks with olive oil and sprinkle with salt mixture.

2. Grill celery for 4 to 6 minutes, turning once to mark both sides. The celery should be softened but still have some crunch.

3. Let cool, then cut on the diagonal into ¼-inch (0.6-cm) slices.

SAUTÉED GREEN OLIVES WITH SPRUCE TIPS

Olives with pits are more flavourful than the pitted ones.

1 Tbsp (15 mL) olive oil
1½ cups (375 mL) large green olives
2 cloves garlic, minced
1 Tbsp (15 mL) dried spruce tips, chopped

1. Heat oil in a saucepan over medium heat, add olives, garlic and spruce tips and sauté until the olives are heated through, about 5 to 6 minutes.

GRILLED HALLOUMI

The halloumi from the Lendrum-Ross farm on Lake Laberge is a favourite in Whitehorse. There are good varieties of halloumi available in the big supermarkets, but whenever you can, search out the artisanal producers in your area.

8 oz (225 gr) halloumi

Olive oil

1 lemon, cut into wedges

1. Preheat barbecue to medium or oven broiler to high. If using oven, place top rack 4 inches (10 cm) from the broiler.

2. Slice halloumi into ½-inch (1.25-cm) slices. Brush olive oil on both sides.

3. On the grill: brush grill with olive oil. Grill halloumi for 2 to 3 minutes per side, or until halloumi is lightly browned and just crisped.
   In the oven: arrange halloumi slices on a lightly oiled baking sheet and place in oven. Broil for 3 to 4 minutes per side, or until done, as above.

4. Remove from heat and squeeze lemon over top. Garnish with extra lemon wedges.

Makes eight servings.

Wild Berry and Gewürztraminer Soup

4 cups (1 L) wild blueberries

1 cup (250 mL) wild lowbush cranberries (lingonberries) or substitute cultivated cranberries

1 cup (250 mL) blackcurrants

3 Tbsp (45 mL) birch syrup

2 Tbsp (30 mL) honey

2 Tbsp (30 mL) lemon juice

2 cups (475 mL) Gewürztraminer, sweetish Riesling or mildly oaked Chardonnay

½ tsp (2.5 mL) salt

½ cup (125 mL) crème fraîche

Mint leaves for garnish

1. Combine all ingredients except crème fraîche in a medium-sized saucepan. Bring to the boil over medium-high heat. Reduce heat and simmer for 15 minutes.

2. Remove from heat, purée soup and press through a sieve, getting as much pulp as possible into the liquid. (Save the remaining pulp for muffins or scones.)

3. Taste and adjust seasoning, adding a splash more wine, lemon juice, sweetener or salt as needed. (Berries vary in sweetness and flavour.)

4. Serve warm, garnished with a spoonful of crème fraîche and mint leaves.

Makes about 8 cups (2 L).

Green Salad with Nectarines and Spruce Tip Oil Vinaigrette

Nectarines from the Okanagan are one of the great pleasures of August. Here the sunny sweetness of the fruit combines nicely with the lemony tang of spruce. For the greens, try a mixture of arugula, mizuna and the crisp inner leaves of romaine lettuce.

6 cups (1.4 L) fresh seasonal greens

2 nectarines, pitted, quartered and sliced crosswise

SPRUCE TIP VINAIGRETTE

6 Tbsp (90 mL) Spruce Tip Oil, recipes on page 230

2 Tbsp (30 mL) white wine vinegar

½ tsp (2.5 mL) freshly ground white pepper

1 tsp (5 mL) coarse sea salt

1 tsp (5 mL) birch syrup

1. Whisk together vinaigrette ingredients. Just before serving, toss with greens and nectarines. Serve at once.

Makes eight servings.

Honey-Mead Glazed Carrots

2 lbs (910 gr) carrots

1 tsp (5 mL) coarse sea salt

2 Tbsp (30 mL) butter

2 Tbsp (30 mL) honey

½ cup (125 mL) mead (or substitute honey ale or lager)

Fresh edible flowers for garnish

1. If carrots are small and tender, wash and slice each once lengthwise. If longer and/or older, wash, slice lengthwise in half and then crosswise into 3.5- to 4-inch (7.5- to 10-cm) pieces. Cut thicker pieces in half lengthwise once more so carrots are an even thickness. Toss carrots with salt.

2. Melt butter and honey in a large cast iron frying pan, whisking to combine. Add salted carrots in a single layer and sauté over medium heat, turning once or twice until carrots start to turn brown and caramelize.

3. Add mead and continue to cook until mead is evaporated and carrots are shiny and glazed.

4. Remove from heat and pile into a serving dish. Garnish with flowers.

Makes eight servings.

Dall Sheep Steaks with Sage Butter

Dall sheep live high in the Yukon mountains, favouring the cliff faces and rocky outcrops that protect them from predators. From the Skagway Road south of Carcross or the Alaska Highway in Kluane they are distant white dots moving far up among the rocks or resting on impossibly angled slopes, and it's a thrill to see them.

The sheep hunt opens every year on August 1. A sheep hunt is logistically challenging, physically demanding and often unsuccessful, which gives rise to contradictory feelings—happiness for the animals that got away and sadness there will be no sheep meat in the freezer this winter. A gift of sheep meat is a fine gift indeed. In the summer of 2013 the guys that work on Peter Heebink's construction crew were successful in their hunt, and shared their bounty with the houseboat diners. We were doubly grateful to hunter and animal.

The boys did their own butchering, and the packages were simply labelled "sheep steak"; I didn't know if they were sirloin tip, backstrap or rib-eye but they were incredibly tender. More and more, I'm convinced that tender cuts of wild meat are best (1) cooked rare and (2) prepared as simply as possible. So that's what we did for the houseboat feast.

1 tsp (5 mL) salt

1 tsp (5 mL) pepper

1 Tbsp (15 mL) pasture sage (*Artemesia frigida*), chopped finely

2 lbs (910 gr) sheep steaks

¼ cup (60 mL) Sage Butter

1. Combine salt, pepper and sage and sprinkle each piece of steak with mixture. Stack two or three pieces together and wrap tightly in plastic wrap. Refrigerate for at least two hours.

2. Heat barbecue as hot as you can get it. Brush grill with oil, arrange pieces of steak on grill and cook for no more than 90 seconds per side. Allow meat to rest for at least 10 minutes.

3. Slice against the grain and on the diagonal into thin slices, arrange on a platter and dot with circles of sage butter.

Makes eight servings.

SAGE BUTTER

¼ cup (60 mL) salted butter, softened

1 tsp (5 mL) dried spruce tips, chopped

1 Tbsp (15 mL) pasture sage, chopped

1. Combine butter and herbs thoroughly, transfer to a piece of waxed paper and roll into a log. Chill for at least an hour.

2. When ready to serve, cut into thin slices and place on warm meat or vegetables. Cut additional slices and serve on ice in a small bowl.

Makes ¼ cup (60 mL).

Note: if using a glass baking dish, make sure it's safe to go directly from fridge to oven.

Turnip Gratin

Late August is the time of abundance in the north, and the Fireweed Market in Whitehorse brims with produce. At that time of year the white onions are creamy and sweet, the turnips as crisp as apples.

I usually cook scalloped potatoes by first making a béchamel sauce to pour over the parboiled potatoes. But fresh turnips have so much juice, it's better to line each layer of vegetables with flour and dots of butter, and pour the milk and cream into the corners of the pan. With this method the juices are absorbed effectively and the end result is creamy, not watery. If you're using older turnips, parboil the slices for 1 minute, plunge in cold water and dry in a tea towel before layering in the pan.

3½ lbs (1.6 kg) white and purple turnips
2 medium fresh white onions
⅓ cup (80 mL) flour
Salt and pepper
⅓ cup (80 mL) butter, divided
1¾ cups (415 mL) 2 percent milk
1¾ cup (415 mL) 10 percent cream
½ cup (125 mL) bread crumbs

1. Peel turnips and slice into ¼-inch (0.6-cm) pieces. Cut larger pieces in half. Slice onions thinly.

2. Butter a 9- × 13-inch (22.5- × 32-cm) pan. Arrange a layer of turnips and a layer of onions in the pan, sprinkle liberally with flour, sprinkle with salt and pepper and dot with butter. Repeat until all the vegetables are used, ending with a layer of onions. Reserve a bit of butter for the crumb topping. (Or get more!)

3. Combine milk and cream and pour into the four corners of the pan; the liquid should come to within ¼ inch (0.6 cm) of the top layer.

4. Sprinkle the bread crumbs over top of the pan and dot with butter.

5. Bake uncovered in a 350F (180C) oven for 45 minutes. Let sit for at least 10 minutes before cutting. Or, if making ahead of the feast, eliminate bread crumbs and butter, cool to room temperature and refrigerate. When ready to serve, sprinkle bread crumbs over top, dot with butter and reheat for 20 to 30 minutes, uncovered, at 350F (180C).

Makes 8 to 12 servings.

Honey Cake with Crème Fraîche

Many honey cake recipes suggest using oil, but I prefer the flavour of butter.

½ cup (125 mL) honey

2 Tbsp (30 mL) whiskey

½ cup (125 mL) freshly made espresso

¾ cup (180 mL) butter, softened

½ cup (125 mL) brown sugar

2 eggs, at room temperature

1¾ cups (415 mL) flour

1 tsp (5 mL) baking powder

½ tsp (2.5 mL) baking soda

½ tsp (2.5 mL) salt

1 tsp (5 mL) cinnamon

½ tsp (2.5 mL) white pepper

½ tsp (2.5 mL) freshly ground nutmeg

Garnish: crème fraîche lightly sweetened with honey, and fresh berries

1. Preheat oven to 350F (180C) and grease a 9-inch (22.5-cm) square pan.

2. Whisk the honey and whiskey into the hot espresso. Set aside to cool.

3. Cream butter, add sugar and beat until light and fluffy. Beat in eggs one at a time.

4. In a separate bowl, whisk together dry ingredients. Beat into the butter and egg mixture in 3 parts, alternating with the cooled coffee and honey mixture.

5. Bake for 30 minutes or until a wooden skewer inserted in the centre of the cake comes out clean.

6. Cool for 15 minutes on a rack before removing from pan. Serve at room temperature with a dollop of sweetened crème fraîche and a scattering of berries.

Makes eight servings.

fika!

MENU

∾

Labrador Tea **104**

Flourless Chocolate Hazelnut Cake **104**

Cranberry-Lemon Squares **105**

Finnish _Pulla_ Bread with Blueberry Filling **106**

Almond and Fireweed Jelly Thumbprint Cookies **107**

BONUS!

Doris Brändström's _Sandsopp_ Soup **108**

∾

The Power of Fika!

In Sweden the coffee break, or *fika*, is taken seriously. You don't just drive through Timmy's for a double-double and a honey cruller, you take the time to go to a café or gather around the table with friends or family, drink a strong coffee with a delicious treat, and chat. Fika is not something you fit in on your way to something else; it's the thing you're doing right now and requires your full attention. Visitors to Sweden are delighted to discover fika—not just the excellent coffee and new and yummy sweets or sandwiches, but the ritual and the celebration of food and friendship.

Fika is not something you fit in on your way to something else; it's the thing you're doing right now and requires your full attention.

Hector and I first had fika without knowing it, at the house of Karin Mellin, a friend of a mutual friend, in Östersund; we were invited for dinner but asked to come at four. We arrived late, and there on the coffee table was a pot of hot coffee, another of hot milk and a spread of three different goodies: whey butter (*messmör*, which tastes like a tangy, caramelized cream cheese) spread between pieces of soft flatbread, a cranberry-lemon sponge cake and beautiful almond rolls. At this point in our culinary travels we were starting to feel bilious, and

I could tell by the way Hector avoided my eye that he too wondered how we were going to consume this small feast *and* dinner, but we tucked in and our hosts smiled at our appetites.

Later we learned that traditionally, it's a matter of pride to offer at least three goodies, and if you're talking cookies, seven is best. The fika habit is taking hold in Canada, as our love affair with Scandinavian cuisine continues, and we see fika turning up on restaurant menus: in the fall of 2013 the Finnish Karelia Kitchen in Toronto featured "At Least Seven Kinds of Cookies" at 75 cents each or nine for five dollars.

Fika can be as elaborate or as simple as you like. We first got together with Chef Susanne Jonsson over a fika of coffee and an almond croissant. We met in the city of Umeå in Norrbotten, at Nya Konditoriet (known locally as NK), an old-fashioned café on an upper floor in a 1920s heritage building. This was a thoughtful choice; a glimpse of an older Umeå, and a comfortable place to have our first in-person conversation about Swedish food, both traditional and modern.

Susanne became our tour guide through Umeå, a lively university town of leafy boulevards and busy squares situated on the wide Ume River, which drains into the Gulf of Bothnia on the Baltic Sea. The streets were clogged with construction, for the city was in the midst of several major civic projects in preparation for 2014,

Reindeer in the woods near Vännäs in Norbotten, Sweden.

when it would be the European Capital of Culture. But Susanne negotiated the city like a pro, and we visited some of her favourite culinary destinations, including a modern kitchen store–deli that sold beautiful rolling pins, but not the spiky kind for rolling out knäckebröd I'd been looking for since Östersund. Dang! We ate lunch at the casually elegant Viktoria, one of the best restaurants in the region. Here Hector ate his favourite meal in all of Scandinavia—rare roast beef in a rich reduction, served on root vegetables with horseradish crème fraîche. Simple, straightforward and delicious. Susanne gave us a great traveller's tip: at really good restaurants, eat

lunch. It's less expensive and just as good an opportunity to see what the chef can do. We ended the day with a tour of the public television station in Umeå's outskirts; Susanne is a contributing chef on *Go'kväll*, Sweden's favourite late-afternoon variety show, where Susanne's specialty is creating nutritious, imaginative dishes for the home cook.

The next day she met us with a pair of warm fleeces to clothe us for our journey farther north; she had raided her closet for us. She had time to escort us through the seasonal farmers' market on a downtown street, where she knew *everybody*, and darted from booth to booth pointing out the cranberry and walnut bread we had to buy, or the women in traditional dress making tunnbröd in a brick oven, or the local goat's cheese we absolutely must sample.

She introduced us to Doris Brändström, who stood smiling behind a counter of pickled wild mushrooms, offering samples of sweet, musky, slightly chewy morsels impaled on toothpicks. Doris is "the mushroom lady;" famous locally for her mushroom knowledge. Behind Doris her equally cheerful colleagues were serving up hot mushroom-stuffed Thai spring rolls and mushroom sausage; clearly, these women loved what they did. When she heard of our interest in mushrooms, Doris invited us to join a mushroom-hunting expedition she was leading the next day. Then it was time to say goodbye to Susanne, and she took us to Brobergs Coffee Shop near the market for a last fika together.

The next day we met Doris on a country road in a spruce forest just beyond a racetrack. We realized how special our invitation was when she introduced us to the rest of the party: Doris's daughter Jenny, her granddaughter Nelli, and Marie and Margaretha, two of her oldest friends. A reporter and a photographer from the local newspaper were there to do a feature on Doris and her mushroom foraging: she had just branched out into a new business selling prepared wild mushroom dishes to local restaurants and cafés.

Doris led us into the woods, where under the open canopy the ground was covered in blueberry bushes, a familiar sight in this abundant land. But we were not there for blueberries; we were looking for the *tröttkanterelle*, or funnel chanterelle (*Craterellus tubaeformis*), which comes into season later than the golden chanterelle, and is prized for its smoky, spicy flavour. We'd heard lots about this mushroom from Maria Edström; it is her favourite. Tina Edström says the flavour of dried funnel chanterelles is more intense than that of golden chanterelles, and she much prefers them.

In the spruce wood near Umeå we roamed through hollows and up hillsides, snacking on blueberries picked in passing, noting familiar flora like juniper, lichen and moss berries and stopping to examine inedible fungi just for interest—these mushroom lovers were keen on every

Pure gold: a bagful of funnel chanterelles collected in the forest near Umeå in Norbotten, Sweden.

species. Doris and I were up on a hill with the reporter looking at a red-banded cortinarius (edible but not palatable) when a shout came from down in the hollow. "Come here!" We scrambled down to find Hector, Marie and Margaretha, grinning from ear to ear, standing beside a river and several tributaries of tröttkanterelles snaking through the undergrowth. Hector was delighted to have discovered the bonanza.

Hector and I entered a mushroom-picking dream and lost track of time and place as we followed the mushrooms through the woods, heads down, focused. After a while we looked up to discover we were totally alone. We meandered out of a hollow, crested a hump of land and there was the gang, seated on coats or logs, sipping coffee and eating blueberry cake.

"It's fika time!" they said. Somebody moved over and patted the ground beside her, somebody else gave us a mug of coffee, and Marie passed the blueberry cake. "Do

The hills above Fish Lake near Whitehorse are a favourite berry-picking spot in fall. But beware the rocky road.

you have fika when you go into the woods?" she asked. I thought about it. Foraging with Hector is about quiet companionship as we gather berries or mushrooms for the larder, but with girlfriends it's a social occasion, when telling stories and laughing about our lives is as important as the berry picking. And we always bring a snack.

"I do have fika." I said. "When I'm berry picking with my girlfriends. My friend Laurel calls it 'Snack.' Sometimes we even bring wine." "Ah, then you must have a sleep before you go home."

Hector had his own version of fika, years ago when he was building our house. Every morning and afternoon he made coffee for the crew on a Coleman stove in the shed. He kept mugs and spoons, sugar and cream on a shelf, and set up folding chairs on the dirt floor. I used to visit the site and find them crowded into the shed, their hands wrapped around pink melamine mugs,

helping themselves to pecan squares or brownies from the cookie tin and shooting the breeze about a construction problem or the time when...Hector said those breaks were number one in creating a happy job site. The power of fika!

We parted from Doris and company with smiles and cheek kisses and promises to keep in touch. Back at our host Anders's house we weighed our mushrooms: 5 pounds, 12½ ounces (2.6 kg). We ate fresh mushrooms simmered in cream that night, to accompany brown trout caught and cooked beautifully by Anders, and he dried the rest of the mushrooms in the sauna.

We had to leave our mushrooms and our friends behind when we left Umeå to travel north, but later I received a mushroom soup recipe from Doris. I've included it here as a bonus, in memory of our mushroom expedition and the fikas we had with our new Swedish girlfriends.

Labrador Tea

Estimate 25 to 30 individual Labrador tea leaves for each cup of tea, or about 1 tablespoon (15 mL), loosely packed.

1. Crush leaves slightly to release oils, cover with boiling water and steep for 10 minutes for a mild and aromatic tea.

Caution: Use Labrador tea in low concentrations and in moderation; it contains narcotic properties and can cause digestive upset in concentrated doses. Pregnant women and those with high blood pressure should be particularly careful.

Flourless Chocolate Hazelnut Cake

Rich and fudge-like, this simple, foolproof cake has only five ingredients. Try it with almonds too. With thanks to Nigella Lawson's Community Recipes forum.

7 oz (200 gr) whole hazelnuts

7 oz (200 gr) dark chocolate

7 oz (200 gr) butter

5 eggs

7 oz (200 gr) sugar

Crème fraîche sweetened with birch syrup, and grated orange peel to garnish (optional)

1. In a 350F (180C) oven, toast hazelnuts for 8 to 10 minutes, until lightly browned and aromatic. Allow to cool slightly, then rub together in a tea towel to remove as many of the skins as you can. When completely cool, grind nuts finely until they resemble coarse sand.

2. Melt chocolate and butter over low heat, stirring occasionally. When melted, add ground hazelnuts and let cool to room temperature.

3. Separate 4 of the 5 eggs into yolks and whites. Beat 4 yolks and 1 whole egg until foamy and thick. Add sugar and beat until dissolved and the mixture is thick and creamy. Add the cooled chocolate and nut mixture and beat well.

4. In a separate bowl, beat egg whites until stiff peaks form. Fold gently into the chocolate mixture until batter is uniform in colour.

5. Pour batter into a lightly greased, 9-inch (22.5-cm) springform pan. Bake in a 350F (180C) oven for 45 minutes, or until the surface feels firm to the touch. The cake may fall slightly in the middle; this only makes it more fudge-like.

6. Cool on a rack. Cut into wedges and serve with sweetened crème fraîche and grated orange peel. Or, wrap wedges in waxed paper and pack into a knapsack for fika on the land. Take napkins.

Makes 8 to 12 servings.

Cranberry-Lemon Squares

Adapted from vanillagarlic.com

This recipe delivers a moist and chewy square that stays fresh for days.

3 eggs at room temperature

1½ cups (350 mL) sugar

½ cup (125 mL) unsalted butter, softened

1 Tbsp (15 mL) lemon zest

1 Tbsp (15 mL) lemon juice

2 Tbsp (30 mL) buttermilk or yogourt

½ tsp (2.5 mL) salt

2 cups (475 mL) flour

2 cups (475 mL) fresh or frozen wild lowbush cranberries (lingonberries) or substitute dried wild or cultivated cranberries

1. Preheat oven to 350F (180C) and lightly grease a 9- × 13-inch (22.5- × 32-cm) baking dish.

2. Beat eggs and sugar together for 5 to 7 minutes until the sugar is dissolved, the colour is pale yellow and the eggs have increased in volume by half.

3. Add softened butter and beat thoroughly for 2 minutes. Add the lemon zest, lemon juice, buttermilk or yogourt, and salt and beat until combined.

4. If you're using dried cranberries, toss them with the flour and work with your fingers to separate any that might be sticking together. Stir flour and cranberries into the wet ingredients with a wooden spoon. If you're using fresh or frozen lowbush cranberries, add half the flour to the batter and incorporate. Toss cranberries with the remaining flour before gently folding into the mix. This will help to keep the berries from bursting and turning the batter pink.

5. Spoon batter into the prepared pan and smooth with a spatula.

6. Bake for 45 to 50 minutes, until a toothpick inserted in the middle is free of crumbs. (Add 5 minutes if the cranberries were frozen.) If the top begins to brown before the cake is ready, place a sheet of foil over top. Cool on a rack before cutting.

Makes about 25 squares, each 2 x 2 inches (5 x 5 cm).

Finnish *Pulla* Bread with Blueberry Filling

Pulla is a moist Finnish yeast bread made with milk, eggs and melted butter, sweetened with a bit of sugar and seasoned with cardamom. The loaf is traditionally braided like challah, but is sometimes formed into small buns with a dip in the middle and filled with jam. That's the version the ladies brought on the Umeå mushroom expedition. This recipe makes two loaves; if you like, braid one half of the dough and make buns with the other.

DOUGH

1⅓ cups (330 mL) milk

1½ Tbsp (22 mL) dry yeast

⅔ cup (160 mL) sugar

2 eggs

1 tsp (5 mL) coarse salt

1 Tbsp (15 mL) ground cardamom

4½–6 cups (1.1–1.4 L) flour, divided

5 Tbsp (75 mL) butter, melted

Canola oil, for greasing

TOPPING

1 Tbsp (15 mL) 35 percent cream

1 egg yolk

2 Tbsp (30 mL) sliced almonds

2 ½ Tbsp (37.5 mL) blueberry jam (optional)

1. Heat milk in a small saucepan just until bubbles begin to form at the sides; cool to 115F (45C) or barely hot to the touch. Transfer to a large mixing bowl. Add yeast and let sit for 10 minutes, or until yeast has bloomed.

2. Beat in sugar, eggs, salt, cardamom and 2 cups (475 mL) of the flour until a stiff batter forms.

3. Add melted butter, stir, and add the remaining flour ½ cup (125 mL) at a time, beating with a wooden spoon, until the dough becomes less sticky and forms a ball.

4. Tip dough onto a lightly floured surface and knead for 10 minutes, adding dustings of flour until dough is silky and no longer sticky.

5. Oil the dough on all sides with canola oil and transfer to a clean bowl. Cover with a tea towel and let rise until doubled in size, about one hour.

6. Deflate dough and knead for 3 minutes, oil again and return to the bowl. Let rise until doubled in size again, about 30 minutes.

7. Gently deflate dough and divide into two equal pieces. To make a braid, divide one of the pieces into three pieces of equal size. Roll each piece into a rope 18 inches (46 cm) long. Lay ropes side by side on the work surface and starting at the top, braid them together. Tuck ends underneath. Repeat with the other piece, or make buns.

   For buns: divide second piece of dough into 8 equal pieces and roll each into a ball. Let balls rest for 5 minutes, then roll each one into a rope 10 to 12 inches (25 to 30 cm) long. Coil ropes into a circle.

8. Transfer loaves or loaf and buns onto baking sheets lined with parchment paper. Cover in oiled plastic wrap and let sit until puffed up, about 20 minutes.

9. Fifteen minutes before baking, preheat the oven to 375F (190C).

10. Whisk cream and egg together and brush loaves thoroughly with the mixture, then sprinkle with almonds. For blueberry pulla, make a depression in the centre of each coiled bun, fill with 1 tsp (5 mL) of blueberry jam, then brush dough with the egg-cream mixture and sprinkle with almonds.

11. Bake until golden brown, about 25 minutes. (If pulla browns too quickly, tent a piece of foil over top of loaf and buns.) Let cool on a rack before serving.

Makes two braided loaves or one loaf and eight buns.

Almond and Fireweed Jelly Thumbprint Cookies

The cookie recipe is based on those delicious Chinese almond cookies you can buy in Asian grocery stores. As an alternative to fireweed jelly, try rose petal or redcurrant. The flower jellies have a more delicate flavour, but the redcurrant provides a bolder contrast to the sweetness of the almond extract.

1 cup (250 mL) butter

1 cup (250 mL) sugar

1 egg, lightly beaten

2 tsp (10 mL) almond extract

2½ cups (600 mL) flour

½ tsp (2.5 mL) baking soda

½ tsp (2.5 mL) salt

1 egg yolk, beaten (for brushing)

5 Tbsp (75 mL) fireweed jelly

1. Preheat oven to 350F (180C) and line two baking sheets with parchment paper.

2. Cream butter until fluffy, add sugar and cream again. Beat in egg and almond extract.

3. Sift dry ingredients into a separate bowl and beat into the butter and egg mixture until blended.

4. Shape dough into 1-inch (2.5-cm) balls and place on baking sheets. Flatten cookies and press a hole into each one with the rounded end of a wooden spoon or your thumb.

5. Bake for 12 to 15 minutes, just until edges begin to brown. You may have to pull the cookies out half-way through and depress the centres once more.

6. Remove cookies from baking tray to a rack. When almost cool, fill each cookie with ½ tsp (2.5 mL) of jelly . Store in a cookie tin, separated by layers of waxed paper.

Makes about 30 cookies.

From top to bottom: Pulla buns filled with blueberry jam. A pulla loaf, braided like challah. Women in traditional dress roll out tunnbröd at the farmers' market in Umeå.

Rivers of funnel chanterelles snake through the boreal forest near Umeå.

Three generations of mushroom pickers: Doris Brändström with her daughter and granddaughter.

Doris Brändström's *Sandsopp* Soup

Doris says this soup is tastiest made with dried *sandsopp* mushrooms, *Suillus variegatus*, the variegated or velvet bolete: not a common subspecies in Canada. Try substituting dried king boletes, a.k.a. porcini mushrooms (*Boletus edulis*), aspen boletes (*Leccinum insigne*) or orange delicious (*Lacterius deliciosus*) mushrooms.

1 oz (30 gr) dried *sandsopp* mushrooms (see above for substitutions)

2 medium shallots, finely chopped

1 clove garlic, minced (optional)

1½ Tbsp (22 mL) butter

3 Tbsp (45 mL) flour

1 Tbsp (15 mL) tomato paste

4 cups (1 L) vegetable stock

1 oz (30 gr) blue cheese

1 cup (250 mL) crème fraîche or 35 percent cream

Salt and pepper to taste

1 tsp (5 mL) lemon juice (optional)

Minced parsley to garnish

1. Crumble the dried mushrooms and soak them in 1 cup (250 mL) hot water until softened. Strain through a sieve and reserve the liquid.

2. Combine soaked mushrooms, shallots and garlic (if using) in a food processor and whizz to a coarse paste.

3. In a medium saucepan, melt butter over medium heat. Sauté mushroom and shallot mixture until browned, about 5 minutes.

4. Sprinkle flour over the mixture, stir and cook for 2 minutes. Add tomato paste, stir in vegetable stock and mushroom water (leaving any gritty bits behind). Bring to the boil, reduce heat to low and whisk in the blue cheese and crème fraîche or cream.

5. Simmer over low heat for about 30 minutes, uncovered, whisking occasionally. Taste and season with salt and pepper. Stir in lemon juice, if using. Sprinkle with minced parsley before serving.

Makes about 4 cups (1 L).

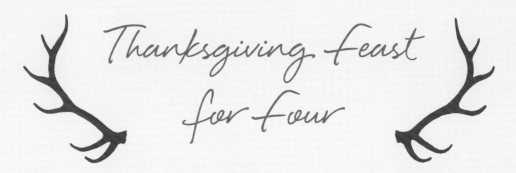

Thanksgiving Feast for Four

MENU

Potatoes Mousseline
with Shaggy Mane Butter **113**

Sautéed Ruffed Grouse Breasts
in Madeira and Cranberry Sauce **114**

Oven-Braised Green Cabbage **116**

Wild Saskatoon Berry and BC Ambrosia Apple
Upside-Down Cake **117**

A Norbotten Thanksgiving

We met Roger Kempanien in a hostel on the outskirts of Gällivare, an iron-mining town in northern Sweden. The first time we saw him he was walking towards us down the corridor, a strong middle-aged man of medium build with a kind, open face, carrying two bowls of steaming dog food. We got acquainted over whiskey in the communal dining room. Roger is a hunter and like every Swedish hunter he has hunting dogs whom he loves and expects much of. He and his dogs were in Gällivare to take part in a competition; the dogs had to do clever things in a difficult, simulated hunt and they had to do them elegantly and well. One of Roger's dogs was a young female who was very smart but had a tendency to lose the plot at crucial moments and go off on a side story of her own. The next day would be her test. Roger hoped she would flush a *fjällripa* on the mountain.

The ripa captures the imagination partly because of where it lives, in the high country, the wilderness, the north.

Fjäll is a word we heard from the beginning of our travels in Sweden, and we knew by the way it was said that it was an important one. Related to the English *fell*, fjäll means mountain or a high place above the treeline, equivalent to our *alpine*, as in "and then we climbed up into the alpine…" Anyone who has ever climbed up into the alpine will know the feeling of freedom and satisfaction that small phrase gives; it conjures memories of long, clear views, adventure and wild beauty. My sister-in-law Tina says, "Fjäll is to me a place to go cross-country skiing over beautiful terrain above tree level. The odd tree you see would be some gnarly windswept little birch tree. Fjäll is connected to the north of Sweden or in our case to Norway, where we used to go alpine skiing. Dad always insisted that we go cross-country skiing the first day of the ski trip 'to get our ski legs,' so we got out 'på fjället' (on the fjäll) every year."

Fjäll is a magic word to say: put an *f* at the beginning of *yell* and enjoy the long opening of the vowel before the tongue taps the roof of the mouth to signify the end of the word. In that open moment you can almost hear a distant yodel calling you to the high country.

As we moved farther north and spent more time in the company of country people we started to hear another word with great frequency and realized it too was important: the word *ripa*, which means ptarmigan. *Ripe* are an important source of food for northern people; the city of Kiruna, a major mining town southeast of Gällivare, derives its name from *giruna*, the Sámi word for ptarmigan. The ripa captures the imagination partly because of where it lives, in the high country, the wilderness, the north. The fjällripa is especially enchanting because its plumage turns snowy white in winter. If it's true that

Rock ptarmigan in their summer camouflage. They are an important source of food for northern people.

the hunter takes on something of the character of the hunted, the hunter of the fjällripa knows insects and willow and crowberries and snow.

Roger's young female dog didn't do so well in the competition; she might have had a chance but it snowed on the fjäll and then it got foggy so the day ended early. That night Roger and some of the other hunters told stories over a couple of whiskies at the dining room table in the hostel, and by the way the young hunters listened to Roger we could tell he was someone they much admired. At the end of the night Roger invited us to visit him in his hometown of Luleå on the Baltic Sea. Perhaps he would cook us a fjällripa.

We found Roger's house in a quiet suburb of Luleå a couple of weeks later, just before Canadian Thanksgiving. Roger and his partner, Birgitta, welcomed us into a home lit with candles and decorated in that simple, clean, pretty way that Scandinavians are so good at.

Travellers will know how nice it is to be in somebody's home after weeks of hostels and restaurants. We stood at the kitchen counter and ate Birgitta's appetizer of flatbread, melted *Västerbottensost* cheese and cloudberry preserves, followed by *Kalix löjrom*, the delicate roe of the vendace, harvested once a year from where the Kalix River empties into the Baltic Sea. As we nibbled, Roger prepared the main course: breast of fjällripa cut into pieces, sautéed in butter with chanterelles and bacon, then braised in a stock made with ptarmigan bones and finished with cream.

It has taken Roger a few years to perfect his recipe and he has a few tips: the broth made with ptarmigan bones is key to communicating the deep flavour of the bird; use no more than two parts cream to three parts stock; don't let the bacon and mushrooms be any more than 20 percent of the whole dish. Roger allotted one whole breast (both halves) for each person. We had lingonberry

Across the top: A miniature fall landscape of lichen and ripening berries. Right: Kalix löjrom, or vendace roe, is harvested where the Kalix River empties into the Baltic Sea. The delicacy is only in season for five weeks in the fall, and for those five weeks is encountered throughout Sweden.

sauce to accompany, and Birgitta made potato cakes with Västerbottensost; we dined by the light of many candles and ended the evening with a singalong of '70s songs. As a parting gift Roger gave me three beautiful cookbooks produced by the Norbotten regional council, where he is a director.

Sweden's fjällripa is our rock ptarmigan, or *Lagopus mutus*, found in the sub-arctic and arctic tundra. I've never eaten a ptarmigan in the Yukon, and until I went to Sweden my culinary experience of the grouse family to which the ptarmigan is related was limited to the spruce grouse. Then in the fall of 2013, a year after our feast with Roger, Cathie Archbould came home with two ruffed grouse and invited me up to her place to cook them for the two of us and our partners.

The breast meat of the ruffed grouse is light in colour and mild in flavour, quite different from the fjällripa or the spruce grouse. In English, one of the colloquial Yukon First Nations names for grouse is "chicken," and can mean all manner of birds from ruffed to sharp-tailed to spruce to dusky grouse, and from willow to white-tailed to rock ptarmigan. Grouse and ptarmigan are members of the order *Galliformes*, as are chickens: science and tradition meet in the Department of Taxonomy.

For this meal I've done some things differently from Roger—taken the mushrooms and incorporated them into the potatoes, made a Madeira-cranberry reduction instead of a cream-based sauce. Nevertheless, in the spirit of friendship and kindness to strangers, here is a boreal Thanksgiving feast for four, inspired by Roger and Birgitta.

Potatoes Mousseline with Shaggy Mane Butter

2 lbs (910 gr) russet potatoes

1 tsp (5 mL) salt

½ cup (125 mL) Clarified Butter, recipe on page 234

½ oz (15 gr) dried shaggy mane mushrooms (or substitute dried porcini)

¼ cup (60 mL) 10 percent cream

¾ cup (180 mL) 35 percent cream

1. Butter a 9- × 13-inch (22.5- × 32-cm) baking dish.

2. Peel potatoes, cut into quarters, rinse and place in a large saucepan. Cover with cold water, add salt and bring to the boil over high heat. Reduce heat to low and cook until potatoes are tender, 10 to 15 minutes. Drain and return the pan to the heat, shaking occasionally, until the potatoes are quite dry and no longer steaming, about 1 minute.

3. Melt the Clarified Butter in a small saucepan over low heat. Break the mushrooms into small pieces and add to the liquid butter. The goal is to infuse the butter with mushroom flavour, which should take about 20 minutes. At this point remove mushroom pieces with a small strainer or slotted spoon and reserve.

4. Press the potatoes through a coarse sieve with a wooden spoon; if you have a ricer or food mill, even better. If you don't own a sieve mash the potatoes with a fork or potato masher, fluffing them up as much as you can.

5. With a wooden spoon, stir half the strained butter and all the 10 percent cream into the potatoes. Whisk the 35 percent cream briefly to incorporate some air, then fold into the potatoes.

6. Transfer the potatoes to the baking dish and spread with a spatula. Pour the remaining butter over top. Test the mushrooms; if the texture is pleasantly crisp, sprinkle them over top, but if they're tough and chewy discard or save them for stock.

7. Bake in a 325F (160C) oven until heated through, about 25 to 30 minutes. (A good way to test is to insert a knife into the middle, leave it there for a moment then touch the knife briefly to the back of your hand. If it's warm, almost hot, the potatoes are ready.)

8. Just before serving, heat the broiler to high and broil the potatoes until lightly browned, 2 to 4 minutes.

Makes four to six servings.

The breast meat of the ruffed grouse is mild in flavour.

Sautéed Ruffed Grouse Breasts in Madeira and Cranberry Sauce

This dish is prepared about 30 minutes before serving, but you soak the cranberries in Madeira for a few hours beforehand. Cook the potatoes and the cabbage in ovenproof serving dishes and time them so that you can bring everything to the table at once and serve family-style. If you don't have Labrador tea and spruce tips in the pantry substitute 1 tsp (5 mL) each dried thyme and rosemary.

½ cup (125 mL) wild lowbush cranberries (lingonberries) or substitute cultivated cranberries

1 cup (250 mL) Madeira

2 ruffed grouse breasts, split and boned (reserve bones for stock)

2 Tbsp (30 mL) each diced carrot, onion and celery

2 Tbsp (30 mL) butter, divided

2 cups (475 mL) chicken or turkey stock

1 tsp (5 mL) Labrador tea leaves

1 Tbsp (15 mL) dried spruce tips

½ tsp (2.5 mL) black peppercorns

1. Two to three hours before you intend to serve, soak cranberries in Madeira.

2. Make the stock: sauté the grouse bones and vegetables in 1 tablespoon (15 mL) butter in a small, heavy saucepan. Add the turkey or chicken stock, bring to the boil and reduce to a low simmer and cook uncovered for an hour. Strain the liquid, measure and return to heat until reduced to 1 cup (250 mL). Set aside.

3. While the stock is simmering, grind Labrador tea leaves, spruce tips and black peppercorns with a mortar and pestle. Dredge breasts in seasonings, cover and return to fridge.

4. Pour Madeira and cranberries through a strainer. Set liquid and berries aside in separate bowls. Reserve 1 tablespoon (15 mL) cranberries for garnish.

5. Thirty minutes before serving, melt remaining tablespoon (15 mL) butter over medium heat in a cast iron frying pan. When butter is sizzling, add grouse breasts and sauté for 3 minutes on each side. Remove from heat and let sit on a plate, uncovered, while you make the sauce. The meat will continue to cook as it rests.

6. Still over medium heat, deglaze the pan with half the reserved Madeira, scraping up any browned bits. Add the remaining Madeira, the stock and the cranberries (except for the berries reserved for garnish), and cook until reduced to a light syrup, enough to hold its shape, but not thickened like cranberry sauce. If you do somehow cook the sauce too long, remove it from the heat and beat in a couple of tablespoons (30 mL) of cold butter.

7. Carve each half breast into four thick slices. Pour a pool of sauce on each of four heated dinner plates and arrange the slices in a fan on top. Sprinkle with the reserved cranberries and serve at once. (Bring any remaining sauce to the table; there won't be much.)

Makes four servings.

In the alpine, the views go on forever.

Oven-Braised Green Cabbage

This dish is adapted from a recipe in Molly Stevens' cookbook, *All About Braising*. The secret to success lies in the long, slow cooking, which releases the cabbage's sweetness. The browning at the end adds colour and a hint of crispiness. The cabbage is best served warm or at room temperature, so it's a great side dish to accompany a main course cooked at the last minute.

1 medium head green cabbage (about 2 lbs/910 gr)

1 large yellow onion cut into eight wedges

¼ cup (60 mL) chicken or turkey stock

¼ cup (60 mL) extra-virgin olive oil

½ tsp (2.5 mL) fennel seeds, cracked with a mortar and pestle

Coarse salt and freshly ground pepper to taste

¼ tsp (1 mL) crushed red pepper

Coarse sea salt or fleur de sel

1. Preheat oven to 325F (160C). Lightly oil a 9- × 13-inch (22.5- × 32-cm) baking dish or a shallow braising dish with a lid.

2. Trim the cabbage, discarding bruised, holey or wilted outer leaves. If the cabbage is too big, it won't fit in the baking dish and it won't braise evenly. Cut the cabbage in half, then cut 8 even-sized wedges and place in single layer on baking dish. Some cabbage will be left over. (Save the remaining cabbage for colcannon or coleslaw.)

3. Separate the onion wedges and scatter over top, tucking some pieces in and among the cabbage. Drizzle over the oil and stock. Combine fennel, salt, pepper and crushed red pepper and sprinkle over top. Cover tightly with foil or the lid of the braising dish and place on a shelf in the middle of the oven.

4. Braise until the cabbage leaves are completely tender, about 2 hours, turning the wedges with tongs after the first hour. It may be tricky to keep them from falling apart, but just try to push them back into a wedge shape. Add a splash of water if the dish is drying out.

5. Once the cabbage is completely tender, remove the foil or lid, increase the temperature to 450F (230C) and roast until the vegetables just start to brown, about 10 minutes. Serve warm or at room temperature, with a sprinkle of coarse salt.

Makes four to eight servings.

Wild Saskatoon Berry and BC Ambrosia Apple Upside-Down Cake

The saskatoon berries can be fresh or frozen, making this a great cake for late fall or early winter when saskatoon season is over but the freezer is stocked. The organic Ambrosia apple, which was developed in the Similkameen Valley in British Columbia by the Mennell family in the late 1990s, took the apple world by storm and is now widely available in Canada. For a great account of their story see *Apples to Oysters* by Margaret Webb.

This is one cake that really must be removed from its pan almost right away. Otherwise the caramelized topping will stick and you won't be able to remove it from the pan, or the steam from the cooling cake will soften the topping and you'll lose that lovely toffee effect. Happened to me once. So disappointing.

If you haven't had too much cream already, serve this cake with whipped cream or crème fraîche sweetened with birch syrup and flavoured with Calvados (apple brandy).

TOPPING

¼ cup (60 mL) butter

¾ cup (180 mL) packed brown sugar

3 Ambrosia apples, cored, quartered and cut into ½-inch (1.25-cm) slices

1 cup (250 mL) saskatoon berries (or wild blueberries), fresh or frozen

CAKE

1½ cups (350 mL) flour

3 Tbsp (45 mL) cornmeal

1½ tsp (7.5 mL) baking powder

½ tsp (2.5 mL) salt

½ cup (125 mL) unsalted butter, softened but still cool

1 cup (250 mL) plus 2 Tbsp (30 mL) sugar, divided

4 large eggs at room temperature, separated

1½ tsp (7.5 mL) vanilla

⅔ cup (160 mL) milk

1. Preheat oven to 350F (180C) and place the rack in the lower third of the oven. Grease bottom and sides of a 9-inch (22.5-cm) round, 3-inch (7.5-cm) deep cake pan. (Do not use a pan with a removable bottom, unless you enjoy both the smell of burnt sugar and cleaning the oven.)

2. Melt butter in saucepan over medium heat, add brown sugar and cook, stirring occasionally for 3 to 4 minutes, until foamy and pale. Pour into prepared cake pan and swirl the pan to distribute evenly. Arrange the apple slices in a swirl pattern, leaving spaces for berries in between and in the centre. Press the berries into the pattern wherever there's room. Set aside.

3. Whisk flour, cornmeal, baking powder and salt together. Set aside.

4. Cream butter until fluffy and gradually add 1 cup (250 mL) of the sugar. Beat until light and fluffy, about 2 minutes in a stand mixer. Beat in yolks and vanilla, scraping the bowl if needed.

5. At low speed or by hand, add the dry ingredients in three batches, alternating with milk. Blend just until the batter is smooth.

6. In a separate bowl, beat the egg whites until frothy. Still beating, gradually add the remaining 2 tablespoons (30 mL) of sugar and beat until egg whites form soft peaks. Fold a quarter of the whites into the batter. Fold in remaining whites until no streaks remain.

7. Pour the batter evenly into the pan and smooth out with a spatula. Bake for about 60 minutes, until top of cake is golden and a toothpick inserted in the middle comes out clean.

8. Cool on a rack for a few minutes, then slide a knife around the edge of the cake to loosen it from the pan. Place a serving platter over the pan and hold tightly. Invert the cake onto the platter. Carefully remove the cake pan.

Makes 8 to 12 servings.

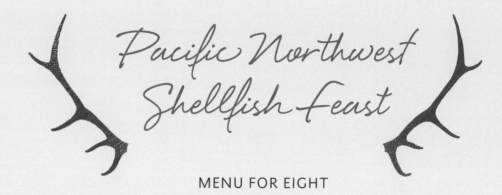

Pacific Northwest Shellfish Feast

MENU FOR EIGHT

Homage to *Västerbottensostpaj*:
Canadian Cheddar Tart **124**

Kale or Chard Risotto **125**

BC Aquavit-Marinated Spot Prawns **126**

Spicy Green Beans **128**

Alaska Spot Prawns in Angelica Sauce **129**

Alaskan King Crab Legs with Wild Sage Butter **130**

Mushroom Sauté **131**

Hazelnut Meringue with Cranberry Filling **132**

Kräftskiva at Tjörn

When my youngest brother, André, was 23 he went to Abu Dhabi to fly airplanes. There he met Tina Edström, who had moved to Abu Dhabi from Sweden to work as a dental hygienist. They got married twice in 1987: once in Abu Dhabi and again in Canada, where we met Tina for the first time, and understood that a force of nature had entered our lives. Tina is variously called the Scandahooligan and the Viking in our family,

The crayfish feast, or Kräftskiva, *is the second big special occasion of the Swedish summer*

and is known among us for her forthright opinions, her generous heart, her love of animals and her ability on the dance floor. She is the oldest of four sisters, and when Hector and I travelled to Sweden in 2012, the sisters threw open their arms, housed us, fed us, showed us around and introduced us to anyone and everyone that could help us in our quest for culinary knowledge.

Tina's sisters Cecilia and Maria Edström both live in Göteborg, and one of the very nicest things they did was delay their annual crayfish feast at the family cabin until we arrived in late August. The crayfish feast, or *Kräftskiva*, is the second big special occasion of the Swedish summer, after Midsummer, and usually takes place sometime in mid-August—the crayfish season opens in early August and runs through to September.

The preferred venue is out on the land, though even IKEA gets into the act by hosting events at its stores, and there is much drinking of aquavit, singing of songs, wearing of paper hats and no-holds-barred, hands-on slurping of crayfish, which don't have a lot of meat, so it's messy. (A Swedish friend said, "We don't eat the crayfish, we drink them.") There are other essential items on the table: *Västerbottensostpaj*, a pie made with *Västerbottensost*, Sweden's most famous cheese; big wedges of *prästost*, or priest cheese, so called because peasants once paid their church tithes in cheese; baskets of *knäckebröd*, salads, potatoes and a special dessert.

Sweden as a nation has been feasting on crayfish since the mid-1800s; before that the spiny inhabitants of river, lake and ocean were exclusive fare, reserved for the aristocracy. In modern times the demand for crayfish is great, but the stock in Swedish inland waters is much depleted, due to habitat infringement and a nasty parasite, so the bulk of the crayfish consumed annually tends to be imported from Turkey, China and the United States.

However, there are still some Swedish crayfish to be found, including at Tjörn, a large island just northwest of Göteborg, where the Edströms' family cabin is located. Maria, her husband, Andreas, their son Frederick, Hector and I piled into the car and took the E6 from Göteborg, crossed the bridge and entered rural Sweden, where neat red and white farm buildings on green fields are interspersed with forest, lakes, and glimpses of the

This page: Prince William Sound in south central Alaska. Next page, counterclockwise from top: The wild and cultivated countryside from above the Edström's cottage on the island of Tjörn. Still life in sunlight: freshly picked golden chanterelles. Egg cheese, or äggost. A family picnic on the dock at Tjörn.

sea, and everything seems organized and beautiful. We surged up a final steep, grassy driveway and arrived at the Edströms' place.

Here the family has created a small haven. The cabin is set high on a grassy hill against a granite ridge. The walls are wood, inside and out, the windows are low and deep-set and there's a big, open brick fireplace in the main room surrounded by cushioned benches. Outside there's an apple tree and berry bushes, there are lingonberries and blueberries in the woods, and in late August, there are chanterelles.

After we unpacked Maria, Hector and I skived off into the woods in search of chanterelles. I mistook a lot of yellowing birch leaves for mushrooms until the golden, almost orange yellow of this most delicious of mushrooms imprinted itself on my retinas. That night we dined on grilled pork, salad and fresh, wild chanterelles sautéed briefly in butter. It was a small feast for five,

and we sat at the long dining table in front of a window looking out at trees, grass and granite. Hector and I felt like we'd arrived.

When I went to bed Maria and Andreas were standing by the stove staring intently into a potful of eggs, milk, sour milk and a tiny bit of sugar. These were the beginnings of *äggost*, or egg cheese, a west coast custard cake that requires a lot of patient stirring before the solids separate from the liquid. The custard is poured into a decorative mould punched with holes so the liquid can drain, and sets overnight. I watched and stirred for a while, and then left them to it. They were up for a long time.

Next day we clambered over grass and rocks to a nearby inlet for a picnic, and on the way back picked the blackberries for the sauce that would be served with the cake. The whole family had arrived. Some of us had been down to the sweet harbour town of Skärhamn to load up on the local saltwater crayfish that Andreas loves. He's

from Umeå, near the Baltic Sea, and prefers the saltwater variety; inlanders tend to like the freshwater variety better. (We had both at our feast.) Cecilia had come with the Västerbottonsostpaj and paper napkins printed with lyrics to all of the songs we would sing that night.

Maria and Cecilia set the table and hung paper lanterns; in the kitchen Andreas split the saltwater crayfish in half lengthwise in preparation for grilling, and made a garlic aioli for the freshwater crayfish he'd bought ready-cooked in Göteborg, to be served cold. Maria worked on potatoes; some combination of sisters and Hector made a salad, I sautéed chanterelles and Cecelia's husband, Staffan, organized the glasses and set out the aquavit bottles on the table. There were five: two Danish, one Swedish, one Norwegian and one Dutch. Each adult's place was set with four glasses, for water, beer, wine and shots of aquavit. We were ready.

At dinner I sat next to Niklas Wennberg, who reclaims vacant city lots for urban agriculture. I may be oversimplifying, but I think he said one of his strategies is to introduce pigs first, who tear up and fertilize the lot and prepare it for the gardens to come. A brilliant side effect is that by the time the pigs are done, those who may have objected to gardens in their midst in the first place think, "Well we survived the pigs, bring on the gardens!" Cue a shot of aquavit!

We wore our funny hats, we dipped cold, cooked crayfish into aioli, we sucked the juices from the grilled crayfish, we drank, we sang, we made a mess of the table, we took a break and then we had dessert.

Andreas carried in the äggost. It was a three-tiered, quivering structure, architectural and fragile: a tour de force. The table broke into applause. We poured blackberry sauce over our individual pieces, and somebody, I think it was Staffan, put down his fork and said, "You know? I love this. I love that we picked the blackberries together and now we are eating them together. Skål!" We raised our glasses and replied, "Skål!" looking into each face around the table.

Several months later, when I was back in Canada, Maria sent me an äggost mould in the mail. I haven't yet had the nerve to try it.

Like the Swedish, Canadians celebrate their favourite shellfish in regional festivals from PEI to British Columbia. Our feasting menu in these pages focuses on a couple of crustaceans of the Pacific Northwest that come into season in the fall: spot prawns and crab. Like the crayfish feast, it's more fun if everyone pitches in, and less pricey too. Assign dishes! Apportion tasks! And have fun.

Opposite, clockwise from top: The pretty harbour town of Skärhamn on Tjörn, on Sweden's west coast, where we found saltwater crayfish; crayfish, sliced and ready for a brief grilling under the broiler; an Alaskan spot prawn; Jill Fredston throws down a shrimp pot.

Homage to *Västerbottensostpaj*: Canadian Cheddar Tart

Västerbottensost is a hard, cow's milk cheese made only in the village of Burträsk in northwestern Sweden, according to a formula surrounded by great secrecy—the recipe is known to a very few and guarded in the company safe. The taste has been compared to a cross between old cheddar and Parmesan with a bittersweet aftertaste—but that description is just enough to torment us, here in Canada, where it's difficult to find this robust and delicious treat.

In Sweden, Västerbottensost is considered the king of cheeses. When Hector and I we were travelling we kept a wedge with us at all times. We ate Västerbottensost in train stations, in hostel kitchens, on hikes, in fancy restaurants and at our hosts' tables, and never tired of it. Chef Susanne Jonsson has written an entire cookbook of recipes based on Västerbottensost, including Västerbottensostpaj, or pie, now a fixture on the crayfish feasting table. (Crayfish don't provide a lot of meat, and need backup; at Tjörn, Cecilia Edström contributed the rich, creamy Västerbottensostpaj that filled the empty corners.) This recipe is based on Susanne Jonsson's, which you will find on the Västerbottensost website. Susanne says, "A fun fact about that recipe is it's one of the most googled recipes in Sweden! Especially around Midsummer and crayfish season!"

PASTRY

½ cup (125 mL) cold, unsalted butter
1⅓ cups (330 mL) flour
1 Tbsp (15 mL) cold water

FILLING

3 eggs
1 cup (250 mL) crème fraîche or 35 percent cream
2½ cups (600 mL) grated old cheddar
1 tsp (5 mL) freshly ground black pepper

1. Preheat oven to 425F (220C).

2. Cut butter into flour until the texture is crumbly; add the water and knead briefly into a smooth dough. Press into a 10-inch (25-cm) flat-bottomed flan tin. Prick the bottom of the shell and bake for 10 minutes. (If pastry puffs up, prick with a fork as soon as it emerges from oven.) Let cool for 10 minutes.

3. Whisk eggs until light and creamy. Fold in crème fraîche or cream, grated cheddar and pepper. Pour into the cooled tart shell.

4. Bake for 20 minutes, until the centre is set. (Note: the filling will puff up considerably in the oven, and then fall as it cools.)

5. Cool on a rack before cutting and serving.

Makes eight servings.

Kale or Chard Risotto

1 Tbsp (15 mL) butter

½ medium onion, finely chopped

2 cloves garlic, finely chopped

1 cup (250 mL) arborio rice

¼ cup (60 mL) dry Riesling

2¼ cups (530 mL) chicken or prawn stock (see prawn stock instructions in BC Aquavit-Marinated Spot Prawns, page 126)

2 packed cups (475 mL) Russian kale, de-ribbed and finely chopped (keep ribs for vegetable stock and freely substitute curly kale or Swiss chard, or arugula, or any fresh, strong-flavoured organic green in season)

½ cup (125 mL) freshly grated Parmesan cheese, divided

1. Melt butter over medium-low heat in a wide, shallow saucepan. Add onion and cook until translucent but not browned, 5 to 7 minutes. Add garlic and cook for another 2 minutes, until aromatic. Add rice, stir to coat in butter, and cook for about 1 minute.

2. Add Riesling, stir once, pat down rice evenly and allow rice to fully absorb the liquid.

3. When the wine is absorbed, add stock ½ cup (125 mL) at a time, stirring and patting rice down each time, allowing rice to fully absorb the liquid before adding the next ½ cup (125 mL).

4. Before adding the last addition of stock, stir in the kale. Add last bit of stock, stir, and when it's fully absorbed, test for doneness. The rice should be creamy and yet still firm to bite. Remove from heat, stir in most of the Parmesan, and cover until ready to serve.

5. Transfer to a warm platter to serve, family style. Garnish with the remaining Parmesan cheese.

Makes eight side-dish portions of just over ¼ cup (60 mL) or four main-course portions.

BC Aquavit-Marinated Spot Prawns

In British Columbia the spot prawn season is open in May through June, and celebrated in festivals from the Lower Mainland to the Okanagan. The Alaskan spot prawn season is brief: one month in October, with occasional small openings in spring and winter, if the annual quota hasn't been caught. The American organization Seafood Choices Alliance and the Canadian Ocean Wise both recommend pot-fished spot prawns as a sustainable choice. Fresh spot prawns are sweet and succulent, but frozen are great too, and available year-round. We buy ours fresh in the fall and vacuum pack them in one-pound packages before freezing. If you're lucky enough to buy them with the heads on then you've got the basis for a really fabulous stock. But if not, the shells will provide sufficient backbone for a flavourful stock and poaching liquid.

Early in the day, peel prawns, leaving the tails on. Save the shells and heads in a separate bowl. Rinse prawns and refrigerate until you're ready to cook them.

Note: if you do intend to serve both BC Aquavit-Marinated Spot Prawns and Alaska Spot Prawns in Angelica Sauce (page 129) at the same meal, peel all the prawns at once and use the entire batch of shells in the stock, without increasing the water, for an even deeper flavour.

STOCK

1 Tbsp (15 mL) unsalted butter

Shells, including heads, from 2 lbs (910 gr) spot prawns

½ cup (125 mL) white wine

½ medium onion, chopped

1 small carrot, chopped

1 stalk celery, chopped

1 Tbsp (15 mL) Labrador tea (or substitute 2 bay leaves)

1 tsp (5 mL) juniper berries

4 cups (1 L) cold water

1. Melt butter in a medium saucepan over medium heat. Sauté the prawn shells in butter until pink and aromatic, about 7 minutes.
2. Deglaze the pan with white wine and add vegetables, Labrador tea and juniper berries. Sauté briefly, then add cold water.
3. Bring to the boil, reduce heat and simmer for 45 minutes.
4. Strain and reserve.

MARINADE

½ cup (125 mL) aquavit

1 Tbsp (15 mL) yellow mustard seeds

1 Tbsp (15 mL) whole coriander seeds, crushed

1 tsp (5 mL) juniper berries, lightly bruised in a mortar and pestle

1 Tbsp (15 mL) finely chopped Labrador tea leaves

1. Whisk marinade ingredients together. Reserve 2 tablespoons (30 mL) for the sauce and set aside.

PRAWNS

2 lbs (910 gr) tail-on spot prawns, shells removed

1. Bring stock to the boil, add prawns and remove from heat immediately. When prawns are no longer translucent (in about 1 minute) remove them from the stock with a slotted spoon and stir them gently into the marinade. Refrigerate for 2 hours.
2. Drain and return prawns to the refrigerator until ready to serve.
3. In a small pot, reduce 1 cup (250 mL) of the stock to 2 tablespoons (30 mL) and reserve for the sauce. Reserve remaining stock for the Alaska Spot Prawns in Angelica Sauce, if making (recipe on page 129).

Coriander, juniper berries and Labrador tea leaves complement the same and similar flavours in Aquavit-Aquavitus from BC's Okanagan Spirits.

SAUCE

⅓ cup (80 mL) Basic Mayonnaise, page 231

2 Tbsp (30 mL) reserved marinade, (see previous page)

2 Tbsp (30 mL) reduced prawn stock (previous page)

1. Whisk all ingredients together. Chill until just before serving.

Makes just over ½ cup (125 mL).

TO SERVE

1. When you're ready to serve, arrange the prawns on a platter surrounding a bowl of sauce. Dip prawns in sauce or spoon over top.

Makes eight servings of three to five prawns per person, depending on the count per pound.

Spicy Green Beans
FOR MY SISTER AND DOUG FESLER

When we made this feast in Whitehorse, my sister was in charge of the green beans. She said, "Ah. This is the bite and the spice I was looking for." The beans are also a tribute to Doug Fesler and Jill Fredston, both avalanche technicians in Alaska before they retired, who took Hector, his brother David and me on a boat trip in Prince William Sound and taught us how to fish for prawns. Doug is crazy for spice and heat. As Jill recalls in her book, *Snowstruck*, in the early days of their partnership Doug told her she could become one of the top avalanche specialists in the country on two conditions: that she eat spicier food and drink more beer.

1½ lbs (680 gr) green beans	2 cloves garlic, chopped
2 Tbsp (30 mL) butter	2 Tbsp (30 mL) lime juice (one large lime)
2 dried serrano chilies, pounded in a mortar and pestle	

1. Top and tail green beans. Bring a medium saucepan of water to the boil, add beans, bring to the boil again and cook for 2 minutes. Drain beans.

2. Just before serving, melt butter in a cast iron pan over medium heat. When it's good and hot, add the chilies and the garlic. Cook for 2 minutes, stirring frequently. Just as the garlic is beginning to brown, add beans and toss to coat with chilies and garlic. Cook for 1 to 2 minutes to heat through.

3. Squeeze lime juice over the beans, toss once more and serve.

Makes eight servings as part of a feast, or four if the only vegetable at a smaller meal.

Alaska Spot Prawns in Angelica Sauce

We came home from Sweden with a precious jar of angelica seeds, bought at Viddernas Hus, a small café specializing in Sámi foods in the town of Jokkmokk, just north of the Arctic Circle. Greta Huuva, who owns and runs Viddernas Hus, is a Sámi elder, a culinary ambassador, a forager and a herbalist. She and her daughter Linn Huuva are committed to preserving and developing Sámi culinary traditions. The café is a haven for locals and travellers seeking simple, delicious fare like reindeer soup and mushroom crêpes.

Greta sat and talked to us for some time when we visited in the fall of 2012, and gave us tasters of pine bark crisp bread and candied angelica. We returned on a Saturday, and Greta very kindly gave me a cooking lesson, demonstrating the angelica cream salad dressing she often serves at the café, and upon which this cream sauce is loosely based. We bought a small bottle of angelica tincture, good for stomach ailments, and Hector adopted it as his new best friend as we continued on our culinary journey. Candied angelica used to be widely available in Canada—my aunt remembers it as a common ingredient in Christmas cake—but angelica products are much harder to find here now. If you can't find angelica, I suggest substituting a combination of coriander seed, anise seed and the merest pinch of cinnamon.

1 lb (455 grams) spot prawns, peeled (reserve heads and shells for stock)

2 tsp (10 mL) angelica seeds, divided (substitute 1½ tsp/ 7.5 mL coriander seed, ½ tsp/2.5 mL anise seed, plus pinch of cinnamon)

2–3 Tbsp (30–45 mL) cold unsalted butter, divided

1 cup (250 mL) prawn stock (see instructions in BC Aquavit-Marinated Spot Prawns, page 126)

1 cup (250 mL) dry Riesling

1 cup (250 mL) crème fraîche

1. Rinse prawns, pat dry and toss in half the angelica seeds, coating thoroughly.

2. Melt 1 tablespoon (15 mL) butter over medium heat in a medium-sized cast iron frying pan.

3. When the butter is sizzling add the prawns all at once and cook just until they turn pink, about 1 to 2 minutes. Transfer prawns quickly to a serving dish. They'll continue cooking as you finish the sauce.

4. Pour prawn stock into the pan, increase the heat to high and reduce the liquid by half. Add Riesling and reduce by half again.

5. When the liquid begins to look thicker and slightly syrupy, add the remaining angelica seeds and the crème fraîche, which will boil up and threaten to overflow the pan, so stir rapidly and constantly and remove the pan from the heat briefly if necessary.

6. Reduce heat to medium and continue cooking until the sauce thickens enough to coat a spoon with a thin film.

7. Remove the pan from the heat and whisk in 1 tablespoon (15 mL) of cold butter. If you'd like a slightly thicker sauce, whisk in the second tablespoon of butter.

8. Pour the sauce over the prawns in their serving dish and garnish with a sprig of mountain ash berries and a silver spoon. Pass the dish around the table with a platter of risotto and a platter of mushrooms. Encourage guests to eat the prawns and sauce on their own, alternating with bites of risotto and bites of mushroom. There will be anarchists who will want to mix everything together. Let them! The spirit of feasting is freedom.

Makes eight servings of two to three prawns per person, depending on the count per pound.

Artemisia frigida *or pasture sage-infused butter is great accompaniment for Alaska king crab legs.*

Alaskan King Crab Legs with Wild Sage Butter

King crab starts appearing for sale in the fall at around the same time as spot prawns. Alaskan king crab is considered a sustainable choice by both Seafood Choices Alliance and Ocean Wise. Most king crab is cooked and frozen immediately upon catching. Our favourite fishmonger recommends taking king crab directly from the freezer and reheating in the oven for 15 minutes.

¼ cup (60 mL) Clarified Butter, recipe on page 234

3 branches wild sage (about 1 tsp/5 mL) or substitute 1 leaf salvia sage

2 lbs (910 gr) frozen Alaskan king crab legs and shoulders

¼ cup (60 mL) water

½ lemon, quartered

1. Combine butter and sage in a small pot and heat slowly over low heat.

2. Preheat oven to 350F (180C). Spread frozen crab pieces on a large, rimmed baking sheet. Pour water into the baking sheet, squeeze lemon over the crab and arrange the spent lemon wedges on the baking sheet.

3. Cover the pan with foil. Bake for 15 minutes, until crab is heated through.

4. Serve immediately on a large platter with the sage butter divided into two bowls for easier access for the whole party. (We have found that the best way to extract crab meat from the shell is to first cut the shell open with kitchen scissors and then use bamboo skewers to spear the meat.)

Makes eight servings.

Mushroom Sauté

Maria likes to add a bit of cream to the pan of cooked chanterelles just before taking it off the heat; this is a point of debate in their household. I asked Andreas about his method. He said, "You cook them in butter. Then you add some salt and pepper." So that's what we did. The next day we found more chanterelles, and cooked them Maria's way for the feast. As Hector and I travelled east and north we continued to find chanterelles in the ICA grocery stores, as well as cranberries, blueberries, blackcurrants and hawthorns, all wild. This was an unbelievable luxury.

But sometimes these mushroom treats come our way in Whitehorse. In the fall of 2013 an email arrived from our friend Lyn Fabio, with a subject line of "fresh goodies at Riverside." Riverside is our local, much-loved, buy-anything store, where you can get organic vegetables of all kinds. Lyn said, "In case you haven't been to Riverside lately"—I had been an hour before—"they have fresh galangal, turmeric, lime leaves, chanterelle mushrooms and horseradish!" We made a beeline back to the store and came home with chanterelles and shiitakes too. We cooked them Maria's way.

8 oz (225 gr) fresh chanterelle mushrooms

8 oz (225 gr) fresh shiitake mushrooms

1 oz (30 gr) dried morel mushrooms, reconstituted for 15 minutes in one cup of water and squeezed dry

1 Tbsp (15 mL) butter

1 Tbsp (15 mL) olive oil

¼ cup (60 mL) 35 percent cream

1. Brush dirt from chanterelles and shiitakes, rinsing and patting dry if needed. Trim the ends from the stems. Tear larger chanterelles into smaller pieces. Leave small chanterelles and shiitakes whole. Slice larger morels into 2 or 3 pieces, leave small ones whole.

2. Melt butter and oil in a 10-inch (25-cm) cast iron frying pan over medium heat until the butter foams. Add mushrooms and stir; they will immediately absorb all the fat. Continue to sauté and stir for 2 to 3 minutes until the mushrooms start to release their liquid and shrink in size.

3. Turn heat to medium-high and continue to cook, stirring occasionally. In about 4 to 5 minutes, when all the liquid has evaporated, the mushrooms will start to stick to the pan. Allow this to happen, stirring just once or twice for the next 2 to 3 minutes to release the mushrooms and brown them evenly.

4. When mushrooms are nicely browned, remove the pan from the heat and add the cream, stirring to deglaze the pan. The cream will allow the mushrooms to cohere, and give them a nice glaze.

5. Transfer to a platter and serve.

Makes eight servings as a side dish.

Hazelnut Meringue with Cranberry Filling

I like this cake best when it's made the day I'm planning to serve it; the meringue can get chewy on day two. That said, several testers said the cake was just as good on the second and even third day, but the whipped cream had lost some of its oomph. To keep the whipped cream stable for leftovers, a little gelatin will help: see the sidebar on opposite page for more information.

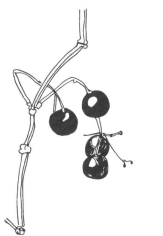

CRANBERRY FILLING

2½ cups (600 mL) wild lowbush cranberries (lingonberries), plus extra for garnish (or substitute cultivated cranberries)

4 Tbsp (60 mL) whiskey, divided (use your favourite—bourbon, rye, Scotch)

¼ cup (60 mL) birch or maple syrup

2 Tbsp (30 mL) brown sugar

WHIPPED CREAM

1½ cups (350 mL) 35 percent cream

¼ tsp (1 mL) unflavoured powdered gelatin sprinkled over 1 Tbsp (15 mL) water (optional)

HAZELNUT MERINGUE

1 cup (250 mL) hazelnuts

4 egg whites, at room temperature

⅛ tsp (0.5 mL) cream of tartar

1 cup (250 mL) sugar

½ tsp (2.5 mL) vanilla extract (substitute the whiskey of your choice)

1. Make the cranberry filling: combine all ingredients except reserved berries and 2 tablespoons (30 mL) whiskey in a small saucepan, heat to bubbling over medium heat, reduce heat and simmer for about 30 minutes, stirring often, until berries have popped and the mixture has thickened somewhat. It will continue to thicken as it cools. Cool to room temperature.

2. In a small bowl, combine reserved cranberries and remaining whiskey for garnish. Set aside to soak.

3. Preheat oven to 350F (180C).

Whipped cream, delicious as it is, doesn't stand up to being made too far in advance. After a few hours it begins to weep, causing cream-filled cakes and pastries to become soggy. The following method, courtesy of *Cook's Illustrated*, will stabilize whipped cream for up to a day, and help it keep its form when piped onto tarts:

To make 3 cups (710 mL) of stabilized whipped cream, sprinkle 1½ tsp (7.5 mL) unflavoured gelatin powder over 1½ Tbsp (22 mL) cool water in a small bowl and let it stand until the powder has dissolved; microwave in 5-second increments if needed. Using a stand mixer or electric beaters, whip 1½ cups (350 mL) chilled 35 percent cream (along with a sweetener like birch syrup if desired) on low speed until small bubbles form, then increase the speed to medium until beaters begin to leave a trail in the cream. Slowly pour in the dissolved gelatin, increase the speed to high and continue to beat until soft peaks form. Use immediately or cover and store in the refrigerator until needed—the cream should stay aloft for 24 hours.

4. Start the meringues: toast the hazelnuts for 8 minutes. Cool slightly, then rub in a clean tea towel to remove most of the skins; don't worry too much about this. Cool to room temperature, then grind the nuts in a food processor until they are the consistency of coarse sand.

5. Reduce the oven heat to 300F (150C) and line the bottom of two buttered 8-inch (20-cm) round cake pans with buttered parchment paper. Alternatively, cut two 8-inch (20-cm) circles of parchment paper, butter them, and put them on a lightly greased baking sheet.

6. Beat the egg whites and cream of tartar until they hold stiff peaks. Add the sugar 1 tablespoon (15 mL) at a time. Fold in the ground hazelnuts and the vanilla with a spatula.

7. Divide the batter between the prepared pans or the circles of parchment paper and spread level.

8. Bake for 1 hour and 15 minutes. If the meringues brown too quickly, tent a piece of foil over each one.

9. Let stand 5 minutes, then run a knife around the inside edge of the pan to loosen. Transfer to a rack to cool.

10. Two hours before you're ready to serve, whip the cream on low speed until bubbles form, then increase the speed to medium, adding the dissolved gelatin, if using, and whipping until firm.

11. To assemble the cake, spread half the cream evenly on one meringue. Drop spoonfuls of the cranberry mixture over top and spread carefully. Place the second meringue over top and spread with the remaining whipped cream. Garnish with cranberries soaked in whiskey. Refrigerate for 1 to 2 hours to set before cutting.

Makes eight servings.

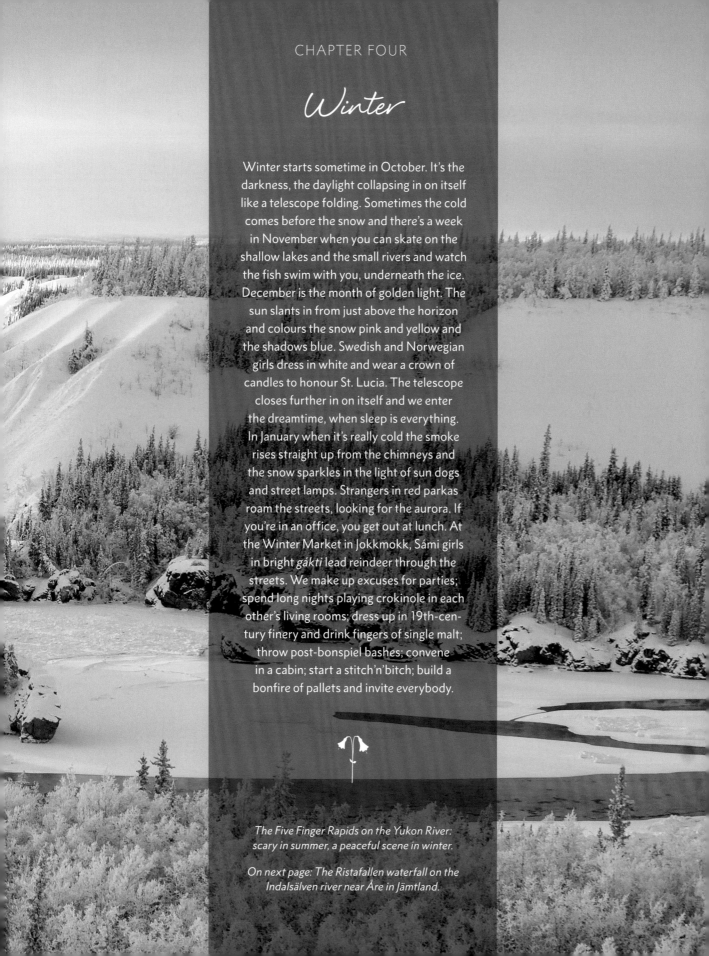

CHAPTER FOUR

Winter

Winter starts sometime in October. It's the darkness, the daylight collapsing in on itself like a telescope folding. Sometimes the cold comes before the snow and there's a week in November when you can skate on the shallow lakes and the small rivers and watch the fish swim with you, underneath the ice. December is the month of golden light. The sun slants in from just above the horizon and colours the snow pink and yellow and the shadows blue. Swedish and Norwegian girls dress in white and wear a crown of candles to honour St. Lucia. The telescope closes further in on itself and we enter the dreamtime, when sleep is everything. In January when it's really cold the smoke rises straight up from the chimneys and the snow sparkles in the light of sun dogs and street lamps. Strangers in red parkas roam the streets, looking for the aurora. If you're in an office, you get out at lunch. At the Winter Market in Jokkmokk, Sámi girls in bright *gákti* lead reindeer through the streets. We make up excuses for parties; spend long nights playing crokinole in each other's living rooms; dress up in 19th-century finery and drink fingers of single malt; throw post-bonspiel bashes; convene in a cabin; start a stitch'n'bitch; build a bonfire of pallets and invite everybody.

The Five Finger Rapids on the Yukon River: scary in summer, a peaceful scene in winter.

On next page: The Ristafallen waterfall on the Indalsälven river near Åre in Jämtland.

A Small Feast for a Late Night

Inspired by *Fäviken*

As December nights grow longer and we live the larger part of our lives in the dark, our natural inclination at 9 p.m. is to switch off the lights and repair to the Land of Nod. But no. Sleep is not permitted. We must stay up, to attend the fourth party that evening, package those gifts destined for distant parts, plan the winter vacation before the seat sale ends, start the hors d'oeuvres for the potluck, pipe green icing onto the shortbreads, sew the final beads onto the moccasins for the youngest niece. It's exhausting! At no other time are we more in need of late-night sustenance than in the days leading up to the longest night of the year.

Here then is a small collection of goodies to help get you through. If by chance yours is a household favoured by visits from Santa, consider leaving a small sample for him. He will thank you.

This selection of treats was inspired by a visit to Fäviken Magasinet in Jämtland, where the feasting starts early and ends late and there is always something magic on the table.

MENU

An Evening at Fäviken

The sound of many footsteps thumping up the wooden stairs announced that a new course was about to be served to the 12 diners gathered in the upper room of an old farmhouse in Sweden. Chef Magnus Nilsson and a sous-chef breached the top stair bearing a roasted leg of lamb and a hacksaw. They strode to a chopping block in the middle of the room and placed the roast upon it. The sous-chef braced himself and grasped either end of the leg of lamb. Chef Nilsson brandished the hacksaw and attacked, sawing through the bone in several furious strokes, sending juices and bone dust flying. The

The experience at Fäviken was different, an entry into haute cuisine that takes the foods and traditions of the forest and countryside, reinterprets them and shocks diners into rethinking their relationship with both food and flavours.

leg fell into two pieces, the chef and sous-chef lifted the chopping block between them and disappeared behind a screen, and in the dining room we wondered what on earth was coming next.

This moment of high drama was just one of several during a four-hour, 23-course meal at Fäviken Magasinet in early September 2012. I had been in Sweden for 10 days, the first stage in a culinary tour of Scandinavia to learn how Scandinavians cooked with the foods of the boreal forest. My husband and I had sampled salted and smoked reindeer, reindeer heart, moose cheese, arctic raspberry jelly, vendace roe from the Kalix River, pickled herring, whole smoked trout, whey cheese and many different kinds of knäckebröd. We already had a notebook full of ideas.

But the experience at Fäviken was different, an entry into haute cuisine that takes the foods and traditions of the forest and countryside, reinterprets them and shocks diners into rethinking their relationship with both food and flavours. I had booked a table three months in advance; there are only 12 seats at each dinner and Fäviken's fame had spread throughout Europe and into North America.

The restaurant is located in a farmhouse on an estate in Jämtland, just below the 62nd parallel in northwestern Sweden. Chef Nilsson, a native of Jämtland, left his career at Michelin-starred restaurants in Paris for his home territory in the late 2000s and came to work at Fäviken, formerly a place where skiers and hunters dined on simple fare like fondue. When a hedge fund millionaire with an interest in contemporary cuisine bought the estate, Nilsson came on board as the sommelier and was running the kitchen within a year.

The 31-year-old chef has developed a reputation for taking the notion of a local cuisine based on hyper-fresh ingredients, foraged and farmed, to culinary extremes. Examples might be deep-fried lichen served with lightly soured garlic cream or thrush heads sliced in half, sautéed in butter and served with their beaks attached. His detractors say he sacrifices gastronomy in pursuit of pushing the boundaries of what's edible. His admirers—among them Bill Buford, former editor of *Granta* and author of *Heat*, and René Redzepi, head chef of Noma in Copenhagen—say he's an inspiration.

The chefs reappeared from behind the screen along with the bartender, the restaurant manager and the remaining kitchen staff and together they swarmed our six tables with the 15th dish of the evening: cubed raw cow heart, wildflower petals, small toasts, herb salt and a dollop of marrow from the sawed lamb bone. Chef Nilsson gave us our instructions: mix the marrow, cow heart and flowers together, spoon onto toasts, sprinkle with herb salt and eat in a very few bites. He nodded, bowed and thumped down the stairs again, the battalion of helpers clattering behind him. Later, we would each be served one thick slice of the lamb with a thin sauce made from herbs, the most familiar dish of the evening.

Johan Agrell, who is sommelier, restaurant manager and part owner of the business, introduced the champagne, mead and four wines that accompanied the meal. On the night we dined, the guests included another writer and a television journalist; we were all taking notes and

Garlic dries in the sun on the stone wall outside the Fäviken farmhouse. It was a thrill to find stone brambles, or Rubus saxatilis, in the woods on the Fäviken estate after enjoying them at dinner the night before.

THE BOREAL FEAST

Opposite page: The view from a guest room in the Fäviken farmhouse. Top left: A walk in the highlands near Åre in Jämtland. Top right: The chopping block in the dining room at Fäviken.

snapping photos. During one course Agrell lost his patience and admonished us, saying it was important to eat while the food was hot.

Some of the flavours were challenging, and some just didn't translate—I couldn't discover the charm of the cow heart and lamb bone marrow, for example—but our table of four found that even when we didn't like a dish we appreciated its effect, which was to stimulate discussion about culinary possibility; about the cultural origins of what tastes good to us and what doesn't; and about what went on in the chef's head. What was he thinking? Why lichen? Why wild trout roe wrapped in a crust of pig blood? Why Root Vegetables Cooked with Autumn Leaves That Have Been Decomposing under the Snow One Winter?

The answer lies partly in the sense of adventure and willingness to experiment that Chef Nilsson and his team seem to have in abundance, and partly in Nilsson's devotion to food that tastes like itself. "When you work as hard as we do at getting the perfect shallot, you want to taste the vegetable," he said. Our meal started with a single fermented young carrot, served on a piece of soapstone, accompanied by a glass of very dry champagne. We moved on to a dip made with blue mussel from off the coast of Norway served with the Swedish staple, thin bread (also known as hard bread or flatbread). Fäviken's interpretation of this classic was made from flaxseeds held together by a paper-thin membrane made with the juice from the soaked seeds and some potato starch.

Throughout the meal we found similar interpretations of Swedish classics—lightly sautéed chanterelles served with raw peas and stone bramble (a berry from the rose family) or mackerel served with raw rowanberries (mountain ash berries) and green barley.

After the meal we repaired downstairs for herb tea, coffee and a digestive or liqueur. I chose duck egg liqueur,

The farmhouse at Fäviken, where the restaurant is located.

made on the premises from the eggs supplied by a farmer called Mr. Duck, who lives nearby and is one of the restaurant's principal foragers as well as one of its most important suppliers. It was delicious: creamy and light and nicely spiked with rum.

Now that the anxiety of producing 23 courses with precision timing was over, the whole place relaxed. The austere manner of chef and staff was replaced by friendly camaraderie, and Nilsson came round to each group of guests to chat. "What did you like? What didn't you like? That's always interesting," he said.

We asked him about the lichen (more a texture than a taste), and he laughed. "That's survival food," he said, and told us about once eating fermented lichen from the stomach of a reindeer. But Nilsson's answer highlights his connection to the traditional foods of Sweden and his efforts to reawaken diners' connection to the natural world. We asked if he tried to recreate the hunter-gatherer experience for diners—if that was why we dug through reconstituted autumn leaves to find our beet and turnip, for example, or why we finished making so many dishes ourselves at the table. He said no, but he could see why we thought so.

Later, in the kitchen, he gave me a sneak preview of his new cookbook, called simply *Fäviken*, for which he

was about to embark on tour, starting in North America. "It was supposed to be 25,000 words and 100 recipes, but it turned out to be 100,000 words and 40 recipes," he said. He pointed at a photograph of his famous Scallop *I Skalet Ur Elden* Cooked over Burning Juniper Branches. "Because really, who is going to cook this at home?" He said it was more important to describe the philosophy that prevails at Fäviken and to inspire in people the desire to reconnect with nature and explore their surroundings. Fäviken and Nilsson are practically household names in Canada now; the book is great reading and familiar territory for Canadians steeped in the foraging and experimenting traditions themselves.

I gave a small bottle of Uncle Berwyn's Birch Syrup to Chef Nilsson. He opened it immediately and tasted the syrup on the tip of his finger. "That's really good," he said and tasted it again. "I thought we were the only ones making this!" Next morning, Johan Agrell, who takes care of breakfast for the overnight guests while Nilsson has a morning at home, came to our table with a special treat. "I tried your birch syrup," he said, and presented us with two delicious, buttery, toffee-like cookies. He had used his grandmother's recipe for the traditional Swedish treat, *kolakakor*. Agrell had substituted birch syrup for the molasses.

Egg Liqueur

Those who love advocaat or Eierlikör will recognize this old favourite, though generally the eggs come from chickens, not ducks. Here the liqueur is spiced with a splash of birch syrup and a scrape of vanilla. Choose amber rum for the best results—darker rum will overtake the fresh, custardy flavour. This a great substitute for eggnog, but not to be taken in the same quantities. Too rich!

5 (chicken) egg yolks

½ cup (125 mL) sugar

½ cup (125 mL) whipping cream

½-inch (1.25-cm) length of vanilla pod, sliced in two

1 tsp (5 mL) birch syrup

½ cup (125 mL) good quality amber rum

1. Beat egg yolks and sugar in small bowl until thick and light.
2. Beat in cream.
3. Scrape vanilla seeds into the mixture and add the birch syrup.
4. Pour mixture into top of double boiler. Cook over simmering water until the mixture thickens, about 10 minutes. Don't let it boil or it will curdle.
5. Remove from heat and strain. Pour in the rum and mix well.
6. Cool to room temperature, then refrigerate in a sealed bottle or jar. Let sit for a day to allow flavours to blend. Serve in small glasses for a holiday treat.

Makes about 2 cups (475 mL). Will keep for up to three weeks in the fridge.

Johan Agrell's *Kolakakor*

½ cup (125 mL) butter

¼ cup (60 mL) sugar

1 Tbsp (15 mL) birch syrup

½ tsp (2.5 mL) baking soda

1 cup (250 mL) plus 2 Tbsp (30 mL) flour

1. Preheat oven to 350F (180C) and line a baking sheet with parchment paper.
2. Cream butter and sugar together until light and fluffy.
3. Sift dry ingredients together.
4. Add birch syrup to butter mixture. Add dry ingredients and mix thoroughly, using your hands as necessary to form a ball.
5. Transfer dough onto a piece of plastic wrap on the counter and shape into a rough 10-inch (25-cm) log. Wrap log and roll with your hands until rounded. Unwrap and slice into about 20 pieces. Arrange pieces on baking sheet.
6. Bake for 15 minutes, or until lightly browned.

Makes 20 cookies.

Håkan Särnåker's Thin Bread

Fäviken's flaxseed bread was a treat, and the recipe is included in Magnus Nilsson's cookbook. This crunchy, nutty version is a good introduction for those who are intrigued by the notion of thin bread and want to explore further. It's gluten-free, and a great staple in any season. Our friend Håkan Särnåker served it on our first night in Sweden. Try it with goat cheese and Spicy Rhubarb Jelly (page 205).

Found in the baking section of the supermarket, corn flour is sold by Bob's Red Mill and Unico, among other brands. Essentially very finely ground cornmeal, the texture of corn flour is floury, not grainy. Don't mistake cornstarch for corn flour; they are different animals. Be aware of the differences between British and North American terminology.

1 cup (250 mL) corn flour
½ cup (125 mL) sunflower seeds
½ cup (125 mL) sesame seeds
¼ cup (60 mL) pumpkin seeds
¼ cup (60 mL) flaxseeds
1 tsp (5 mL) fennel seeds

1 tsp (5 mL) anise seeds
1 tsp (5 mL) ground juniper berries
Sea salt to taste
¼ cup (60 mL) canola oil
1 cup (250 mL) boiling water

1. Cut two sheets of parchment paper to fit 9- × 13-inch (22.5- × 32-cm) baking trays.

2. Stir dry ingredients together. Add oil and stir to combine.

3. Add boiling water and mix thoroughly. The dough will be quite runny at first, thickening as the corn flour absorbs the water.

4. Using a spatula, spread as thinly and evenly as you can onto the sheets of parchment paper. Don't worry if there are small gaps in the dough. (It's easier to spread the dough on the paper before moving it to the baking tray.)

5. Bake at 300F (150C) for 1 hour.

6. Turn the oven off, prop the door open and leave the bread in the cooling oven for 20 minutes.

7. Remove from oven and cool on baking trays. When at room temperature, break the bread into large pieces. Will keep for several days in an airtight container.

Makes about four dozen pieces.

A Forage Party

A Feast of Hors d'Oeuvres, Inspired by Ramshackle Theatre's Theatre in the Bush

MENU FOR EIGHT

Forage! At Theatre in the Bush

Those who grew up in northern communities will be familiar with the wild bash in the woods known as the bush party. There is always a bonfire, and dancing, and singing of songs, and more often than not, high drama of a personal or public kind. In recent years Brian Fidler, artistic director of Ramshackle Theatre in White-horse, has taken the ritual and mad magic of a bush party and distilled it into an interactive, multidisciplinary event called Theatre in the Bush.

Theatre in the Bush happens for one night at the fall equinox in a small section of the boreal forest just south of Whitehorse. At the box office, a little plywood ticket booth with a mason jar for the cash, theatregoers select a token such as a rosehip, a cranberry or a pine cone to help them find the group they will spend the evening with. Groups of 10 to 20 gather at the main bonfire and when the performances start, follow their guide along winding pathways lit with torches and lanterns to each performance site in rotation; at any time there might be 50 to 100 people roaming through the trees, and when they stop, audiences of 10 to 20 at each of seven performances happening simultaneously.

The performance sites are named for their feature or location, such as "The Bowl," a natural amphitheatre, or "The Rise," a ridge above the Yukon River, or "Wind-blown Trees," a clearing by a fallen spruce. Performers select their site by lottery a week before the event, and sometimes develop their piece in response to the site. Performers are expected to create an interactive,

10-minute show, and the time limit is strict. On theatre night Brian rings a bell at the beginning and the end of each 10-minute period to signal the performance is over and each group should move on to the next one.

There are installations on the pathways between sites whose practical purpose is to slow a group down if it's going to be too early for the next performance, and whose other purpose is to astound with beauty. In 2013 many theatregoers went back a second time to marvel at Tara Kolla-Hale's giant chandelier of paper houses, lit from within and hung from a spruce tree. And there's a whole alley of installations too, where parties spend 10 minutes exploring on their own during the guided tour. In 2013 they could shake it up at Sarah Moore's greenhouse dancehouse lit with Christmas lights, or dress up in costumes and snap a picture in Genevieve Doyon and Alistair Maitland's *Animated Photo Booth*, or visit Gisli Balzer's sculpture garden, or listen to a sound-scape by Baptiste.

In 2013 I staged an event called *Forage!* with Hector and a couple of friends. The *Forage* site was Wall Tent; we had the wall tent as a staging area and a bonfire too, with a whole stack of pallets and dead branches piled at the ready nearby, and ample space in the clearing to spread out our foraging materials.

Our nearest neighbours were Hazel Venzon at The Bowl, who got everybody talking to each other in *Hello, How Are You, F-You*, and Susan Walton and Emily Wood-ruffe at the Cutline just up the hill, who waved their

For a bright and fizzy cocktail, pour 1 tablespoon (15 mL) of cranberry liqueur into the bottom of a glass, add Prosecco and stir in some cranberries.

arms and twinkled their legs in elegant stylized patterns against a backdrop of blue tarp in a carnival booth. They were dressed in swimming attire, including bathing caps and nose plugs, and their theatrical offering was entitled *Synch or Swim*. Up at the Rise, Eric Epstein performed a set of sad cowboy campfire songs and passed a bottle of bourbon around; he came down to visit us at our bonfire during the breaks and passed the bourbon there too.

By the time attendees walked under the *Forage* sign strung between two pine trees they were in the mood for interaction, which was good. Their task at *Forage* was to pair off, decide who would be sweet and who savoury, build a dessert or an appetizer and then tell each other all about it. It was up to them if they gave their partner a taste or not, and they could, if they wanted, write down their recipe on a card and pin it to the clothesline.

Sophia Marnik was keeper of the savoury station, and Tara Kolla-Hale the sweet. I stood by at the edge of the fire with a cast iron pan to fill custom orders of bison marrow or moose steak. At each station, spread out on tree stumps and lit by candles, we had arranged little bowls and plates with small items of food and divided them into categories of base, middle, topping and garnish. The idea was to select one item from each category and build an appetizer or a dessert. You couldn't go back for seconds, so you had to commit. We said, "There are

no bad recipes and no critics." The important thing was to talk about what you did and why, to compare the way your thing tasted against your expectation, to conjure memory and share experiences.

"There are no bad recipes and no critics."

We sat by the fire and listened to the foragers chat about their concoctions. A husband and wife pressed side by side on the bench by the fire and examined their treats. "What did you get?" said one. A couple of French gals checked on the ingredients of the thin bread; an anglophone asked where the circumflex went on "fraîche." Sophia and Tara replenished the stations and Hector tended the fire. We each managed to sneak away once or twice to see another performance and visit the installations. And then the final bell rang to end the evening. Suddenly there were 60 people at our site.

We announced that all restrictions were lifted, that people could eat anything they wanted and go back for seconds, and *Forage* turned into a giant cocktail party, with conversations happening all over the site and tired theatregoers staring into the fire, foraged treat in hand.

Then it was time to shut down the site. We could hear the dying chatter of the audience walking back to the main bonfire for one last farewell before heading home.

Northern lights over the city of Whitehorse. Aurora borealis occur year round but are best viewed in winter. When the lights appear in the sky, the message goes out over phone lines and social media: Great northern lights over the city RIGHT NOW! And we run into the street to see them.

We took down the *Forage* sign and packed away the leftovers. I pushed the last wheelbarrow of supplies up the path to the truck. Hector said goodbye and drove off and I went back to the main bonfire. Hardly anyone was left. In Sarah Moore's greenhouse dancehouse a ladder and bucket stood in the middle of the floor, and Christmas lights dangled from the ceiling, half taken down. Over the loudspeaker came the sad and sweet strains of Ron Hynes singing "Sonny's Dream."

Forage! took place in late September, but a forage party is worth considering for the festive season, when there are new people among the old friends at the gathering, and some of us are shy. Telling someone about your creation or asking them about theirs is a great way to start up a conversation. There's a good food story lurking in everyone!

Here are some examples of the items at the *Forage!* stations:

SAVOURY

Bases: boiled, sliced Yukon Gold potatoes, Håkan Särnåker's Thin Bread (page 144), Spruce Tip Focaccia (page 156), sliced, roasted beets

Middles: Smoked Arctic Char Liver Pâté (page 154), Bison Marrow (page 150), Goat Sausage with Shaggy Mane Mushrooms, Juniper and Wild Blueberries (page 152), salmon candy

Toppings: crème fraîche, apple and Calvados jelly, Salmon Roe (page 241), Soapberry Jelly (page 216)

Garnishes: spruce tip salt, lowbush cranberries, preserved lemon slices, Pickled Spruce Tips (page 226)

SWEET

Bases: rose petal shortbreads, Johan Agrell's *Kolakakor* (page 143), cranberry scones, puff pastry shells

Middles: Mocha Mascarpone Mousse (page 166), Spruce Tip Crème Brûlée (page 157), chèvre sweetened with birch syrup, chocolate and cranberry ganache

Toppings: crème fraîche, rose petal jelly, Vodka-Soaked Cranberries (page 159), Simple Wild Raspberry Jam (page 217)

Garnishes: Candied Spruce Tips (page 209), rose petal sugar, mint leaves, nasturtiums and violas

Here are some of the recipes and comments people pinned on the clothesline:

FROM THE SAVOURY STATION:

Ramshackle Toast: Focaccia, moose steak, beets, spruce salt, cranberries

Susan and Em's Delight: Thin bread, morel mushrooms, crème fraîche ("Very subtle, smooth, with a light woodsy aftertaste.")

Potato, salmon, chèvre

Focaccia bread, chèvre, salmon roe, preserved lemon

Spruce tip focaccia with arctic char pâté with apple jelly and spruce tip salt ("*C'est bien!*")

Graham Potato Sambo: Potato, moose sausage, soapberry, spruce salt

FROM THE SWEET STATION:

Rose petal shortbread, chocolate mousse, thimbleberry jam, mint

The Stephanie: Cranberry scone, chocolate mousse, raspberry jam, rose petal sugar

Rose petal shortbread, crème brûlée, cranberries, candied spruce tips

Shortbread, chocolate mousse, raspberry jam, mint leaf ("Yum!!")

Cranberry scone, chocolate mousse, raspberry jam, flower

Puff pastry, crème brûlée, thimbleberry jam, candied spruce tips

Rose petal shortbread, ganache, candied spruce tips

Delicious: *Kolakakor*, crème brûlée, rose petal jam, mint

Sweet Delight: Cranberry scone with sweet chèvre, topped with rose petal jelly & garnished with candied spruce tips

Bison Marrow with Smoked Fleur de Sel

Bone marrow is the soft tissue in the hollow centres of long bones like the femur and the tibia. The marrow of elk, moose, deer, bison and caribou has long been an important source of fat for indigenous people in northern countries, but it features in southern cuisines too: think of the Vietnamese pho or Italian osso bucco. Marrow has been showing up on restaurant menus long enough that foodies are getting bored, but I've noticed that here in the Yukon it's not so common.

Marrow is definitely an acquired taste; to be blunt, you have to like meat-flavoured fat. (I've never had a problem with that!) The trick with marrow is cooking it long enough that it softens and separates from the bone but not so long that it melts away. The most common methods are to roast the bones for 18 to 20 minutes in a hot oven (450F/230C) or stand them upright in water and simmer them for 8 to 10 minutes. The marrow is generally extracted with a long, thin spoon with a narrow bowl (there are beautiful antique versions available online) and eaten on toast.

However, when the bone is straight you can gently push the marrow through to emerge in one cylinder. In this case a good way to cook it is coated in flour and then sautéed in a cast iron frying pan over medium-low heat for 8 minutes or so. (At Theatre in the Bush we did this at the very edge of the fire.) I learned this trick from British chef Valentine Warner, who came to Whitehorse to do a cooking show. I replicated the dish at Theatre in the Bush (eliminating the Dijon mustard and red wine vinegar) and it was a big hit. The smoked salt, the Spruce Tip Focaccia toast and the watercress or arugula provide a sharp, bite-y contrast to the creamy, fatty marrow. In order to get enough *straight* marrow bones for this recipe you might need to buy two bags of bones at the butcher's, but then you can roast the more crooked or irregular ones, dig out the marrow with a knife and spread it on focaccia or use the roasted bone and marrow for stock.

1½ lbs (680 gr) straight bison marrow bones, 4–6 bones (or substitute organic beef bones)

2 Tbsp (30 mL) flour

1 Tbsp (15 mL) butter

1 Tbsp (15 mL) canola oil

8 or so slices of Spruce Tip Focaccia, recipe on page 156

2 handfuls arugula or watercress, washed and dried

1 Tbsp (15 mL) Spruce Tip Oil, recipes on page 230 (or substitute olive oil)

1 tsp (5 mL) lemon juice

1½ tsp (7.5 mL) Smoked Fleur de Sel, recipe on next page

1. Soak the marrow bones in cold, salted water for several hours or overnight to draw out the blood and loosen the marrow from the bone. Rinse and pat dry. Using your thumb, gently push the marrow at one end until it emerges at the other. After the initial resistance it should be fairly easy. Keep the bones for stock.

2. Dredge each cylinder of marrow thoroughly in the flour. Heat butter and canola oil in a cast iron frying pan over medium-high heat. Start the marrow at medium-high and turn to medium after a couple of minutes to avoid burning the flour. (Though it may seem counterintuitive to use butter and oil, it's there to crisp the flour coating on the marrow.)

3. Cook the marrow for 7 or 8 minutes, turning carefully, until the outsides are crisp. Test by cutting into one end; if the fat is soft and somewhat translucent the marrow is ready. Drain on paper towels. Transfer to a cutting board and slice each cylinder lengthwise.

4. Toast the focaccia under the broiler (or on a grill over the fire) while the marrow is cooking. Toss the watercress or arugula in oil and lemon juice.

5. Arrange the marrow, toast and greens on a platter and pass the Smoked Fleur de Sel. Place the greens on the toast, top with marrow and sprinkle with fleur de sel. And make sure to have at least one bite of the marrow, unadorned.

Makes six servings as an appetizer.

SMOKED FLEUR DE SEL

There are many sources of excellent Canadian sea salt and fleur de sel, and one of them is in the Pacific Northwest: Vancouver Island Salt Co. In addition to their flavoured salts, consider purchasing the plain versions, then experimenting with different flavours on your own.

I have a Bradley smoker with a temperature control so I can cold-smoke, but hot- smoking in a box smoker with an electric coil in the bottom or in a modified gas barbecue will also work. In a box smoker put the salt on the top rack; in a barbecue keep the temperature as low as possible.

To modify a gas barbecue into a smoker soak 3 cups (710 mL) wood chips overnight in cold water and wrap them in foil. Remove one side of the grill, turn the gas on as low as possible, open the foil package at the top and place it directly on the flames. Keep the temperature low so the wood chips don't flame but just smoke. Place the item to be smoked on the other side of the grill.

Suggestion: even if you live in the city, consider banding together with a bunch of friends and buying a smoker, which can then move from household to household as needed, or become the catalyst for a neighbourly smoke-fest. The only thing you need is one backyard with an outdoor electrical outlet.

¼ cup (60 mL) fleur de sel or coarse sea salt (flavour salt in small batches until you're sure you like it and will use it)

1. For smoker: line a grill basket with a piece of parchment paper; turn the oven off if you can and open the vent halfway.

   For barbecue: place the parchment paper on a piece of foil with the edges curled up.

2. Spread the fleur de sel evenly on the parchment paper. Lay a second piece of parchment paper over top to protect the salt from vent drippings or flakes.

3. Smoke for 1 hour, taste-test and smoke for another hour if necessary. Stir occasionally to redistribute the salt for even smoking. The flavour will be subtle, not hit-you-over-the-head.

4. Remove salt from the smoker and spread out on a parchment-lined baking tray to dry for a couple of hours. Transfer to a glass jar and store in the cupboard.

Makes ¼ cup (60 mL).

Goat Sausage with Shaggy Mane Mushrooms, Juniper and Wild Blueberries

We are lucky in the Yukon; we have goat farmers who live on Lake Laberge and provide us with beautiful cheeses like halloumi, chèvre and feta from May to December and fresh goat meat in the fall.

To make these sausages you'll need a hand-cranked or electric meat grinder and sausage horn; the alternative is to make sausage patties. There are sausage-making attachments available for most commercial mixers, worth the investment if you think you might want to pursue sausage-making or charcuterie. The great thing about homemade sausage is you control the ingredients.

The blueberries are roasted at low heat to intensify the flavour and reduce the liquid; this way, you avoid turning the sausage entirely blue, although the finished product will definitely have an indigo hue. The juniper berries are roasted to enhance the flavour and reduce bitterness.

½ cup (125 ml) blueberries

1 tsp (5 ml) juniper berries

½ oz (15 gr) dried shaggy mane mushrooms (or substitute porcini or morel mushrooms)

1 tsp (5 mL) butter

1 tsp (5 mL) olive oil

1 lb (455 gr) goat meat, preferably from the neck

4 oz (110 gr) pork fat, refrigerated

3 feet (0.9 m) sausage casing, either brined or dry-preserved with salt

2 cloves garlic, minced

1 Tbsp (15 ml) wild sage (*artemisia frigida*) or substitute cultivated sage (*salvia officinalis*)

2 Tbsp (30 mL) red wine

Salt and pepper to taste

PREPARING THE INGREDIENTS

1. Roast the blueberries: preheat oven to 150F (65C). Spread blueberries on a baking sheet lined with parchment paper. Roast berries for about 1 hour and 30 minutes, so that they are still somewhat moist. Remove from oven and let cool before attempting to remove berries from the parchment paper. They tend to stick. Be patient.

2. Roast juniper berries in a cast iron frying pan over low heat until they are shiny and aromatic, about 10 minutes. Remove from heat, cool and grind with a mortar and pestle.

3. Soak shaggy mane mushrooms in boiling water to cover until soft, about 15 minutes. Squeeze mushrooms to remove excess liquid, and reserve liquid for stock or soup. Heat butter and olive oil in the same pan you used for the juniper berries. Sauté the shaggy manes over medium heat until golden. Remove from heat, cool and chop roughly.

4. Cut the goat meat from the bone. Remove the sinew and gristle, but not the fat. Cut the meat into cubes. (Reserve the neck bone for stock.)

5. Remove the skin from the pork fat and cut into cubes. (Refrigerate the fat again unless you're going to use it immediately.)

6. Soak the sausage casing in fresh water for 15 minutes. Fasten one end of the casing to the tap and run water through to rinse the insides. Cover with fresh water and set aside.

MAKING THE SAUSAGE

1. Combine meat and fat, add garlic, sage and crushed juniper berries and mix thoroughly.

2. Place a bowl underneath the meat grinder. Press the meat and fat mixture through the grinder fitted with a plate with ¼-inch (0.6-cm) holes.

3. Once the ground mixture stops coming through the holes, stop the machine, unplug it, remove the attachments and clear the screw and blade of meat and fat. Mince any larger pieces with a sharp knife and add to the bowl of ground sausage meat. Wash the attachments and prepare for the sausage-making stage.

4. To the newly ground mixture, add the blueberries, shaggy manes, red wine, salt and pepper and mix thoroughly. Make a small taster patty and cook for 5 minutes over medium heat. Taste and adjust seasoning if necessary.

5. Attach the sausage-making horn to the mixer. Bring the bowl of water and sausage casing over to the mixer, and feed the whole length of casing carefully onto the horn, leaving about 5 inches (13 cm) dangling off the end. You'll be tempted to tie a knot in the bottom now, but don't; if you do the casing will fill up with air before the sausage meat starts coming out.

6. When the first bit of meat emerges from the horn, wait until it reaches a length of 3 inches (7.5 cm), turn off the machine and tie off the bottom of the casing. Turn the machine back on and fill the entire casing; you can help by gently stroking the meat downwards in the casing as it fills. Your trusty sous-chef's extra pair of hands is a great addition to the project.

7. Near the end the sausage meat will emerge more and more slowly and then stop altogether, but there will still be quite a bit of meat that hasn't come through. Unplug the mixer, detach the horn from the mixer while keeping the casing attached to the horn's end, and press the remaining meat through the horn with the end of a wooden spoon while you hold the horn. Be gentle with the wooden spoon so as not to rip the casing.

8. Pinch the casing between your fingers at sausage-length intervals—usually 5 to 8 inches (13 to 20 cm). The pressure will push meat away from either side of your fingers. With your hands on either side of the pinch, twist the sausage in opposite directions, gently. Repeat down the whole length of the sausage. Cut each link in the middle of the twisted bit of casing; the cut seals the casing closed.

9. Dry the sausages on a rack overnight in the refrigerator; the skin will become tight and somewhat shiny. Pack in butcher's paper or waxed paper and plastic. The sausages will keep for three days in the fridge or two months in the freezer.

GRILLING THE SAUSAGES

1. Simmer sausages over very low heat until they rise to the surface, usually about 10 minutes.

2. Broil at high heat or grill on the barbecue for five minutes.

3. Let sit for a few minutes, then slice each sausage on the diagonal into six. (The ends are traditionally reserved for those who are working in the kitchen or setting the table.)

Makes about 6 × 6-inch (15-cm) sausages. Cut into slices, makes 12 servings as an appetizer.

Smoked Arctic Char Liver Pâté

I have to thank Jennifer Hess for teaching me about Arctic char livers. For many years Jenn worked at Icy Waters Arctic Charr aquaculture company near Whitehorse. (She fillets a fish with a few graceful strokes of the knife and it's beautiful to watch.) While still at Icy Waters, Jenn developed her own business, FishWitch Smokehouse, in order to create and sell value-added products made with the light-fleshed char that isn't as attractive commercially. She made char candy, several varieties of smoked char, and in latter years, she started smoking char livers.

I first tasted her smoked Arctic char livers in the summer of 2013 and was blown away. The flavour is like that of smoked oysters, with the buttery texture of foie gras. The livers are delicious on their own or sliced thinly, placed on a round of radish and topped with wasabi cream. At Klondike Kate's in Dawson City, chef Jeffrey Mickelson serves them with rhubarb compote and crème fraîche. The pâté cranks it up a notch; it's creamy, smoky, briny and very rich. (I gave a small ramekin to a neighbour and the next time I saw him he kissed me in the street.) Try the pâté on Rice Crackers (page 237) with Spicy Rhubarb Jelly (page 205) or Soapberry Jelly (page 216), or serve with Finnish Black Bread (page 235) and Red Onion Compote (next page). Admittedly you are not going to find Arctic char livers easily in downtown Vancouver or Montreal, but ask your fishmonger. You never know. In January of 2014, Icy Waters was developing char livers as a product line. In the meantime, try the pâté with smoked chicken livers.

SMOKED ARCTIC CHAR LIVERS

The livers are brined for 10 to 15 minute in a fairly weak solution before smoking; as Jenn says, the livers are soft tissue and easily penetrated by the brine. Too much salt will turn the livers into "tiny salt licks." You'll need a grill basket with small mesh for the smoker; the livers are small and will fall between the bars of a regular grill.

4 cups (1 L) cold water
3 Tbsp (45 mL) sea salt
1½ lbs (680 gr) raw Arctic char livers

1. Whisk salt and water together until salt is dissolved. Add livers and soak for 10 to 15 minutes.

2. Drain into a sieve and rinse livers under cold running water. Pat dry with paper towel.

3. Oil the grill basket and place livers on it in a single layer. Set the oven temperature in your smoker at 125F (50C) and use alder chips. Allow the smoker to come up to temperature and fill with smoke before putting the livers in.

4. Open the smoker's vent halfway to let steam escape. Hot-smoke the livers; they will develop a pellicle as they smoke. Turn the livers over during the first hour of cooking. Start testing for doneness after 1 hour; the interior should have a soft, smooth texture and the colour should no longer be pink. They may take as long as 2 hours, but check frequently after 1 hour.

5. Cool on a rack. Reserve 1 pound (455 gr) of livers for the pâté and enjoy the remainder as they are. Experiment!

A dark and snowy path leads upwards to winter light.

PÂTÉ

1 lb (455 gr) Smoked Arctic Char Livers (see previous page)

8 oz (225 gr) unsalted butter, softened

½ tsp (2.5 mL) mace or grated nutmeg

2 tsp (10 mL) dry mustard

½ tsp (2.5 mL) ground allspice

½ tsp (2.5 mL) toasted juniper berries, crushed

3 green onions, finely chopped

½ tsp (2.5 mL) garlic, minced

¼ cup (60 mL) cognac

2 Tbsp (30 mL) parsley, finely chopped

⅓ cup (80 mL) 35 percent cream

1. Place all ingredients except cream in the bowl of a food processor and process until the pâté is completely smooth. Add cream, scraping down the sides of the bowl with a spatula. Store in an airtight container; the pâté will keep for one week in the refrigerator.

2. Note: the livers are high in oil, which sometimes seeps to the top of the pâté after a few hours. In that case, blot the surface with paper towel and whisk the pate with a fork before transferring to a ramekin to serve.

3. Serve at room temperature with toasted fingers of Finnish Black Bread (page 235) and Red Onion Compote.

Makes about 1½ lbs (680 gr).

Red Onion Compote

1 medium red onion

1 tsp (5 mL) olive oil

2 Tbsp (30 mL) brown sugar or birch syrup

2 Tbsp (30 mL) red wine

2 tsp (10 mL) balsamic vinegar

Sea salt to taste

1. Peel onion, cut in half and slice thinly lengthwise. Sauté in olive oil over medium-low heat in a cast iron frying pan until softened, 5 to 7 minutes.

2. Add sugar or syrup and caramelize lightly. Add wine and vinegar and cook slowly until liquid has evaporated. Cool to room temperature and store in the refrigerator for up to a week.

Makes about ½ cup (125 mL).

Spruce Tip Focaccia

This recipe assumes you have a sourdough starter on hand. To learn how to start a starter from scratch, see Sourdough Boot Camp in *The Boreal Gourmet*.

1½ cups (350 mL) active sourdough starter (it's best if the starter has been refreshed twice before you start)

2 cups (475 mL) warm water (80F/27C)

3 Tbsp (45 mL) coarsely chopped dried spruce tips, divided

3–3½ cups (710 mL– 830 mL) all-purpose flour, plus more for kneading

¼–½ cup (60–125 mL) Spruce Tip Oil, divided, recipes on page 230 (or substitute olive oil)

1 Tbsp (15 mL) coarse sea salt

1. Add warm water to starter and mix thoroughly with a wooden spoon. Beat in 2 tablespoons (30 mL) spruce tips (reserve the rest for the top). Add the flour to the starter 1 cup (250 mL) at a time, stirring thoroughly after each addition until the dough comes together; it should be wet and sticky, so hold off on the last ½ cup of flour if necessary. (The wetter the dough, the bigger the holes in the focaccia.) Let the dough rest for 20 minutes in the bowl under a tea towel.

2. Beat ¼ cup (60 mL) Spruce Tip Oil and salt into the dough with a spoon; the oil will not absorb fully at once, but keep beating until it does. Dump the dough onto a lightly floured surface and knead for 8 to 10 minutes, using a dough scraper to lift it from the surface and fold it over. It will be quite floppy. The dough is ready when you can pinch a piece of dough and it will stretch for 1 inch (2.5 cm) or so before breaking off.

3. Form the dough into a ball, oil it and let it rise in a bowl until it's doubled in size. This will take from 4 to 12 hours, depending on the temperature in your kitchen, so plan accordingly. If you're making dough at night, refrigerate it overnight to avoid over-proofing and return to room temperature before continuing.

4. Once the dough has risen, lift it away from the sides of the bowl with a scraper and ease the whole ball carefully onto a baking tray lined with parchment paper.

5. Stretch and press the dough with wet hands until it's an even thickness of about 1 inch (2.5 cm). Poke deep holes into the dough at regular intervals, drizzle with additional Spruce Tip Oil and sprinkle with the remaining spruce tips. Let rise for 30 minutes.

6. Place a pan of water in the bottom of the oven and preheat to 450F (230C).

7. Bake the dough for 20 to 30 minutes; when the crust has formed on both sides and sounds hollow if you tap the bottom, it's ready. Cool thoroughly on a rack before cutting into it.

Makes one 10 × 14-inch (25 × 36-cm) focaccia.

Spruce Tip Crème Brûlée

Crème brûlée is a classic restaurant dish that has become easier to accomplish in the home kitchen with the advent of the culinary torch. I highly recommend the purchase of this device, which retails for under $50. I have given up on producing the requisite caramelized top under the grill in my kitchen stove, after a few flaming disasters. My nerves can't take it. For the sugar topping, I've had the best results with organic raw cane sugar or regular granulated white sugar.

1 cup (250 mL) 35 percent cream

2 cups (475 mL) 10 percent cream

¼ cup (60 mL) fresh or frozen spruce tips

6 egg yolks

⅓ cup (80 mL) plus 3 Tbsp (45 mL) sugar, divided

2 tsp (10 mL) Spruce Tip Liqueur, recipe on page 158 (optional)

1. Preheat the oven to 325F (160C).

2. Bring cream and spruce tips to the boil over medium-high heat. Remove from heat and cover, letting the spruce tips steep for 15 minutes.

3. Beat egg yolks until they've thickened slightly, then add ⅓ cup (80 mL) sugar and beat until light and creamy. Whisk in Spruce Tip Liqueur.

4. Strain the cream mixture into a measuring cup and pour slowly into the egg mixture, beating constantly. If the mixture foams up and increases in volume, stir slowly with a wooden spoon to break the bubbles, until the mixture subsides.

5. Set eight ½-cup (125-mL) ramekins in a roasting pan and evenly divide the cream mixture between them.

6. Fill the roasting pan with boiling water until it comes halfway up the sides of the ramekins.

7. Bake for 35 minutes. The centres should still be slightly wobbly.

8. Cool completely on a rack, then cover with plastic and refrigerate for several hours or overnight.

9. About 30 minutes before you're ready to serve, remove from the fridge. If condensation has dripped onto the custard, blot the surface carefully with a tea towel or paper towel.

10. Sprinkle sugar over top in a thin but even layer. The easiest way to do this is to pour about a teaspoon onto the first custard and gently shake the ramekin to evenly coat the surface. Pour the excess sugar onto the next custard, and so on, until each one is covered.

11. If you are brave, set the oven on broil and move the top rack so that it's about 3 inches (7.5 cm) from the element. Give the broiler 2 or 3 minutes to heat up, then slide the custards underneath on a baking tray. Watch like a hawk. The tops will bubble and then caramelize very quickly; it should take no more than 2 to 3 minutes.

    Alternatively, set the culinary blowtorch on medium and rotate the flame over each custard until the tops are brown and speckled.

12. Serve at room temperature. The crust softens over time, so once caramelized it should be served within a few hours.

Makes eight ½-cup (125-mL) servings.

Spruce Tip Liqueur

My first effort at this mild and spruce-y after-dinner drink tasted neither mild nor spruce-y, but more like Pine-Sol. The trick is to use just one part spruce tips to three parts vodka, a tip generously provided by David Curtis of Dawson City. The other trick is to use good quality vodka. The cheap stuff just doesn't cut it.

1 cup (250mL) fresh or frozen spruce tips

3 cups (710 mL) good quality vodka

1 cup (250 mL) sugar

1 cup (250 mL) water

1. Pour spruce tips and vodka into a clean 4-cup (1-L) jar. Store in a cool, dark place for 3 weeks, turning the jar every 2 or 3 days.

2. Strain through a sieve lined with cheesecloth, then strain through a coffee filter and transfer to a clean jar. Store in a cool, dark place for 6 weeks to 3 months before sampling. Stop here for a delicious aquavit, or continue to the next step for liqueur.

3. Boil sugar and water together until sugar is dissolved.

4. Cool syrup, then add to the strained vodka to taste and stir until combined.

5. Store in a sealed jar or bottle in a cool, dark place for at least 3 months.

6. Uncork and serve after dinner in a schnapps glass. You can also drizzle over ice cream, or add soda water and ice for a refreshing cooler.

Makes about 3 cups (710 mL) aquavit or 4 cups (950 mL) liqueur.

Cranberry Liqueur and Vodka-Soaked Cranberries

A tray of boreal liqueurs: egg, cranberry and spruce tip.

This recipe makes a sweet–tart liqueur that is good at three months and better after a year. Vodka-soaked lowbush cranberries are its delicious by-product, an excellent pantry item to have on hand as a garnish for game, smoked fish, desserts and fancy cocktails or for use in sauces, salads and stuffing. Lowbush cranberries will keep in the refrigerator for a year or longer, with or without vodka; they're high in benzoic acid, which acts as a preservative.

2 cups (475 mL) wild lowbush cranberries (lingonberries) or substitute cultivated cranberries

3 cups (710 mL) good quality vodka

1 cup (250 mL) sugar

1 cup (250 mL) water

Optional flavourings: a 1-inch (2.5-cm) wide strip of lemon peel and/or 1-inch (2.5-cm) piece of ginger, peeled and chopped

1. Wash berries, shake dry and pour into a clean, dry jar with a screw-top lid.

2. Pour vodka over berries. Seal and store in a cool, dark place for 10 days to 3 weeks. Shake the jar gently every day.

3. Strain through a sieve lined with cheesecloth, then through a coffee filter. Reserve the berries and store in a covered container in the refrigerator. They will keep for a year or longer.

4. Make a simple syrup by combining sugar and water, adding optional flavours if you like. Bring to the boil, remove from heat and cool. Strain. Add to the cranberry vodka until it's sweet enough for your taste, and store the vodka in a cool, dark place for at least 3 months.

Makes about 3 cups (710 mL).

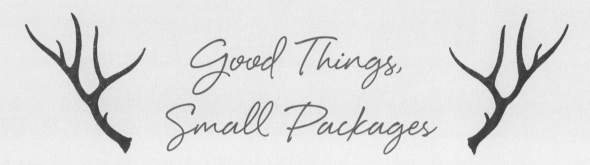

Good Things, Small Packages

MENU

Boreal Sweets to Celebrate the Season

Baking rises to the fore at this time of year. From Watson Lake to Old Crow, kitchen lights burn late into the night as we pore over cookbooks and cruise the food blogger sites, hunting for new treats to complement the old favourites, dazzle the cookie exchange or shine on the potluck table. Who among us hasn't been up past midnight, wrestling with that candy, cookie or tiny tart that looks so pretty in the picture but is proving impossible to reproduce? It's a season of triumph and despair, of last-minute saves and sad admissions of defeat.

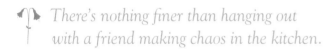

There's nothing finer than hanging out with a friend making chaos in the kitchen.

Happily, most of our friends are engaged in the same pursuit, and we know some of their successes are going to come our way. There are a couple of keeners in my social network, and every winter solstice a beautiful package of goodies appears on my back porch. It might be hanging from the doorknob or tucked underneath the bench, and could appear as early as 5 p.m. or as late as 10 p.m. One solstice I went to bed at midnight with sadness in my heart: no package. But when I checked again in the morning, there it was, hidden behind the broom. Hooray! The season had begun.

Since 2008, Whitehorse residents Michelle Rabeau and Guiniveve Lalena have generated a seasonal big bang of baking energy in Guiniveve's kitchen. They meet in the dying days of the sun, when the air is crisp and the light is golden, to stir, beat, pulse, mix, coat, sugar, bake and decorate goodies. These they package in appealing and ingenious containers and deliver personally to the door of each person on their list of 20 or so. Their aim is to bake, package and deliver in one day, which sometimes means a 12-hour day, but it's worth it. At this time of year, they say, there's nothing finer than hanging out with a friend making chaos in the kitchen.

Each year the contents of the solstice package are different, and might include a tiny crème brûlée, a clutch of shortbread cookies, a scattering of meringues, a lemon square, a truffle, a pecan tart and a couple of savoury oatmeal biscuits. One year the surprise ingredient was cinnamon butter, made with the leftovers from Guiniveve's partner's 40th birthday, when he received a gift of 40 pounds of butter. Guiniveve processed enough cinnamon butter to fill 20 250-mL jars.

Guiniveve and Michelle have a few working principles for their kitchen marathon. Top of the list is having a good time. "If you're going to do this, choose someone you really want to hang out with," they advise. Next is, know your friends and accommodate their food allergies and sensitivities. Michelle always includes at least one gluten-free recipe, and the "no-nut" families' boxes are kept separate from the rest.

Michelle always likes to do something lemony and something chocolatey; Guiniveve's standby is biscotti.

Guiniveve and Michelle assemble all the goodies before divvying them up into packages.

Items like the cinnamon butter or crème brûlée are "easy to make, pretty to package, and they take up space in the box," said Michelle. The crème brûlée provided the necessity of a cautionary warning one year, after a giftee left his package at the office over the holidays and returned to disaster. "We've learned to tell people to open and eat right away," said Michelle.

The baker gals agree that, based on the principle that KFC is the first item to run out at a potluck, it's important to include a treat that is trashy but irresistible. Hence pieces of Rolo candy, melted into the holes of a twisty pretzel and then pressed with a pecan so the whole thing fuses together. "People loved those!" said Guiniveve. (Michelle burst out with what can only be described as a cackle.)

Variety is key. "When you think about how a box looks, there are the self-contained items, like the brûlée, the sprawly things like nuts or meringues, and then the cookies—you don't want to have too much of one thing," said Guiniveve.

Guided by this principle, and with approval from these two intrepid bakers, I've taken a few of their favourites from over the years and "borealized" them with northern ingredients—birch syrup, Labrador tea, wild berries and espresso coffee from our local coffee roasters.

The gals say this list is looking pretty good, though there are only six items compared to their usual seven. I sent a note asking their advice for filling in the gaps. Michelle replied, "I would suggest something simple—chocolate chip cookies, quick truffles, etc, as part of our philosophy of making it fun/easy." Guiniveve replied, "We have a philosophy?"

Of course they do! They make delicious things for their friends to celebrate a magical time of year, and they have a great time doing it. What could be better? Cooks, start your engines!

Birch Syrup Spiced Pecans

1 lb (455 gr) pecan halves, or about
4 cups (950 mL)

½ cup (125 mL) birch syrup

½ cup (125 mL) raw sesame seeds

2 tsp (10 mL) coarse salt

1 egg white at room temperature

1. Preheat oven to 300F (150C) and line two baking sheets with parchment paper.

2. Toss pecans in birch syrup, making sure they're thoroughly coated. Add sesame seeds and salt. Mix thoroughly.

3. In a separate bowl, beat egg white until soft peaks form. Add to pecans and mix thoroughly once more.

4. Spread nuts in a single layer on the baking sheets.

5. Bake for 30 minutes, stirring every 10 minutes. If the nuts start to smell as though they're done before 30 minutes are up, trust your nose and remove them from the oven.

6. Separate nuts as they cool. Even when cool, the nuts will be slightly sticky. This is part of their charm.

Makes 4 cups (950 mL).

Boreal Jelly Candies

Candy-making requires patience, attention and nerve, especially when the thermometer is stuck at 212F (100C) and the candy smells like it's starting to burn. I've learned to take the mixture off the heat when that happens, and consider it done. It usually works. That said, it's worth noting that heat rises slowly to 220F (104C), then leaps ahead. Watch closely. I keep a glass of cold water at hand, as well as the thermometer, and test for readiness by periodically dropping the mixture off a spoon into the water. See the sidebar for a complete list of temperature equivalents for soft-ball, firm-ball, hard-ball and thread stages. Remember to compensate for altitude when making candy; the boiling point is lower the higher you go above sea level.

STAGES IN CANDY-MAKING

Thread: 223F to 234F (106C to 112C)
(Syrup)

When dropped into cold water, the syrup forms a coarse thread that can't be formed into a ball.

Soft ball: 234F to 240 F (112C to 116C)
(Fudge, pralines, marzipan and fondants)

The syrup forms a soft, malleable ball that flattens when removed from the water and held in the hand.

Firm ball: 242F to 248F (117C to 120C)
(Caramels, marshmallows)

The ball doesn't flatten when removed from the water but will flatten when squeezed between the fingers.

Hard ball: 250F to 266F (121C to 130C)
(Nougat, marshmallows, gummies, brittle and rock candy)

The ball is rigid but can still be squeezed between the fingers.

Soft crack: 270F to 290F (132C to 143C)
(Saltwater taffy, butterscotch)

The syrup forms hard threads that, when removed from the water, are flexible enough to bend.

Hard crack: 295F to 310F (146C to 154C)
(Toffee, lollipops)

The syrup forms brittle threads that, when removed from the water, will break if bent.

CARAMELIZED SUGAR

Clear Liquid Stage: 320F (160C)
The water has boiled away and the remaining sugar is a light amber liquid.

Brown Liquid Stage: 338F (170C)
The liquefied sugar has caramelized and turned brown.

Burnt Sugar: 350F (177C)
The sugar takes on a burnt, bitter flavour. Beware.

Rhubarb Ginger Jellies

When frozen chopped rhubarb thaws, there's usually a fair amount of juice. Reserve this juice when thawing the rhubarb, topping it up with another liquid if necessary.

4 cups (950 mL) frozen chopped rhubarb, thawed

2 Tbsp (30 mL) fresh ginger, chopped

½ cup (125 ml) lemon juice (about 3 lemons)

Grated zest of 1 large lemon

2½ cups (600 mL) rhubarb juice, topped up with water, white wine or apple juice if necessary

2–3 tsp (10–15 mL) agar powder

2 cups (475 mL) sugar, plus extra for sprinkling

1. Butter an 8-inch (20-cm) square pan and line it with a piece of buttered parchment paper, leaving two ends hanging over the edges.

2. Bring the rhubarb, ginger, lemon juice, zest and rhubarb juice to a boil in a saucepan, reduce heat and simmer for 10 minutes.

3. Remove from heat and strain the mixture into a bowl through a sieve, pressing on the solids with a wooden spoon.

4. Stop when all of the liquid is extracted, but before the mixture resembles a purée. (Save the solids to include in muffins, or add to a pie or crisp mixture.)

5. Measure the liquid. You should have about 3 cups (710 mL). You'll need 1 teaspoon (5 mL) agar powder (or 2 teaspoons/10 mL agar flakes) for each cup (250 mL) of liquid.

6. Remove ½ cup (125 mL) liquid and whisk in the agar powder. Set aside.

7. Place the remaining liquid in a clean saucepan, add the sugar and stir to dissolve. Turn heat to medium, bring to boil and cook, stirring periodically, until the mixture reaches the firm-ball stage (248F/120C). If the mixture starts to smell as though it might burn, remove from heat and stir vigorously. Do not cook further.

8. When the mixture is ready, remove from heat, stir in the agar mixture, reduce heat to medium-low and cook, stirring constantly, for 2 to 3 minutes.

9. Pour into the prepared pan, cool to room temperature, then chill in the pan for 8 hours.

10. Turn out onto a clean surface coated with a layer of sugar. Peel off parchment paper and sprinkle the surface with more sugar.

11. With a sharp knife, trim the edges so you have a clean square. Cut into 64 pieces by dividing evenly into eighths both ways. Have wet and dry cloths handy to clean and dry the knife periodically.

12. Dry the jellies on a rack over a baking sheet for a couple of hours. Sprinkle with more sugar before storing flat in a container. Separate layers with a piece of waxed paper.

Makes 64 × 1-inch (2.5-cm) jellies.

WILD BERRY JELLIES

To make this variation of **Rhubarb Ginger Jellies**, substitute equal quantities of **mixed berries** for the rhubarb and **berry juice** for the rhubarb juice. Reduce the **lemon juice** to **2 tablespoons (30 mL)** and eliminate the zest. Add **sugar** to taste, as the berries will probably be less tart than rhubarb—start with **1 cup (250 mL)** and test.

Salted Lowbush Cranberry Toffee

1½ cups (350 mL) wild lowbush cranberries (lingonberries) or substitute cultivated cranberries

½ cup (125 mL) 35 percent cream

3 Tbsp (45 mL) butter

1 cup (250 mL) brown sugar

About 1 tsp (5 mL) coarse sea salt

1. Butter an 8-inch (20-cm) square pan and line it with a piece of buttered parchment paper, leaving two ends hanging over the edges.

2. Cook cranberries for five minutes over medium heat, just until the juice starts to appear.

3. Remove from heat, strain, blend and press through a sieve. (Use the pulp for muffins, smoothies or mixed into your morning oatmeal.)

4. Combine cranberry juice in a wide saucepan with cream, butter and sugar and heat to boiling over medium heat.

5. Cook at medium heat, stirring constantly, until the mixture reaches the firm-ball stage, 248F (120C) on a candy thermometer.

6. Pour into the prepared pan, spreading with a spatula. Cool for about 10 minutes, then sprinkle the top with your favourite coarse salt.

7. When the toffee has completely cooled, turn out of the pan and peel off the parchment paper.

8. Cut into 1-inch (2.5 cm) squares. Wrap in pieces of waxed paper (about 4 inches/10 cm square) and twist the ends, just like Halloween candy wrapping.

Makes 64 pieces of toffee.

Mocha Mascarpone Mousse

Adapted from the Coffee and Chocolate Mousse Cups recipe in *Gordon Ramsay's Sunday Lunch*. The texture is best when the mousse is served at room temperature. If you are packaging the mousse as a gift, see the instructions for stabilizing whipped cream in the sidebar on page 133.

8 oz (225 gr) dark chocolate, 70 percent cocoa

8 oz (225 gr) mascarpone cheese

¼ cup (60 mL) icing sugar

½ cup (125 mL) strong espresso, cooled

1⅓ cup (330 mL) 35 percent cream plus ½ cup (125 mL) for garnish

Chocolate-covered espresso beans (for garnish)

1. Break the chocolate into small pieces and melt in a double boiler over simmering water. Let cool to room temperature.

2. Beat the mascarpone and icing sugar together until smooth, then beat in the cooled espresso and melted chocolate.

3. In a separate bowl, whip 1⅓ cups (330 mL) of cream until soft peaks form. Fold the cream into the mocha mixture until well combined and spoon into cappuccino cups or ramekins.

4. Chill if you're not serving right away, but remove from fridge 30 minutes before serving to bring to room temperature.

5. Just before serving whip the remaining cream until stiff peaks form and place a dollop on each mousse, then top with two chocolate espresso beans.

Makes 4 cups (950 mL).

Bakeapple Rugelach

Adapted by Sarah Agnew from The Cookie Lover's Cookie Book *by Richard Sax*

I met Sarah Agnew at the Sturgeon Lake Sailing Club the summer I was 11 and she was 12, and we became fast friends. In our early teens we spent many summer evenings baking cookies or cupcakes in the kitchens at our cottages. (Our mothers thought this a grand activity.) At 16 we graduated to dining out; Toronto's restaurant scene was flowering and we pored over the reviews in *Toronto Life* magazine and explored Greek, Italian and French cuisine. A few years ago Sarah and her husband finished building a house and studio on the west coast of Newfoundland, and spent a year there. Sarah and I wrote letters from one fierce climate to another, bonding anew over snow, long winter nights and dreams of wild berries.

Sarah says: "When Hanukkah rolled around in Newfoundland last year, I wanted to make a holiday treat with a local flavour. The blueberries that grow outside our kitchen door were long finished and the partridgeberries too few for my purpose, so I reached for the jar of bakeapple jam that was languishing in the cupboard. I'm not a big bakeapple fan (although it's pretty good on top of cheesecake) but a little cinnamon and some chopped walnuts brought out the caramel-y baked apple-y flavour that give this berry its Newfoundland name. Thanks to my neighbour for the jam, and the recipe bloggers who led me to Richard Sax's perfect rugelach recipe!"

SOUR CREAM PASTRY DOUGH

2 cups (475 mL) all-purpose flour

1 cup (250 mL) cold unsalted butter, cut in small pieces

1 egg yolk

¾ cup (180 mL) sour cream

BAKEAPPLE FILLING

1 cup (250 mL) bakeapple (cloudberry) jam

¼ tsp (1 mL) ground cinnamon

⅓ cup (80 mL) walnuts, finely chopped

TOPPING

2 Tbsp (30 mL) unsalted butter, melted

3 Tbsp (45 mL) granulated sugar

1. For dough: place flour, butter, egg yolk and sour cream in large bowl. Beat with electric mixer at low speed until dough just comes together. Wrap in plastic wrap and chill until firm, overnight or longer.

2. For filling: in a bowl, stir together the jam, cinnamon and walnuts.

3. Preheat oven to 350F (180C). Divide dough into 4 pieces. Place 3 pieces in refrigerator and roll 1 piece on a lightly floured surface to an even 9-inch (22.5-cm) circle (trim if need be). Spread a quarter of the filling over the circle of dough.

4. With sharp knife or pizza cutter, cut circle into 12 neat wedges. Beginning with outside edge, roll wedges up tightly towards the centre. Place rolls on an ungreased baking sheet, tucking centre points underneath, spacing about ½ inch (1.25 cm) apart. Repeat with remaining dough and filling. Keep assembled rugelach refrigerated while you work on the remainder.

5. For topping: brush rugelach very lightly with butter; sprinkle with sugar.

6. Bake until golden brown, about 30 minutes. Transfer to racks to cool.

Makes four dozen cookies.

Smoked Labrador Tea Shortbreads

This recipe, adapted from Vanilla Rooibos Tea Cookies at food52.com, makes a crispy, crunchy shortbread. The Labrador tea adds a truly boreal note, with flavours that suggest cardamom and lemon.

⅓ cup (80 mL) Labrador tea leaves, lightly crushed in a mortar and pestle.

⅓ cup (80 mL) sugar

1⅓ cup (330 mL) flour

1 Tbsp (15 mL) milk

1 tsp (5 mL) birch syrup

½ cup (125 mL) salted butter

1½ Tbsp (22 mL) turbinado sugar

1. Place a cast iron pan over medium heat. When pan is hot, add Labrador tea leaves, stir to distribute and toast until they become fragrant, 2 to 3 minutes. Remove from heat, transfer to a bowl and let cool.

2. Combine the tea and the sugar in the bowl of a food processor and pulse until the tea leaves are powdered.

3. Add the flour and pulse until combined. Then add the milk, birch syrup and butter and whizz until a dough forms—this could take a couple of minutes. Pinch a piece of dough together, and if it seems too powdery, add another teaspoon (5 mL) of milk. Remember that the dough will come together as you work it with your hands.

4. Turn the dough onto a clean work surface, gather it together and knead briefly. Divide into 2 pieces and roll each piece into a log 1½ inches (3.8 cm) in diameter.

5. Sprinkle turbinado sugar onto the work surface and roll each log in the sugar, covering the entire surface of the log.

6. Wrap log in plastic or waxed paper and chill for 30 to 45 minutes.

7. Fifteen minutes before baking, turn oven to 375F (190C) and line a baking sheet with parchment paper.

8. Remove log from fridge and cut ⅓-inch slices off the log, rotating the log as you go to ensure that cookie slices stay round.

9. Transfer cookies to the prepared baking sheet, leaving a ½-inch (1.25-cm) space between each one. They don't spread but need breathing room to crisp up.

10. Bake for 12 minutes, until cookies are just starting to brown. Leave on the cookie sheet to cool for 5 minutes, then transfer to racks.

Makes three dozen cookies.

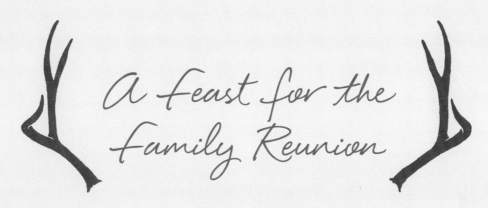

A Feast for the Family Reunion

MENU FOR 10

From Saguenay-Lac-St-Jean to Whitehorse to Parksville: Tourtière is a Moveable Feast

For most Canadians a tourtière is a pie made with flaky pastry and a combination of ground pork, ground beef, onions, herbs and spices, popular at Christmas. Not so in Saguenay-Lac-Saint-Jean. For people from that region, that kind of meat pie is not a tourtière but a *pâté à la viande*. It may be eaten at Christmas, but it's not a tourtière. The tourtière is another matter entirely, a rich construction of four different kinds of meat cut into cubes, potatoes, onion, herbs and broth, encased in pastry and cooked for at least six hours in a roasting pan or Dutch oven big enough to feed a family of 10 or 15.

 Marlynn remembers her grandmother's tourtière as the best and her mom's as second best, but these days, she says, "Really I like mine the best," which is as it should be.

Marlynn Bourque of Whitehorse and Whistler, BC, grew up on the Saguenay River in a town called Jonquière, now renamed Kénogami. When she was little the whole family gathered at her grandmother's house to celebrate *réveillon* and Christmas, and her grandmother made tourtière for the feast on Christmas Day. (And sometimes on New Year's Day too.) That tourtière "was always big, there were so many kids and people," said Marlynn. Her mother makes tourtière and Marlynn does too, and they're different from each other and from her grandmother's.

Marlynn sat down with me one December afternoon at the Baked Café in Whitehorse and walked me through her recipe, trying to estimate quantities for a dish she does by instinct. Every family's tourtière is different, she noted, and depends on the meat that is readily available, wild or domestic or both, and the traditions that have evolved in the family kitchen over generations. Those traditions might include the use of Bisto or Bovril to flavour the stock, a pastry made with lard and additions of milk or brown sugar or egg, but always baking powder (that's from my mom, said Marlynn), a combination of red meat (beef, venison, moose, rabbit), white meat (chicken, duck, pigeon) and pork. Marlynn said fatty pork is best, and the potatoes should equal the meat. The herbs could be thyme or basil, and the addition of sweet spices like allspice berries is allowable, though not traditional. "I personally wouldn't do that," said Marlynn.

The meat, onion and herbs are mixed together to season overnight, and the next day the potatoes, cut in the same-sized cubes as the meat, are added to the mix. The entire cooking vessel is lined in pastry, in go the meat and potatoes and then cold water or stock is poured in to just below the level of the meat. The dish is put into a 400F (205C) oven for an hour and then the temperature turned

Above: A cross-country skier sets off across an alpine lake in the White Pass area south of Carcross, Yukon Territory. Right: Dried rosehips and pine branches decorate a winter solstice table.

down to anywhere from 325F (160C) to 275F (135C) for at least six hours of cooking. Marlynn said, "Six hours is a good thing and eight hours is a good thing."

When Marlynn homesteaded with her own family on the Annie Lake Road south of Whitehorse she rendered the fat from her own pigs and kept it in peanut butter jars in the root cellar. In those days she made her tourtière entirely from meat she raised or hunted and the vegetables she grew. "It was really fun to make a tourtière from all of that." The last time she made one was in summer, with some moose she had on hand and blue potatoes; she cooked it in the oven of her mobile home as she and a couple of her kids drove down the coast from Whistler. A tourtière is a moveable feast.

Armed with Marlynn's advice I went down to my sister's place in Parksville on Vancouver Island with a cooler

A view of Whitehorse from the clay cliffs on a December afternoon.

full of moose, grouse and rendered pork fat to make our own tourtière for a solstice celebration three days before Christmas. My brother Paul, a mad and creative cook, was visiting from Toronto, so we had the familial critical mass needed to undertake a large cooking project. Essentially we winged it, as Marlynn's recipe was more a general direction than a marked trail. It took five of us three days to make our tourtière, including shopping and stock-making. The end result was so good it was ridiculous, a juicy meat pie where every bite was tender, each kind of meat had its own characteristic flavour and the potatoes were soft and buttery.

At Marlynn's suggestion, to accompany our meal we made the traditional salad of leaf lettuce, green onions, salt and pepper, dressed with 35 percent cream. We added a bit of buttermilk for sharpness, because you're allowed to create new traditions. The final element on the table was a simple cranberry sauce. The five of us ate half the tourtière in one sitting, and four of us finished it off the next night. From this we deduced a six-litre tourtière would provide 10 feast-like portions, with no regrets next day. Paul suggests a bottle of fat red burgundy to accompany, and two are better than one.

BEEF, BISON OR MOOSE STOCK

Most butchers sell pork or beef bones; at our local butcher we can sometimes get bison as well. If you ever do a farm-gate purchase of a domestic animal, the farmer will probably ask if you want the bones and the offal. Say yes.

3 lbs (1.4 kg) moose, bison or beef marrow bones

Salt

2 Tbsp (30 mL) olive oil

1 medium white onion, chopped

1 fennel bulb, chopped

1 medium carrot, chopped

2 stalks celery, chopped

1 large leek, chopped

½ cup (125 mL) red wine

2 bay leaves

3 cloves

1 tsp (5 mL) juniper berries, crushed

5 peppercorns

1. Preheat oven to 400F (205C). Soak bones in cold, salted water (about 1 tablespoon/15 mL salt per litre of water) for 15 minutes to draw out some of the blood and remove impurities; drain, rinse and pat dry. Spread bones on a rimmed baking sheet.

2. Toss vegetables in oil and spread on a rimmed baking sheet. Roast vegetables and bones in the oven until browned and aromatic, anywhere from 30 to 40 minutes.

3. Place vegetables and bones in a large saucepan and cover with 13 cups (3 L) of cold water. Deglaze each baking sheet with a few tablespoons of the red wine and add the scrapings to the pot along with the remaining wine. Add bay leaves, cloves, juniper berries and peppercorns.

4. Over medium-low heat, bring the stock to a slow simmer, uncovered. The bubbles should be large and slow and barely break the surface. Skim off any scum that rises to the top.

5. Simmer uncovered for 4 hours. Strain into a very large bowl through a colander lined with cheesecloth. Remove fat—either by chilling overnight and skimming off the hardened fat, or in a fat separator.

6. When the fat is removed, pour stock into a clean saucepan and reduce by half over low heat.

7. Let cool to room temperature. Decant into storage containers and refrigerate or freeze, reserving 3 cups (710 mL) for the tourtière.

Makes 6 cups (1.4 L) stock.

Tourtière for 10

SAGUENAY-LAC-SAINT-JEAN TOURTIÈRE

For our Parksville tourtière we made a lot of pastry and filling, because we weren't sure what we were doing, and ended up with one 24-cup (6-L) tourtière, three nine-inch (22.5-cm) pies and two five-inch (13-cm) square single-serving pies. That's a ton of tourtière! Here I'm going to provide the recipe for just the 24-cup (6-L) amount of pastry and filling, more reasonable for first-timers.

LA PÂTE

Instead of using commercial lard I rendered pork fat from a local pig we'd purchased in Whitehorse in the fall—this was time-consuming but rewarding. The rendered fat was beautiful: snowy white, aromatic and good enough to spread on toast. For instructions on how to render pork fat, see the note on page 177.

5 cups (1.2 L) all-purpose flour

1 Tbsp (15 mL) baking powder

2 tsp (10 mL) salt

1½ Tbsp (22 mL) brown sugar

1 lb (455 gr) rendered pork fat or commercial lard, chilled

1 egg yolk

½ cup (125 mL) milk

1. Whisk together dry ingredients. Cut pork fat into the flour mixture with a pastry cutter or two knives until the fat pieces are the size of peas and there are some larger pieces here and there.

2. Combine egg yolk and milk and stir into dough with a fork just until it holds together.

3. Shape dough into a rough ball, cover with plastic and refrigerate at least 1 hour. You can do this step the day before you make the tourtière.

FILLING

The right amount of stock to use was disputed in Parksville. My brother Paul felt the pie could have used a touch more. Marlynn's instructions were to fill the stock up to within about ½ inch of the top of the filling, but other cooks cover the meat. Friends who grew up near Saguenay-Lac-Saint-Jean say the idea is for the stock to be fully absorbed by the time the tourtière is cooked. So I've stuck with what we did.

1½ lbs (680 gr) beef (preferably a marbled cut)

1½ lbs (680 gr) pork tenderloin (preferably with some fat attached)

1 lb (455 gr) moose

8 oz (225 gr) grouse breast, duck leg or breast, or chicken legs or breast, removed from the bone

2 yellow onions, diced

2 cloves garlic, minced

2 Tbsp (30 mL) fresh thyme, leaves removed from stems (or 1 Tbsp/15 mL dried)

1 tsp (5 mL) ground black pepper

2 lbs (910 gr) russet potatoes

1 tsp (5 mL) salt

3 cups (710 mL) Beef, Bison or Moose Stock, recipe on page 173

1 egg, beaten (for brushing)

1. Cut meat into ¾-inch (2-cm) cubes and combine with onion, garlic and thyme. Add ground black pepper and refrigerate 8 hours or overnight.

continued on next page

Photos from top to bottom, left to right: The fat is added to the flour. The fat is cut into the flour. After chilling in the fridge, the dough is rolled out. The dough is pressed gently into the bottom and up the sides of the dish. The filling is added and the stock poured in. The sides of dough are folded over the top and gently sealed. Ta da! The finished tourtière.

Tourtière for 10 *continued*

2. When ready to assemble, preheat oven to 400F (205C) and grease a covered 24-cup (6-L) roasting pan or Dutch oven. Remove the dough from the fridge about 10 minutes before you're going to roll it out.

3. Peel potatoes, wash, dry and dice into ¾-inch (2-cm) cubes. Combine with meat mixture and add salt.

4. Cut off one quarter of the dough. Roll out the larger piece on parchment paper. Check the size against your cooking vessel to make sure you'll have enough.

5. When it is large enough to line the bottom and sides with some overhang, flour the top of the dough so that it won't stick to itself. With a spatula, loosen any dough that might be stuck to the counter, and fold the dough into thirds, like an envelope.

6. Drape the envelope of dough crosswise over the pan. Peel the parchment paper from the outside of the dough envelope. You'll need help to lift the dough briefly while you peel the paper from the underside, and then you'll need to lift the uppermost flap of dough to unpeel the parchment paper underneath.

7. Let the folded envelope settle gently into the pan, then unfold the flaps. The entire piece of dough will now be sitting loosely in the pan. Press dough gently into the bottom and sides of the pan and patch any holes. Cut the overhanging pieces so that there's just a lip remaining over the rim of the pan.

8. Fill the pastry with the meat and potato mixture, leaving an inch (2.5 cm) of headroom at the top. Pour stock over until it reaches ½ inch (1 cm) below the top of the filling.

9. Roll out the remaining piece of pastry to fit the top of the pan. Lay it over the meat mixture. Fold the overhanging pasty over the top, making a tight seal.

10. Brush pastry with the beaten egg and cut three or four vents in the pastry to allow steam to escape.

11. Cover pan with lid and bake for 1 hour. Reduce heat to 300F (150C) and bake for another 2 hours, then reduce again to 275F (135C) and bake for another 2 hours. Remove lid and bake for a final hour, for a total baking time of 6 hours.

12. Let the tourtière sit for 20 minutes before serving to allow juices to fully absorb. Serve at the table so everyone can enjoy the magic moment when the interior is revealed.

Makes 10 servings.

To render pork fat, remove the skin from a piece of fatback and dice the fat into small pieces. Place it in a heavy saucepan on low heat, or in a Dutch oven in a 170F (80C) oven. For every pound (455 gr) of fat, add ½ cup (125 mL) of water. Start with the pan covered, but once the fat has melted enough to coat the bottom of the pan, take the cover off; the water will evaporate.

Pour off the accumulated fat into a heatproof glass container every 30 minutes, or when it reaches a level of ⅛ inch (0.13 cm) to ¼ inch (0.6 cm). Add a tablespoon (15 mL) of water to the remaining solids, cover the pot until the bottom is coated with fat, then remove the lid once again so the water will evaporate. Repeat until there is just a small amount of connective tissues left in the bottom of the pan; these are the cracklings, which at this point will look like large, relatively dry bread crumbs. Allow fat to cool to room temperature, then refrigerate until you're ready to use.

It can take up to eight hours to render 1½ pounds (680 gr) of fat, so be patient. Fat rendered near the end of the process will be slightly yellower in colour; this simply means it's taken on some colour from the cracklings. Once you've poured off all the rendered fat, turn up the heat slightly and cook the cracklings until they're browned. Drain cracklings on paper towels and refrigerate or freeze for future use on salads.

Leaf Lettuce Salad

1½ heads leaf lettuce, washed, dried and torn	½ cup (125 mL) 35 percent cream
8 green onions, thinly sliced	Sea salt and freshly ground pepper to taste
2 Tbsp (30 mL) buttermilk	

1. Toss lettuce and onions in a large salad bowl. Whisk together buttermilk and cream, pour over top and toss again. Grind sea salt and pepper over top, toss again and serve immediately.

Makes 10 servings.

Simple Cranberry Sauce

2 cups (475 mL) wild lowbush cranberries (lingonberries) or substitute cultivated cranberries	¾ cup (180 mL) sugar
	1 tsp (5 mL) apple cider vinegar
	½ tsp (2.5 mL) sea salt

1. Combine all ingredients in a small saucepan. Simmer over medium-low heat until thick, about 30 minutes.

2. Cool to room temperature and chill—Marlynn says the cranberry sauce is best cold, and we think she's right.

Makes about 2 cups (475 mL).

Boreal Christmas Cake

Every family has its own version of Christmas cake, and every version is fiercely defended by its loyal advocates. With this cake I throw my hat into the ring. It has evolved over several years in the north, and has received (ahem) rave reviews from friends and tasters. On our tourtière night in Parksville, dessert was mandarin oranges and a slice of cake, and that's all we needed. This recipe will make one 9-inch (22.5-cm) round, one 9- × 5-inch (22.5- × 13-cm) loaf and two 4- × 2-inch (10- × 5-cm) mini-cakes. Because it's so easy, I make my own candied citrus peel.

For best results, make the Christmas cake six weeks before you plan to serve.

FRUIT

1½ cups (350 mL) brandy or cognac

2 cups (475 mL) currants

2 cups (475 mL) sultanas

2 cups (475 mL) organic Turkish apricots, chopped

1½ cups (350 mL) Candied Orange and Lemon Peel, recipe on next page

1 cup (250 mL) Thompson raisins

1 cup (250 mL) dried cranberries

½ cup (125 mL) crystallized ginger, chopped

1 cup (250 mL) whole wild lowbush cranberries (lingonberries), fresh or frozen (or substitute cultivated cranberries)

2 Tbsp (30 mL) birch syrup

1. Combine spirits, all dried fruits (not the whole cranberries) and ginger in a large bowl, stir and let sit overnight.

2. Cook the whole cranberries and birch syrup in a small saucepan over medium heat until thick, 20 to 30 minutes. Cool to room temperature. (You can do this step ahead and refrigerate overnight.)

CAKE

2½ cups (600 mL) all-purpose flour

1 tsp (5 mL) freshly ground nutmeg

1 tsp (5 mL) cinnamon

½ tsp (2.5 mL) ground cloves

1½ tsp (7.5 mL) baking powder

½ tsp (2.5 mL) salt

1 cup (250 mL) butter, softened

1½ cups (350 mL) brown sugar

4 eggs at room temperature

Prepared fruit and brandy mixture

Prepared cooked whole cranberries

2 cups (475 mL) pecans, chopped

Brandy for drizzling cakes

Homemade Marzipan, recipe on page 180 (optional)

Royal Icing, recipe on next page (optional)

1. Preheat oven to 300F (150C). Place a pan filled with hot water on the bottom rack. Grease one 9-inch (22.5-cm) round pan, one 9- × 5-inch (22.5- × 13-cm) pan and two 4- × 2-inch (10- × 5-cm) mini-cake pans and line the sides and bottoms with parchment paper.

2. Whisk together dry ingredients, except pecans.

3. Cream butter and sugar together until light and fluffy. Add eggs, one at a time, beating after each addition.

4. Beat in dry ingredients with a wooden spoon, one third at a time.

5. Stir in fruit and brandy mixture, cooked whole cranberries and pecans.

6. Spoon into prepared pans and smooth the tops with a spatula dipped in water, pressing down slightly to ensure the pan is evenly filled.

7. Bake the mini-cakes for 1 hour and the loaf and round cake for 2 to 2½ hours. If the tops are browning too quickly, place a sheet of foil loosely over top. The cakes are done when a toothpick inserted into the middle comes out clean.

8. Cool cakes in their pans on a rack for 30 minutes. Carefully turn out onto racks and cool completely.

Boreal Christmas Cake continued

9. When the cakes have cooled to room temperature, wrap them in brandy-soaked cheesecloth and then tightly in plastic. After a week, unwrap cakes, poke holes in the top with a bamboo skewer and drizzle in 1 tablespoon (15 mL) of brandy. Repeat every week until 1 week before you're going to crack into the cakes. For longer-term storage, continue to add brandy once a month; store tightly covered in cheesecloth and plastic in a cool, dark place for up to a year. (My brother André did this for a year with a cake I sent to him in Abu Dhabi. He said it was the best Christmas cake he'd ever had.)

10. If you wish, cover with a layer of Homemade Marzipan and decorate with Royal Icing (for instructions, see sidebar, next page).

Makes one 9-inch (22.5-cm) round, one 9- × 5-inch (22.5- × 13-cm) loaf and two 4- × 2-inch (10- × 5-cm) mini-cakes.

CANDIED ORANGE AND LEMON PEEL

3 medium organic lemons

3 medium organic oranges

1½ cups (350 mL) sugar plus extra for tossing, if desired

1½ cups (350 mL) water

1. Quarter and peel lemons and oranges—it's easiest to separate the flesh from the peel with your fingers. Scrape any remaining flesh from the peel with a small spoon. (Some recipes ask you to remove the pith as well; I find the slight bitterness from the pith adds depth to the candied peel.)

2. Slice peel into ¼-inch (0.6-cm) strips, transfer to a saucepan and cover with water. Bring to the boil, reduce heat and simmer for 10 minutes. Drain water, leaving peel in the saucepan.

3. Add sugar and water to the saucepan and mix thoroughly. Bring to the boil again over medium heat, reduce heat to medium-low and cook for 40 to 50 minutes until peel is translucent.

4. Remove peel from syrup using a slotted spoon (reserve the citrus-flavoured syrup for use in cocktails). Drain peel on a rack set over a baking sheet. You may have to separate pieces that have stuck together. When peel has cooled, toss in granulated sugar, if you like (I didn't) and transfer to a jar for storage. (Dipped in dark chocolate, these make a great addition to the seasonal sweets tray.) Will keep in the refrigerator for 3 weeks.

Makes about 2 cups (475 mL) candied peel.

ROYAL ICING

As you probably know, this icing becomes hard and shiny and will set like cement around any decorations you choose to put on top of the cake, such as dried fruit and nuts in pretty patterns.

2 large egg whites at room temperature

2 tsp (10 mL) brandy or cognac (or substitute lemon juice or vanilla)

3–3½ cups (710–830 mL) icing sugar, sifted

1. Beat egg whites until stiff. Add the cognac, 1 teaspoon (5 mL) at a time.

2. Gradually beat in the sifted icing sugar, about ½ cup (125 mL) at a time until the icing falls back on itself in a stiff ribbon when you lift out the beater. Taste; if the flavour of the icing sugar is too pronounced, add a few drops more brandy or cognac.

3. Spread immediately onto marzipan-covered cake and press decorations into the top. When not using, place a damp tea towel or plastic wrap over the bowl to keep the icing soft.

4. Refrigerate cakes for at least 12 hours before wrapping or cutting. Dip knife in hot water before cutting.

Makes about 2½ cups (600 mL) of icing, enough for a thin layer for each of the four cakes.

DECORATING

If you're giving away cakes as gifts it's great to go one step further and coat them with marzipan and ice them with Royal Icing. You can either buy marzipan from a deli or make your own. The deli staff will tell you which is the best product for cake decorating. To coat the Boreal Christmas Cakes with a thin layer of marzipan you'll need about 14 ounces (400 gr); count on about 6 ounces (170 gr) each for the round cake and loaf, and about 1 ounce (30 gr) for each of the mini-cakes.

Bring the marzipan to room temperature and roll it out on the counter to a size that will coat the top and sides of your cake. Have some icing sugar on hand to dust the rolling pin. Brush the cake with a bit of melted jelly: try redcurrant or highbush cranberry. Lift the sheet of marzipan onto the cake and press it into the top and sides. Place on a baking sheet lined with parchment paper and refrigerate until you're ready to ice the cake.

HOMEMADE MARZIPAN

4 cups (950 mL) blanched almonds

2 cups (475 mL) granulated sugar

1 cup (250 mL) water

6–8 Tbsp (90–120 mL) cognac, orange juice or kirsch

2 egg whites

½–¾ cup (125–180 mL) icing sugar, plus extra for dusting counter

1. Grind the almonds very fine, stopping just before the oil separates from the nuts and you have almond butter.

2. Mix granulated sugar and water in a saucepan big enough to accommodate all the ingredients, bring to the boil and cook at high heat until the temperature reaches 240F (116C), the "soft ball" stage. Watch carefully once the thermometer registers 220F (104C); heat rises quickly after this point.

3. Cool the syrup to 110F (43C). Put the pot on a damp tea cloth for stability, and whisk the almonds into the syrup a few spoonfuls at a time, changing to a wooden spoon when the mixture stiffens. Add the cognac or other flavouring and stir vigorously until ingredients are creamy. Refrigerate for 12 hours.

4. Dust a flat surface with icing sugar, turn the almond paste out and knead it as you would bread dough, sprinkling icing sugar as needed to keep it from sticking. Stop kneading when the paste becomes easy to handle but is still a bit sticky. The almond paste is perfectly useable (and delicious) at this point, for use in stollen or other Christmas treats. Or carry on and make marzipan, slightly sweeter and a little more malleable.

5. Whip egg whites until they hold stiff peaks and mix into almond paste. Sift the icing sugar into the mixture and mix thoroughly. Sprinkle icing sugar on the counter and knead the marzipan until it is pliable yet firm enough to hold its shape.

Makes about 2 lb (910 gr) marzipan.

January Matryoshka Painting Party

MENU FOR 12

The Matryoshka Party

For my birthday, which occurs in January, I've hosted a matryoshka doll painting party at my house every year since 2008. I order about 20 blank wooden doll sets from Russia or the US; it varies from year to year but usually they're about four and a half inches high and there are five dolls in each set, the smallest around an inch high. The night before, a few of us set up in the basement and sand the dolls, then paint them with a primer of white glue diluted with water.

 I'm not a crafty person and my dolls are always a bit of a mess, but who cares?

When the guests, all women, arrive next day, they find a couple of long tables coated in plastic and at each place, a primed doll, a selection of paintbrushes, a dry cloth, a yogourt container full of water and a palette, usually the lid from the yogourt container. We line up tubes of acrylic paint in the centre of the table, and try to remember to return them once we've finished with them. (One of the matryoshka stalwarts is Whitehorse artist Meshell Melvin, who helps us with things like mixing the right colours for flesh tones and generally keeps us in line.)

We start at noon and end at 6 p.m. People come and go, in between ferrying kids to soccer games or the rink, taking their mothers shopping, or teaching an art class at the elementary school. The personnel change every year, but there's a core group that's always there. We've had brand new babies as guests, old dogs that sleep quietly in the corner, young barky dogs that someone is sitting, and once we had a brother-in-law.

We drink wine and tea and soda, people bring snacks and there's always a pot of soup on the stove. I used to make a supper, too, and we'd continue long into the evening, but most of us can only carve out so many hours in the day, so now whoever wants to hang around afterwards does, with the understanding that dinner is not forthcoming. Those who stay light candles downstairs and maybe nip upstairs now and then to do one last thing on their dolls in the now empty room.

I look forward to the matryoshka party almost as much as Christmas. I love the chatter and the silence and the sudden bursts of laughter, the feeling of permanence and impermanence, and the designs people come up with every year. I'm not a crafty person and my dolls are always a bit of a mess, but who cares? There's nothing like painting a matryoshka doll with a roomful of women for eliciting joy and a soupçon of humility.

Here are a few geographically appropriate recipes to be getting on with if you ever decide to embark on this adventure yourself, ending with a magnificent matryoshka doll cake. For information on where to order blank dolls see the Products section on page 243.

Wild roses and birch trees decorate a matryoshka painter's dolls from two different years. The table gets messier as the day progresses.

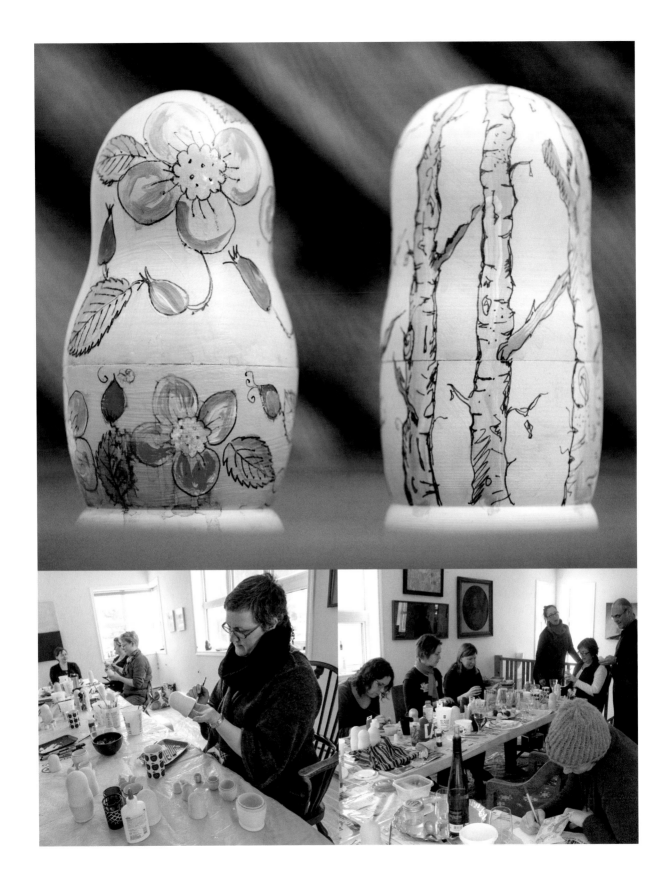

Karjalanpiirakat with Roasted Cauliflower Filling

The morning after Hector and I arrived in Helsinki we turned a corner onto the waterfront to discover a lively scene of booths, tents, tables and crowds of cheerful guys in dark sweaters speaking Russian and filling their gym bags with delicacies and souvenirs. Fishing boats were tied up along the pier stern first, their aft decks covered with awnings or blue tarps and decorated with branches of birch and mountain ash. Their owners stood in the wells selling seafood of all kinds but especially herring—fried, smoked, salted, brined, pickled, in cream sauce, tomato sauce, mustard sauce and in any other sauce you can imagine—and offering samples. We had stumbled upon the annual Baltic Herring Fair, held in the first week of October and attracting visitors from the shores of the Gulf of Finland from Saint Petersburg to Tallinn. We felt the thrill of strangeness; we were no longer in Scandinavia. This was a Baltic culture, unfamiliar and exciting.

We strolled along the plaza, listening to the new languages that lifted and settled and rose around us and sampled tiny Baltic vendace coated in flour and fried in butter in huge, rounded skillets. We ate lampreys and gravlax and pickled herring and these little tarts we loved whose name we couldn't quite catch. When I came back home I discovered what they were: *Karjalanpiirakat*, a traditional pie from the North Karelia district of Finland, originally made with a filling of long-cooked barley and now, most commonly, with a kind of savoury rice pudding, and occasionally mashed potatoes or turnip.

When I rolled out and pinched these pastries at home for the first time I felt as though I were participating in a ritual performed in Finnish kitchens for centuries, one that combined basic, inexpensive farmhouse ingredients into an ingenious, nourishing and satisfying treat for the family. This recipe is a natural for community baking. It takes one person working alone about two hours from start to finish, but will go much faster and be way more fun with a couple of friends taking turns rolling, filling and pinching. Vanessa Marshak, formerly of Whitehorse, says, "The family has banded together a few times to make these. Oh, the egg butter!"

I've departed from tradition here for the filling and used a roasted cauliflower purée, which was much in evidence on Scandinavian restaurant menus in the fall of 2012. Try the purée in other contexts too, as a vegetable accompaniment to roasted meats or as a dip for raw and roasted vegetables.

The traditional topping for these pastries is the egg butter to which Vanessa refers, spooned over top just before eating. To make egg butter, mash hard-boiled eggs and soft butter with a fork, in proportions of 2 tablespoons (30 mL) butter to every egg, and add lots of salt.

FILLING

2 heads cauliflower, chopped into florets

2 Tbsp (30 mL) olive oil

1½ tsp (7.5 mL) sea salt, divided

1 head garlic

¾ cup (180 mL) vegetable or chicken stock

¾ cup (180 mL) 35 percent cream

Black pepper

1. Preheat oven to 375F (190C) and line two baking trays with parchment paper.

2. Toss the cauliflower with olive oil and half the sea salt. Slice off the top of the head of garlic so the flesh is exposed. Drizzle oil over top of the garlic, and coat the outside with a touch of oil.

3. Divide the cauliflower between the two baking trays. Place the head of garlic on one of the trays. Roast, uncovered for 45 minutes until cauliflower is browned and fully cooked and garlic is soft.

4. Remove from oven and let cool slightly before puréeing cauliflower with the stock, cream, the remaining salt and garlic. (Just squeeze the garlic from its casing into the bowl.) Taste and adjust seasonings. Set aside.

PASTRY CRUST

Note: this dough is quite stiff but rolls out beautifully.

2¼ cups (530 mL) all-purpose flour

1½ cups (350 mL) rye flour

1 tsp (5 mL) salt

1–1½ cups (250–350 mL) cold water

FOR BRUSHING:

2 Tbsp (30 mL) butter, melted

½ cup (125 mL) milk

1. Whisk together flours and salt in a medium-sized bowl. Add 1 cup (250 mL) cold water and mix with a wooden spoon and then with your hands. If the dough doesn't come together into a ball, add more water 1 tablespoon (15 mL) at a time.

2. Once the dough is uniformly moist and will form into a rough ball turn it onto the counter and knead for 4 to 5 minutes. This is a workout.

3. Let dough rest for 10 minutes then form into a long roll. Cut the roll into 24 even pieces. Flatten each piece into a disc, sprinkling rye flour onto the counter as needed to prevent sticking. Cover the discs with a tea towel as you work.

continued on next page

Previous Page: The Uspenski Orthodox Cathedral dominates the skyline from its chunk of rock on Katajanokka peninsula, its dome and spires spied at every turn from the Helsinki Market Square where the annual Baltic Herring Fair is held. Scenes from the herring fair: A vendor enjoys his own wares; an acre of funnel chanterelles for sale; a working harbour at rest, with the cathedral twinkling in the distance. Above: Karjalanpiirakat in a stall at the herring fair, and in a Whitehorse kitchen.

Karjalanpiirakat with Roasted Cauliflower Filling (continued)

4. Roll each disc out into a thin circle about 5 to 6 inches (13 to 15 cm) in diameter. The circles should be no thicker than ⅟₁₆ inch (1.6 mm), and it will not be difficult to get there. Stack circles as you go, sprinkling a bit of rye flour on each to prevent sticking, and keep them covered with a tea cloth.

5. Preheat oven to 450F (230C) and line three baking sheets with parchment paper. Mix the melted butter and milk.

6. Working with 8 circles of dough at a time, fill each one with 3 tablespoons (45 mL) of cauliflower filling in a streak down the middle of the circle, almost touching the edge at the top and bottom but leaving lots of space at either side.

7. Pinch the top of the circle together with your fingers, and then crimp each side in four to five spots with thumb and two fingers, ending with a final pinch at the bottom. You'll end up with an open, flat-bottomed boat with pointed bow and stern and crimped gunnels, and the filling exposed in the middle.

8. Transfer the pastries to a baking sheet, cover with cloth and repeat until all 24 pastries are complete. Brush each one thoroughly with the butter and milk mixture (reserve mixture for second brushing).

9. Bake for 8 minutes, remove from oven and brush again; this keeps the pastry from getting hard. Bake for another 7 minutes and remove from oven. Cool briefly on a rack and serve while still warm, when they're at their best. These pastries freeze well; just reheat straight from the freezer, wrapped in foil, at 450F (230C) for 10 minutes.

Makes 24 pastries.

Beet and Blueberry Borscht

1 medium onion, chopped

1 Tbsp (15 mL) canola or olive oil

1 red pepper, chopped

2 stalks celery, diced

1 lb (455 gr) beets (about 4 medium), peeled and diced

4 cups (1 L) wild blueberries

1 cup (250 mL) organic, unfiltered apple juice

3 cups (710 mL) chicken or vegetable stock

2 Tbsp (30 mL) balsamic vinegar

2 Tbsp (30 mL) pure birch syrup (or substitute maple syrup)

Salt and pepper to taste

Goat milk yogourt, for garnish.

1. In a medium-sized saucepan, sauté onion in oil over medium heat until softened, about 5 minutes. Add red pepper and celery and sauté another 5 minutes. Add beets and blueberries. Stir.

2. Add apple juice and stock, cover, and bring to the boil. Turn heat to low and simmer until beets are soft, about 40 minutes.

3. Add vinegar, birch syrup, salt and pepper. Remove from heat.

4. Blend into a purée. For a rougher texture leave as is, but if you'd like a smoother, creamier soup press through a sieve.

5. Before serving, check seasoning and if necessary, add a splash more vinegar. Garnish with a dollop of goat milk yogourt.

Makes about 6 cups (1.4 L).

Matryoshka Cake

Get ready. This is a major construction project. Clear the agenda for the day you plan to assemble and decorate the cake, and make the two 9- × 13-inch (22.5- × 32-cm) cakes the day before.

Tara Kolla-Hale did this all by herself for the 2013 matryoshka party, and then we did it together in order to show you how. If you're not an artist, as I am not, don't worry. Just go for a very simple design.

OLD-TIMER'S CHOCOLATE CAKE

A rich, moist cake. Tara says: "This recipe was given to me by a Yukon old-timer. She had gotten it from a friend of her family's when she was married, with a note that said, 'This cake proves to your mother-in-law that her son is in good hands!'"

Halve the recipe for a simpler, single layer cake.

3½ cups (830 mL) all-purpose flour

3½ cups (830 mL) sugar

1½ cups (350 mL) cocoa

1 Tbsp (15 mL) baking soda

1 Tbsp (15 mL) baking powder

2 tsp (10 mL) salt

4 eggs at room temperature

2 cups (475 mL) milk

1 cup (250 mL) canola oil

1½ Tbsp (22 mL) vanilla

2 cups (475 mL) boiling water

1. Preheat oven to 350F (180C). Grease and flour two 9- × 13-inch (22.5- × 32-cm) baking pans and line the bottom of each pan with greased parchment.

2. Whisk together dry ingredients in the bowl of a stand mixer. Stir in remaining ingredients except for water on low speed and beat for 2 minutes at medium speed.

3. Add boiling water at low speed, beating only until combined. The batter will be very thin. Pour into prepared pans and bake for 40 to 45 minutes until a toothpick inserted in the middle of the cakes comes out clean. Cool in pans on a rack. After 30 minutes, remove each cake from pan in one piece. The cake is very moist, so be sure it is thoroughly loosened from the cake pans before attempting to remove it. To remove cake, place a baking sheet over top of each baking pan and flip the pan upside down.

4. When the cakes have cooled to room temperature, wrap in plastic and store at room temperature until you're ready to ice and assemble.

Makes a double-layer 9- × 13-inch (22.5- × 32-cm) cake.

continued on next page

Matryoshka Cake continued

CHOCOLATE GANACHE ICING

10 oz (285 gr) dark chocolate, at least 70 percent cocoa

2 cups (475 mL) 35 percent cream

6 Tbsp (90 mL) butter

1. Break chocolate in small pieces into a bowl.

2. Bring cream and butter to a boil over medium-high heat and pour over chocolate.

3. Place a plate over the bowl and wait for 5 minutes for the chocolate to melt.

4. Beat thoroughly until smooth and creamy. Cool to room temperature and then refrigerate to a spreadable consistency.

Makes about 4 cups (950 mL), enough to generously ice the Matryoshka cake.

DECORATION

⅔ cup (160 mL) Simple Wild Raspberry Jam, recipe on page 217

1 lb 6 oz (620 gr) Homemade Marzipan at room temperature, recipe on page 180

Icing sugar for dusting

Food colouring gel in desired colours

Vodka for thinning

ASSEMBLY

1. On a piece of parchment paper draw a rectangle the same size as the cake pan and within it, draw a matryoshka doll outline. Cut out the outline. Lay it on each cake in succession and cut with a serrated knife to make two doll-shaped cake layers. Reserve the scraps in case you have to fill in any holes where the cake stuck to the pan.

2. Transfer the first layer to a large serving platter, with the help of a couple of spatulas. Fill any holes with scraps of cake and spread the top with raspberry jam. Spread the top of the second layer with ⅔ cup (160 mL) ganache and flip it onto the first layer. You will now have two layers of cake with raspberry jam and ganache sandwiched between them.

3. Trim the edges of the two layers so they're even. With the serrated knife held at an angle, trim off the sharp edge around the top layer to create a rounded effect. (The rounding will become more noticeable once the marzipan layer is on.)

4. Patch the top of the cake with scraps as necessary, then ice the entire cake with ganache. Refrigerate, uncovered, while you roll out the marzipan.

continued on next page

Matryoshka Cake continued

5. Roll the marzipan: start with the marzipan at room temperature. Work it with your hands into a smooth ball, then flatten the ball with the palm of your hand into an oval. Dust the counter and rolling pin with icing sugar. Roll the marzipan into an oval about ¼ inch (0.6 cm) thick, 17 inches (43 cm) long and 14 inches (36 cm) wide, dusting counter and rolling pin with icing sugar as necessary.

6. Bring the cake out of the fridge onto the counter beside the sheet of marzipan. Working from top to bottom, fold the marzipan in three, and lay it horizontally over the middle of the cake. Unfold so that the marzipan is draped over the entire cake. Press the marzipan gently into shape, following the contours of the cake. Fold marzipan at the corners of the body section as though you're wrapping a present. Trim the excess marzipan with a sharp knife so that all the edges are clean. Reserve one largish piece of rolled-out marzipan to use as a colour tester.

7. Smooth the marzipan with a wet hand to remove any traces of icing sugar. Refrigerate while you prepare the food colouring.

8. Assemble food colouring, paintbrushes, vodka, small bowls for mixing and a couple of bowls of water for cleaning brushes. For each colour, start by mixing ¼ teaspoon (1 mL) of gel and ¼ teaspoon (1 mL) of vodka, stirring vigorously with a small spoon or whisk. Sometimes the gel separates into small globs; add vodka drop by drop after the first ¼ teaspoon (1 mL) and press the blobs with the back of the spoon periodically to break them up. We found that between ½ teaspoon (2.5 mL) and 1 teaspoon (5 mL) of each colour, after thinning, was sufficient for the cake. Test colours by brushing them onto the sheet of reserved marzipan.

9. Lightly score the cake with your design using a skewer or toothpick: a smaller circle on the head for the face, a larger circle in the body for the apron, and the knot and tails of the kerchief.

10. Paint the body, leaving a round space in the middle for the apron, and then paint the kerchief on the head, leaving a round space for the face. Paint the knot and tails of the kerchief. (Refrigerate between stages as necessary to make sure the cake stays firm.)

11. Next paint in the flowers in the apron, draw the face in black, and finally, outline the face, the kerchief ends and the apron in black. Finish by decorating the kerchief with three dots in a triangle. If you are nervous (as we were), keep it simple, and if you make a mistake, dab the colour with a clean paper towel. Refrigerate the cake until you're ready to serve.

12. Before serving, wipe the platter clean with a damp cloth and decorate with flowers or evergreen sprigs. Then deliver to the table and enjoy the accolades.

Makes 25 to 30 servings.

CHAPTER FIVE

The Boreal Pantry

A walk through the boreal forest is a walk through a living feast. Getting to know the plants, berries, flowers and trees in this most beautiful of biomes is a life-long pleasure. When building a boreal pantry there are many stages along the way: learning about habitat, harvesting, cleaning, storing, preparing and finally, (hooray!) eating and celebrating. It can be hard work, but every stage has its particular reward. You develop a different way of seeing. You learn to be patient. You learn not to take anything for granted, to share the bounty, to leave some for the birds and animals, and to be grateful for everything the forest gives you, whether it's a windy picnic with your girlfriends, soft moss under your knees among the spruce trees, or freezing fingers in the September dusk because you can't stop picking cranberries. Then, it's so satisfying to open the cupboard and survey jars full of the boreal foods you have gathered yourself and turned into syrups, jams, vinegars or liqueurs. Every jar and every bottle tells a story: the people you were with that day, the late August swim in the lake by the border, the outspoken raven in the spruce tree, the bear spied on the distant ridge. It's all there. You've brought it home with you, and you will again. When you eat the forest, you love the forest, and when you love the forest you help to protect and preserve it,

Cloudberries, or Rubus chamaemorus, *are native to the alpine and arctic regions of the circumpolar north.*

The Boreal Pantry

What's in Season?

Snow comes early and stays late in the north and sometimes it can seem there are not four seasons but two: snow and not-snow, or snow and less-snow. In fact seasonal changes are constant and subtle. Traditionally, Yukon First Nations people moved camp according to intimate knowledge of seasonal changes and animal migration. In his book *Canada's Boreal Forest*, J. David Henry reminds us that the Eastern and Woods Cree who inhabit the boreal forest divide the year into six seasons: spring, break-up, summer, fall, freeze-up and winter. For Sámi reindeer herders there are eight seasons based on the rhythms of the herd, the search for food, the rut and the harvest. Part of the daily joy of living in a northern climate is watching for the small changes that take place from month to month in the forest, the sky and the water.

Part of the daily joy of living in a northern climate is watching for the small changes that take place

Predicting harvest-readiness is a tricky thing in an area as large as the Yukon, let alone Canada or the global boreal forest. Variables such as latitude, altitude and weather confound us. Though not exhaustive, this section is meant to remind you when to start paying attention, with the understanding that it might be a while before the longed-for plant or berry or mushroom appears.

A well-used berry picker owned by Karin Mellin of Östersund, Jämtland. Every year Karin and her family pick kilos and kilos of berries in the abundant Swedish forest.

Keeping a diary is helpful. In 2010, in a notebook he labelled "Gatherings," my husband started recording the date and location of the plants and berries we typically harvest. Now, three years later, we have a useful record of annual variations, and a fun reminder of where we went and what we found.

GUIDELINES FOR ETHICAL FORAGING

With thanks to Amber Westfall, who composed this list of guidelines. Amber is a herbalist, teacher and proprietor of The Wild Garden in Ottawa, Ontario (www.thewildgarden.ca)

1. Make sure you have a 100 percent positive identification. Ideally, reference more than one field guide, or better yet, go out with an experienced forager.

2. Do not over-harvest. Be mindful of how many remaining plants are needed to ensure the stand will continue to flourish and thrive. Learn about how the plant reproduces. By seed? Rhizomes? Slow-growing bulbs? Think about what other animals, insects and people might be using those plants.

3. Know the poisonous plants in your area and what to avoid.

4. Harvest away from busy roads and rail lines. Avoid contaminated areas and areas that have been sprayed with chemical fertilizers or pesticides. The edges of farm fields, unless organic, are not appropriate for harvesting for this reason.

5. Know the history of the area you are harvesting from. Be wary of empty lots and avoid land previously used for industrial purposes.

6. Do not harvest on private property without permission.

7. Do not harvest on protected land, fragile or at-risk environments or in provincial or national parks.

8. Learn which plants are threatened or at-risk and do not harvest them.

9. Learn which plants are prolific and which plants are invasive. These are ideal for harvesting.

10. Whenever possible, replant root crowns and rhizomes, and spread seeds (except invasives).

11. Only harvest the appropriate part of the plant at the proper time of day and in the proper season.

12. Use clean, appropriate tools to reduce the spread of disease. Make neat, clean cuts at growing nodes to allow the plant to heal well and continue growing.

13. Leave some of the best specimens to go to seed and reproduce. If we take all the best plants and leave behind weak or diseased specimens, we are selecting for future plants that will be weak and subject to disease.

14. Have as little impact on the surrounding area as possible. Fill in any holes, re-cover bare dirt with leaf litter and try to leave the area better than you found it.

15. Don't waste the plants that you harvest. Use and process them promptly while still fresh and compost any parts that are not used.

SPRING

Trees and shrubs: Birch leaves, wild rose leaves and raspberry leaves begin to appear in late April to mid-May. The birch sap begins to run any time from early to late May. Uncle Berwyn's Yukon Birch Syrup appears in stores in late June. Yukon Brewing's Birch Beer is brewed anytime from mid- to late June and is generally available all summer.

Plants and herbs: April–May, dandelion roots and leaves, fireweed shoots, yarrow greens; May–June: lungwort, lamb's quarters, wild onion, pasture sage, Labrador tea.

Buds and flowers: May–June, Spruce buds, or tips, can appear any time from mid-May to late June. Rose petals follow soon after. Dandelion flowers start to bloom in mid-June, yarrow flowers in mid- to late June.

Fruits: Rhubarb, rhubarb, rhubarb, and that's about it until mid-July. (I know rhubarb's not a fruit, but we treat it like one.)

Mushrooms: The morel harvest begins as soon as the snow recedes in last year's burn areas.

Fish: From mid-March to mid-April ice fishing yields lake trout, burbot, pike and Dolly Varden. On Atlin

Lake the whitefish harvest begins in late March and ends in late April or early May. In early June the lakes have not yet turned, and lake trout are close to the surface. Halibut season begins in March and ends in mid-November.

SUMMER

Plants and Herbs: Pineapple weed, lamb's quarters, plantain, *Artemisia tilesii*, coltsfoot.

Berries: Soapberries, strawberries, cloudberries, raspberries, saskatoons, redcurrants, blackcurrants, Arctic raspberries; blueberries, near the end of August.

Mushrooms: Orange delicious, aspen and birch boletes, king boletes, agaricus, oyster, hedgehog, Hawk's Wing, shaggy manes in late August through mid-September.

Fish: Sockeye salmon, followed by king salmon in July–August and coho and chum in August–September. The lake trout have gone deeper. Pike, grayling, inconnu, whitefish (though they can get wormy).

Facing page, top: Hikers and a trusty friend explore the hills in the Tombstone Mountains on the Dempster Highway. Facing page, bottom: A hiker turned berry picker finds cloudberries on the Dempster Highway. Left: The boreal pantry grows over time, as we become more familiar with berries and herbs and learn what to do with them.

FALL

Berries and Fruit: Lowbush cranberries and highbush cranberries, moss berries, Arctic raspberries, rowanberries, crabapples, rosehips.

Game: Elk, Dall sheep, caribou, moose, bison, grouse.

Fish: Halibut, chum salmon, lake trout, coho, black cod.

Shellfish: Alaskan spot prawns; Alaskan sidestripe prawns, king crab.

NOTES ON FORAGING

In *Stalking the Wild Asparagus*, Euell Gibbons points out that just as we have learned to recognize and differentiate between a head of cabbage and a head of lettuce on the supermarket shelves, we can learn to recognize and differentiate between plants in the wild. Foraged, wild foods are a source of nutrition, healing and flavour available to all of us. But foraging is a learned behaviour, and requires time, preparation, patience and a good measure of caution.

It's a good idea to familiarize yourself with the principles of safe and ethical foraging before going out into the wild. That way you'll continue to have good experiences, your knowledge will grow, and so will your appreciation, even love, for the boreal forest or other eco-region that provides the bounty.

The Boreal Pantry

This section is organized into categories, and within each category, recipes are arranged according to when the main ingredient comes into season. So, for example, a wild ingredient like lowbush cranberries will appear in more than one section, and perhaps not where you would first expect it—please consult the index of this book to find recipes by ingredient. I've tried not to duplicate recipes that appear in *The Boreal Gourmet*; so if you're looking for a plain blueberry jam or basic highbush cranberry jelly recipe, check there too.

NOTES ON JELLY- AND JAM-MAKING

Jelly- and jam-making can be the most perplexing of kitchen adventures, best undertaken with a sense of humour and a willingness to go boldly forth. Sometimes your mixture reaches the gelling stage after a mere 15 minutes of cooking; other times you give up in despair and resign yourself to syrup, only to discover it has turned into jelly after a month in the cupboard.

In truth, jelly-making is an unruly art. There are many variables that affect the setting point: the balance of fruit, pectin, sugar and acid, the size of the pot, the heat under the pot, the humidity that day. A failed jelly or jam makes excellent syrup or sauce, and this is a comfort. But even so, sometimes we just want it to work. So here is a bit of science and a few tips that may provide assistance for your next foray into jelly- or jam-making.

PECTIN

Pectin is essential to gelling, and it needs help from both sugar and acid; hence the inclusion of sugar and lemon juice in so many recipes. The acid helps to extract the pectin from the fruit, and the sugar increases pectin's ability to gel by absorbing water; in the absence of water the pectin molecules bind more easily. Sugar and acid also contribute to the longer-term preservation of the jelly or jam.

Pectin and acid occur naturally in fruits in different measure, depending on the fruit. Both pectin and acid decrease as the fruit ripens. Mixing underripe and ripe fruit is a good strategy for a successful gel; so is combining fruits that have a higher pectin or acid content with those that have less. Think of cranberry-blueberry jam, for example, or crabapple-rhubarb jelly, or pear and redcurrant jelly.

Here's a quick look at the pectin and acid contents of some fruits:

- High pectin and acid: *crabapples, green apples, cranberries, redcurrants, blackcurrants, gooseberries, rosehips, soapberries, tart plums* and *grapes*
- High pectin, low acid: *sweet apples* and *quinces*
- High acid, low pectin: *rhubarb, strawberries, raspberries, cherries* and *pineapple*
- Low pectin and acid: *peaches, pears* and *blueberries*

Combining fruits, adding lemon juice or vinegar for extra acid, and cooking for anywhere from 10 to 30 minutes in an open pot (the "open-kettle" method) will generally yield a jam or jelly that sets; it just takes patience, and you have to accept that there will be some loss in yield. However, you can also get help from commercial pectin.

COMMERCIAL PECTIN

Commercial pectin is extracted from citrus peel or apples and is available in both liquid and powder forms. There are several varieties available under different brand names. Many require a high proportion of sugar to fruit to work properly, sometimes as much as 7 cups sugar to 4 cups fruit. We're warned, with good reason, not to fool around with the proportions suggested in the recipes that accompany these products: the pectin needs that much sugar to be activated. Similarly, liquid and powdered pectins can't be used interchangeably. Remember that commercial pectins have a limited shelf life. Check the best-before date before you embark.

If, like me, you object to using a lot of sugar for reasons of both health and flavour, you will be happy to know there are several alternatives out there. Bernardin makes a "No Sugar Needed" powdered pectin that requires little to no sugar to gel, and honey or sugar replacements such as Splenda can be substituted as sweeteners. The recipes that accompany the product call for unsweetened fruit juice (apple, white grape, cranberry, apricot) in addition to fruit.

Pomona's Universal Pectin is another pectin that requires minimal sugar and works just as well with honey or sugar replacements. The pectin is derived from pure citrus and is activated by calcium rather than sugar. Each package comes with an envelope of powdered pectin and a smaller one of calcium. The instructions for use are clear and straightforward. I've found both Bernardin and Pomona's very useful for making herb and flower jellies, whose delicate flavours would be lost with too much cooking or too much sugar. Unlike other commercial pectins, Pomona's has an unlimited shelf life.

There is one caveat, and I have to thank Mary Lou and Connie Sumberg of Pomona's Pectin for pointing this out. Appropriate levels of lemon juice or vinegar must

A scattered colony of apple trees thrives in the yards of downtown Whitehorse; some are crabapples, others are hardy apple or apple-crab varietals. Some were planted decades ago by the original property owners and are still going strong. One of my neighbours bought her house in winter, when the entire property was covered by a metre of snow. That spring after the snow melted she found a small apple tree in the backyard. She was so moved she burst into tears.

be added to flower and herb jellies to ensure food safety. Botulism spores can survive in an oxygen-free, low-acid environment, even after the food has been processed in a boiling water bath. When in doubt, add lemon juice. Pomona's recommends adding 1 tablespoon (15 mL) of lemon juice per cup (250 mL) of mashed, low-acid fruit, and 2 tablespoons (30 mL) lemon juice per cup (250 mL) of water in a water-based infusion such as for herb jelly.

For the food science geeks: foods with a pH of 4.6 or lower are considered high-acid and can be safely canned in a boiling water bath. Most fruits and berries have a pH of 4.6 or less, but the pH level of the entire final product needs to be 4.6 or less, not just the ingredients that went into its making. Adding garlic or onion to a cranberry chutney will change its pH. Foods such as tomatoes, figs or mangoes that have a pH level of close to 4.6 need extra acid for safe canning. For information on the pH levels of common foods, see Useful Websites on page 243.

I've found the shelf life of jellies and jams made with less sugar and Pomona's pectin tends to be shorter once the jar is opened. I make herb and flower jellies in ½-cup (125-mL) rather than 1-cup (250-mL) jars. Another Pomona's tip: if you're following the recipe guidelines in the package and find your jelly or jam is too stiff, reduce the amount of pectin by ½ to 1 teaspoon (2.5 to 5 mL) per batch.

Pomona's Pectin was developed in the 1980s by a jelly and jam–lover who wanted to find a way of using less sugar. Today, Pomona's is still a family-run business with a troubleshooting hotline and an extremely helpful website. (See the Sources and Suppliers section on page 242.)

HOMEMADE PECTIN

Homemade pectin derives from the juice of crabapples or tart apples like Granny Smiths; a homemade pectin recipe is included on page 202. Essentially a concentrated apple juice, homemade pectin doesn't act as predictably as commercial pectin but it will help a jelly or a jam set. The strength of homemade pectin can be determined through a simple alcohol test. (The same test will also reveal how much pectin is present in any fruit juice you're going to make into jelly.) Each batch of homemade pectin will be different, opening the door to experimentation. Note that commercial apple juice can't be substituted for homemade, fresh apple juice for making pectin.

A Recipe for Homemade Pectin

4 lbs (1.8 kg) crabapples (or substitute unripe Granny Smiths)

4 cups (1 L) water, or enough to cover

2 Tbsp (30 mL) lemon juice

1. Wash crabapples, cut out any blemishes and remove stems. The crabapples and apple-crabs tend to be small, so don't bother quartering them, but do quarter the larger Granny Smiths if you're using them.

2. Cover apples with water and bring to the boil. Add lemon juice. Reduce heat and simmer for 30 minutes, or until apples are completely soft.

3. Strain through cheesecloth into a clean bowl. Squeeze the cheesecloth gently at the end if you don't care if your juice is clear; otherwise let the liquid drip for 2 hours before the next step.

4. Place the juice in a clean saucepan and bring to the boil over medium-high heat. Perform the alcohol test (see sidebar opposite) to test for gelling ability. If you're satisfied with the result, pour the juice into jars. If not, reduce the juice further, stirring frequently, and test until you're satisfied. Note: when I first made pectin I didn't know about the alcohol test and just winged it; don't be afraid to do the same.

5. Use the pectin right away, store in the fridge for a week, freeze for up to 6 months, or can in sterilized jars and process in a hot water bath for 10 minutes, adding 2 minutes per 1,000 feet (305 m) above sea level.

Makes about four 1-cup (250-mL) jars.

ALCOHOL TEST

Note: don't taste the results of this test—the alcohol is poison.

Combine 1 tablespoon (15 mL) of cooled, homemade apple juice with 1 tablespoon (15 mL) of rubbing alcohol in a clean jar with a lid. Shake gently. The alcohol will pull the pectin together into a more or less cohesive gel. Lift out some of the gel with a fork. If the gel is cohesive and stays on top of the fork in one blob, there is ample pectin present. If the jelly separates into two or three blobs, or hangs down from the tines of the fork, there is enough pectin for a loose gel. If the jelly is composed of many smaller blobs, there is less pectin present. In order to increase the amount of pectin present, cook down the apple juice a bit more.

Jam- and Jelly-Making Tips

PREPARING JARS

1. Start by washing your jars and lids in clean, soapy water and rinsing well.

2. Sterilize the jars by putting them in the canning pot as you heat the water to boiling.

3. To prepare lids, bring a small pot of water to the boil, remove from heat, put the lids in and return to the element set at low. Dip screw-top portion of lids in the boiling water bath just before screwing them onto the jar.

4. Don't re-use sealing lids. It's okay to re-use screw tops but discard any that are rusty or dented.

MAKING JAM OR JELLY

1. Make small batches at a time—start with 4 to 6 cups (1 to 1.4 L) of juice.

2. Use a wide, heavy-bottomed saucepan that's deep enough for the jam or jelly to boil rapidly without overflowing; about 3 litres (3 quarts) is a good size for small batches.

3. Bring juice to the boil, add the sugar, and then reduce heat to medium-high or medium.

4. Stir the jam or jelly frequently as it cooks; this keeps it from adhering to the bottom of the pan and scorching.

5. For jellies made without commercial pectin, start testing about 10 to 15 minutes after you've added the sugar, and be patient.

6. Use the testing method you're most comfortable with (various methods are discussed on page 204).

STORING

1. Fill jars to within ¼ inch (0.6 cm) of the top. Run a sterilized knife around the inside of the jar to remove air bubbles. Wipe rims clean; any drops left there will interfere with the seal. (I dip a piece of paper towel into the boiling water bath for this job.)

2. Ensure the water in the boiling water bath covers the jars by 1 inch (2.5 cm).

3. Compensate for the lower boiling point of water at higher altitudes by adding minutes to the boiling time: the rule of thumb is a minimum of 2 minutes per 1,000 feet (305 m) of altitude above sea level.

4. After processing jars in a boiling water bath, put them on a wooden board or in a pan lined with a towel and set them aside, undisturbed, for a few hours or overnight. Resist tipping the filled jars to see if the jelly has set; tipping just slows down the process.

5. Listen for the "pop" that indicates a vacuum seal. (A vacuum-sealed jar will have a slightly concave lid.) When jars are cool, press down on each lid. If a lid pops back the jar hasn't sealed properly and must be refrigerated.

John Lenart of Klondike Valley Nursery & Market Garden has supplied several trees to downtown Whitehorse residents in recent years. Since 1986 John has lived on a small homestead on the Klondike River just south of Dawson, experimenting with apple varietals, pears, cherries, plums and ornamental trees. His property is only accessible by boat; if you see his red canoe on the gravel bar across the river from the highway you know he's at home. In the summer of 2013 Hector and I visited the gardens and purchased a couple of apple-crab for our front yard, and we are hopeful they will yield fruit in a couple of years. We plan to get a crabapple too, for the beauty and for the jelly. In the meantime some generous neighbours bring kilos of crabapples from their tree over to our house every fall, enough for lots of different jellies, juice, apple vodka, homemade vinegar and homemade pectin.

Jams, Jellies, Syrups and a Salsa

JELLY TESTING METHODS

The wrinkle test: Place a small plate in the freezer when you start the jelly-making process. When you think the jelly's getting close, pour a teaspoonful onto the plate and chill for one or two minutes. Take out the plate and push the pool of jelly with your fingertip; if it wrinkles, it's ready.

The sheet test: With a spoon, lift a small amount of jelly from the pot and let it cool slightly before tipping it back into the pot from the edge of the spoon. In the early stages of cooking there will be one light and syrupy drop but when the jelly is nearly done two drops will form on the edge; when the drops run together to form a thick sheet, the jelly is ready.

The temperature method: This method depends on two things: (1) an accurate, calibrated candy thermometer, and (2) knowledge of the water-boiling temperature at your altitude.

Calibrate your thermometer by bringing water to a boil, clipping the thermometer to the side of the pot, ensuring it's immersed but not touching the bottom, and leaving it there for five minutes while the water boils. Compare the results to the boiling point of water where you live, and add or subtract degrees accordingly. So, if water boils at 212F (100C) where you live, and your thermometer reads 208F (98C) after five minutes, you'll know you need to add 4F (2C) for an accurate read.

For jelly- or candy-making, subtract 2F (0.5C) from the sea-level temperature for every 1,000 feet (305 m). Unless otherwise stated, home canning recipes generally use sea-level temperatures as the standard; for jelly that's 220F (104C).

This section is ordered chronologically, according to when the herb, fruit, flower or jelly is in season, more or less. We start off with rhubarb (early May) and end with crabapples (late September and into October).

Late April: young shoots in tiny earth-filled pots bask on sunny windowsills across the north, revving up for the transplant to the greenhouse or into the garden under the cold frame, while cooks and gardeners dream of the meals to come. But outside crumbling snow still dominates the landscape in silty piles, and we yearn for the moment when rhubarb thrusts its snout up through the hard earth and declares that winter is over. By mid-May, long before planting time, the rhubarb is ready and raring to go, suggesting crisps and chutneys and salsas and salads. If the gardener is diligent about pinching off the flower, the rhubarb will continue feeding the family with sweets and savouries right into September. Indeed if we're not careful the rhubarb will take over, the situation currently unfolding in my yard, where dandelions and rhubarb duke it out every year and the rhubarb is winning.

Whitehorse resident Christine Cleghorn is familiar with this predilection of rhubarb for world domination; she calls rhubarb "the J.R. Ewing of the backyard." She too welcomes the first sighting of rhubarb. "It always shows up first," she says, "usually right around the time I think the snow is never going to leave and I can't handle any more people complaining they can't ski anymore and the biking isn't good yet. Rhubarb kind of rides in and saves the day." Christine is the inspiration for the Rhubarb Pavlova with Birch Syrup Ice Cream recipe on page 38, a dish she says tells your guests you've gone the extra mile. The three rhubarb pantry items that follow will rack up points as presents to friends or presentations on your own table.

Spicy Rhubarb Jelly

Adjust the heat in this jelly by using the lesser amount of hot pepper. Substitute jalapeno pepper if serrano is hard to find, but remember it's not as hot. If you don't have lowbush cranberries in the freezer in May, try substituting one slice of beet for colour.

6 cups (1.4 L) fresh or frozen rhubarb

¼ cup (60 mL) wild lowbush cranberries (lingonberries) or substitute cultivated cranberries (optional, for colour)

Water to cover—about 4 cups (1 L)

1–2 Tbsp (15–30 mL) serrano pepper, chopped

1 Tbsp (15 mL) fresh ginger, minced

1 Tbsp (15 mL) lemon zest

¼ cup (60 mL) lemon juice

3 tsp (15 mL) Pomona's Universal Pectin powder

1½ cups (350 mL) sugar

3 tsp (15 mL) calcium water, prepared according to package directions

1. Bring rhubarb, cranberries, pepper, ginger, lemon zest, juice and water to the boil, reduce heat and simmer until the rhubarb is thoroughly cooked.

2. Strain into a bowl through a jelly bag or sieve until dripping stops.

3. Measure juice; there should be about 4 cups (1 L). Discard solids.

4. Mix the pectin powder with sugar and set aside. Add calcium water to the juice, bring to the boil and add sugar-pectin mix. Cook for two minutes, whisking vigorously to dissolve pectin, bring to the boil again and remove from heat.

5. Pour into sterilized jars and process in a boiling water bath, adding 2 minutes per 1,000 feet (305 m) above sea level.

Makes about four 1-cup (250-mL) jars.

Rhubarb Chipotle Salsa

Great with grilled vegetables, tortilla chips or barbecued steak.

1 Tbsp (15 mL) olive oil

1 medium onion, finely chopped

2 cloves garlic, minced

2 Tbsp (30 mL) chipotle pepper in adobo sauce, chopped

4 cups (1 L) chopped fresh or frozen rhubarb

½ cup (125 mL) packed brown sugar

½ tsp (2.5 mL) salt

1. Sauté onion in oil in a saucepan over medium heat until translucent, 7 to 10 minutes. Add garlic, stir and sauté another 2 minutes. Add remaining ingredients to the saucepan, stir and cook until rhubarb is tender, about 10 minutes. (If rhubarb is fresh you may need to add 1 tablespoon/15 mL of water or lemon juice to loosen up the mixture.)

2. Remove from heat and cool to room temperature. Cover and refrigerate. Will keep for one week.

Makes about 2 cups (475 mL).

Rhubarb and Blood Orange Jam

Blood oranges don't come into season until late January, so if you want to try this one, remember to save a 4-cup (1 L) bag of chopped rhubarb in the freezer over the winter. Or make the jam in May using fresh rhubarb and thin-skinned oranges such as Valencia, usually available in May, June and July.

4 cups (1 L) frozen rhubarb, thawed, with juice

Water to cover—about 2 cups (475 mL)

2 blood oranges

1½ cups (350 mL) sugar

1. Combine thawed rhubarb, rhubarb juice and water in a medium saucepan. Bring to the boil over medium-high heat, reduce to a simmer and cook until rhubarb is soft but not mushy—about 5 minutes for frozen, thawed rhubarb and 10 minutes for fresh. Strain into a bowl. Reserve rhubarb and return the juice to the saucepan. There should be about 2 cups (475 mL).

2. Wash the oranges and cut a thin slice from both ends of each one. Slice in half. Remove central line of pith and seeds by cutting a V into the centre with a sharp knife. Cut into quarters and slice thinly.

3. Add sugar to juice over medium-high heat, stirring to dissolve, then add orange slices. Bring to the boil; reduce to medium low and cook uncovered until the oranges are translucent, about 30 minutes.

4. Add reserved rhubarb, increase heat to medium-high and cook for 3 to 5 minutes, stirring often, until the gelling point is reached. (At this stage it happens quickly.) Test for doneness (see page 204 for testing methods) and if the jelly is ready, proceed to the next step.

5. Pour into sterilized jars and process in a boiling water bath, adding 2 minutes per 1,000 feet (305 m) above sea level.

Makes about five 1-cup (250-mL) jars.

Yarrow blooms among the purple lupines on a sunny summer day.

Yukon Herb Jelly

Yarrow blossoms from late June to mid-July, around the same time as pineapple weed, and *Artemisia tilesii* leaves are green and abundant then. Yarrow is quite pungent when fresh, and so is the *Artemisia*, but the flavours mellow considerably after drying. Dry small bundles of these herbs by tying with string and suspending from a rope or string away from direct sunlight. Store dried herbs in jars in a cool, dark cupboard once they're thoroughly dried. Experiment by substituting for the more usual thyme, oregano and rosemary in savoury dishes.

Try this jelly on toast spread with a bit of chèvre, on cheese trays, as an accompaniment to pâtés such as Smoked Arctic Char Liver Pâté (page 154), or as a condiment with roasted or grilled meat.

½ cup (125 mL) loosely packed, dried yarrow blossoms and leaves

¼ cup (60 mL) loosely packed, dried *Artemisia tilesii* leaves

¼ cup (60 mL) tightly packed dried pineapple weed, stems, leaves and flowers (three bushy plants)

4 cups (1 L) unsweetened white grape juice or homemade crabapple juice

½ cup (125 mL) lemon juice

1 package Bernardin No Sugar Needed pectin

1 cup (250 mL) sugar

1. Combine herbs and grape juice in a medium pot. Bring to the boil over high heat, turn to medium-low and simmer for 5 minutes. Remove from heat and steep for 30 minutes.

2. Strain into a bowl through a sieve lined with cheesecloth. Return to clean saucepan, add lemon juice and pectin, whisking to dissolve, and bring to a rolling boil over high heat.

3. Add sugar, whisking once again, bring to a rolling boil and boil for 1 minute.

4. Remove from heat, skim off foam and pour into sterilized jars. Process in a boiling water bath for 10 minutes, adding 2 minutes per 1,000 feet (305 m) above sea level.

Makes about four 1-cup (250-mL) jars.

Spruce Tip Jelly

In the Yukon we collect the new green tips from the branches of white and black spruce trees anytime from mid-May to mid-June, depending on how much sun and rain there's been, and the latitude and altitude. Spruce tips are packed with vitamin C, have a fresh citrusy flavour, make an excellent tea and can be used in sweet or savoury dishes. And, they grow on different kinds of spruce across the country, though they'll come into season earlier in southern latitudes. I encourage you to keep an eye out for them in the spring; they look like bright green paintbrush tips with a small brown husk at the end.

When you're picking, remember that this is the tree's new growth and pick sparingly from each branch and from each tree. Remove the small brown husk from the tip as you pick by knocking it gently with your fingers, or pick husks off at home before processing. Spruce tips can be stored in resealable bags in the freezer or air-dried out of direct sunlight in a well-ventilated room, and stored in jars in the spice cupboard. Use dried spruce tips in breads or as a seasoning the way you would rosemary. Experiment with fresh or frozen spruce tips as a herb, as a vegetable, in sugars or salts, or in cakes and cookies. Use them to flavour olive oil, and turn them into jellies, syrups or liqueurs.

4 cups (1 L) spruce tips, fresh or frozen

4 cups (1 L) water

1 cup (250 mL) sugar

3 tsp (15 mL) Pomona's Universal Pectin powder

3 tsp (15 mL) calcium water, prepared according to package directions

½ cup (125 mL) lemon juice

1. Cover spruce tips with water in a medium saucepan and bring to the boil. Reduce heat and simmer for 20 minutes.

2. Cool to room temperature and refrigerate spruce tips in juice overnight to allow the flavour to fully develop.

3. Strain into a bowl through a sieve lined with cheesecloth and then through a coffee filter; this will remove some of the cloudiness from the juice. You should have about 4 cups (1 L) of juice.

4. Mix pectin and sugar together and set aside. In a clean saucepan, combine calcium water, lemon juice and spruce tip juice, mix well and bring to the boil.

5. Add sugar and pectin mix, stir vigorously for a couple of minutes, return to the boil and remove from heat.

6. Pour into sterilized jars and process in a boiling water bath, adding 2 minutes per 1,000 feet (305 m) above sea level.

Makes about four 1-cup (250-mL) jars.

Left to right: A jam and two jellies: Lowbush Cranberry and Rosehip Jam, Fireweed Jelly and Spruce Tip Jelly. The boreal forest in late summer. An abundance of fresh, green spruce tips.

Spruce Tip Syrup

2 cups (475 mL) water

2 cups (475 mL) sugar

2 cups (475 mL) spruce tips

1. Bring sugar and water to the boil. Add spruce tips; reduce heat to medium and simmer, covered, for 30 minutes.

2. Taste; if the flavour is pronounced enough for you, strain through a sieve lined with cheesecloth, bring to the boil in a clean saucepan and pour into sterilized jars.

3. For a bolder flavor, cool the syrup to room temperature without straining and refrigerate overnight. Next day bring to the boil again to thin the syrup, strain through a sieve lined with cheesecloth and return to the boil in a clean saucepan. Pour into sterilized jars.

4. Cool, refrigerate and use within a month.

Makes two 1-cup (250-mL) jars.

Candied Spruce Tips

1 cup (250 mL) Spruce Tip Syrup	1 cup (250 mL) fresh or frozen and thawed spruce tips

1. Combine syrup and spruce tips in a small saucepan. Bring to the boil, reduce heat and simmer for 5 minutes. Strain through a sieve, shaking to remove excess liquid. Cool syrup to room temperature and store in fridge for other uses.

2. Spread spruce tips on a baking sheet lined with parchment paper or on a food dryer tray. Dry for 3 to 4 hours in a 150F (65C) oven or for 6 hours in a food dryer at 95F (35C), until spruce tips are dry but still chewy. Store in the refrigerator and use within three months.

Makes 1 cup (250 mL).

Fireweed

Fireweed (*Chamerion angustifolium*) starts to flower from the bottom up, around mid-July, and often the bottom blossoms are fading before the top buds have opened. The picking season can therefore be quite long, good news if it's your first time making fireweed jelly—if you're not successful you still have time to pick more blossoms and try again. When picking blossoms, remember to leave the seedpods behind, and don't pick all your flowers from one plant or one patch, for the sake of the bees and other insects. Finally, if you pick the blossoms from the stems you'll save time cleaning later.

Fireweed jelly and syrup have a subtle, floral flavour, easily overpowered by too much sugar. For this reason I would only use Pomona's Universal Pectin or Bernardin No Sugar Needed pectin.

The fireweed petals will lose their colour during boiling, and the water may turn a brownish colour, but the addition of lemon juice will bring the pale magenta back again. My fireweed juice was quite cloudy; I've since learned that if you allow the liquid to sit in the fridge for a couple of days before making jelly, the pollen and other sediments will settle.

Fireweed Jelly

4 cups (1L) packed fireweed flowers, without stems

2 cups (475 mL) water

2 cups (475 mL) unsweetened white grape juice

3 tsp (15 mL) Pomona's Universal Pectin powder

2 cups (475 mL) sugar

½ cup (125 mL) lemon juice

3 tsp (15 mL) calcium water, prepared according to package directions

1. Bring fireweed flowers, water and grape juice to the boil over gentle heat and simmer for 10 minutes, or until the flowers have lost their colour.

2. Strain into a bowl through a jelly bag or a sieve lined with cheesecloth. Measure juice; it should come to 4 cups (1 L). Either cover and leave in the fridge for a couple of days to allow the pollen to settle, or proceed to next step.

3. Mix pectin and sugar together and set aside. In a clean saucepan, combine the lemon juice and the fireweed juice. Add calcium water to the saucepan, whisk and bring to the boil.

4. Add the sugar and pectin mixture to the saucepan, stir vigorously for a couple of minutes, return to the boil and remove from heat.

5. Pour into sterilized jars and process in a boiling water bath for 10 minutes, adding 2 minutes per 1,000 feet (305 m) above sea level.

Makes about four 1-cup (250-mL) jars or eight ½-cup (125-mL) jars. Note: since there is reduced sugar in this jelly, the shelf life is shorter once the jar is opened. I tend to make this jelly in smaller jars.

Fireweed Syrup

Fireweed Syrup lends its colour and delicate floral note to summery drinks like gin and tonic or Prosecco. Mix 2 tablespoons (30 mL) of Fireweed Syrup with 1 teaspoon (15 mL) of lemon juice and top it up with soda water for a cool midday refresher. Try the syrup over vanilla ice cream or on Finnish Pancakes (page 11).

4 cups (1 L) packed fireweed flowers, stems removed

2 cups (475 mL) water, divided

2 cups (475 mL) unsweetened white grape juice

1 cup (250 mL) sugar

½ cup (125 mL) lemon juice

1. Combine flowers, half of the water and all of the grape juice in a saucepan. Bring to the boil over gentle heat and simmer until the flowers are white, about 10 minutes. Strain juice into a bowl through a sieve lined with cheesecloth.

2. Make simple syrup: combine sugar and remaining water in a small saucepan and bring to the boil. Simmer until the sugar dissolves and remove from heat.

3. Return fireweed juice to a clean saucepan. Add lemon juice and simple syrup, bring slowly to a boil and simmer until syrup has thickened enough that it drops from a spoon back into the pot in a slow drip.

4. Pour into sterilized jars and process in a boiling water bath for 10 minutes, adding 2 minutes per 1,000 feet (305 m) above sea level.

Makes about four 1-cup (250-mL) jars or eight ½-cup (125-mL) jars. Opened jars of syrup will last about a month in the fridge, so choose your jar size depending on how fast you will use it.

Northern Berries

Countries of the circumpolar north share a passion for wild berries. This love isn't exclusive to the north, of course, but when you don't have local access to the hard and soft tree fruits of more southern regions berries take on a special importance. They're what we have, and we celebrate them by going out into the bush in berry-picking parties, giving berries as gifts to elders and neighbours who can't go out on their own, sharing recipes and exchanging endless glass jars of preserves and jellies, chutneys and marmalades. In the Yukon, where First Nations people thrived for thousands of years on a diet of wild foods, it's impossible not to imagine the imperative of the coming winter, and the importance of the berry harvest for sustaining the family, when you're on your knees in a hollow among the spruce, picking lowbush cranberries. Berry picking is an act of the body and of the imagination that connects us to each other and to the past. In Scandinavian countries the whole family goes into the woods with buckets and baskets, and the farther north you travel, the more important berries become on the plate, in stories and in myth.

Motorcyclists love to venture up the Dempster Highway, but are sometimes defeated by mud.

Berry picking is an act of the body and of the imagination that connects us to each other and to the past.

Cloudberries

In the summer of 2013, Hector and I had only one opportunity to travel up the Dempster Highway in search of cloudberries (*Rubus chamaemorus*), and that was just before the Dawson City Music Festival in the third week of July. We knew we were probably going to be too early for the berries but we packed a cooler and camping gear, jumped into the car and set off for the Arctic Circle, 1,405 kilometres away. It may seem crazy to take such a long road trip in search of a berry that might not even be in season yet, but we were driven by memories of cloudberries in Scandinavia and we really wanted to get to know them in our own territory.

The cloudberry is known by many names amongst northern peoples: salmonberry or yellow berry in the northern Yukon and NWT, bakeapple in Newfoundland, *hjortron* in Sweden, *molter* or *viddas gule* ("highland gold") in Norway and *lakka* in Finland. The cloudberry is an aloof and reticent berry—a lover of tundra, bogs and high altitudes, difficult to get to and highly resistant to cultivation. It can take seven years for a plant to fruit, and the berry is only suitable for picking for a few short days before it turns mushy and loses its flavour. This makes the cloudberry a precious commodity, equally loved for its taste, its rarity and its bright beauty.

In Norway strict rules govern the picking of cloudberries and the penalty for breaking the rules is stiff: fines, even imprisonment. The berry is an important item of trade in Norway, Sweden and Finland, gathered by expert foragers who are willing to brave the mosquitoes and muskeg of the north country; we met one family

Distant hills and long views are part of the Dempster's magic.

who had picked 75 kilos and sold them to buyers and restaurants in Stockholm. As Canadians know, IKEA sells cloudberry jam in its food store, and the Finnish make a cloudberry liqueur that even Swedish people say is the best on the market.

Wherever you go, cloudberry lovers are fiercely protective of their patches and share little information. Hector and I knew we were on our own on the Dempster, and were careful not to ask "Where are the cloudberries good this year?" but rather, "Are they in season yet?" At the interpretive centre in Tombstone Territorial Park we came in for a lot of good-natured teasing from Dawsonites who consider the Dempster their cloudberry backyard, and rightfully so. Dawson berry pickers make an annual pilgrimage up the Dempster for cloudberries in late July, just as Whitehorsians travel south to Fraser, BC, for blueberries in August.

It was intriguing to be that far north in July and see the difference between the flora there and in our usual stomping grounds near Whitehorse. Along the pathways in the Tombstone campground the forest floor was lush with coltsfoot, lungwort and *Artemisia tilesii*, the latter in varieties I had never seen before, some of them almost sweet to the taste. One of our Whitehorse friends was staying over in campsite 19, where there were "tons of cloudberries," she said, "you must come and see." I was still getting to know cloudberries and tended to confuse their leaves with the leaves of young coltsfoot, but when I saw them together at campsite 19 it became much easier. There were cloudberry plants, in some number, but the berries were still pale red and tightly packed within a sheath of four tiny leaves. As the berries ripen the colour changes to golden orange and the leaves open and retreat down the stalk. These berries were at least four days and maybe as much as a week away from readiness.

The question became, would our luck be better or worse, the further north we went? Some (heated) discussion ensued but finally we agreed: let's just do it. I had never been north of the Tombstone campground on the Dempster, so it wasn't just the berries for me, it was the fabled Blackstone Uplands, and the Ogilvie and Richardson Mountains that were calling.

As we drove I rolled pieces of coltsfoot leaf into balls and set them on the dashboard to dry in the sun; I wanted to try turning them to ash and using them as a salt substitute as suggested in *Edible & Medicinal Plants of Canada*. We crossed the Blackstone River and drove through the Blackstone Uplands, long sweeps of tundra, dwarf birch and willow and a skyline punctuated by limestone tors reaching up into the blue, which was rapidly becoming grey. The feeling of space and ancient animal, human and geological history is strong up there. We didn't talk much, mesmerized by the landscape. Then the rain moved in on us in sheets and sheets; by the time we were through Windy Pass and near the Engineer Creek Campground we'd had enough, so we stopped for the night with the other refugees from the rain, one of whom was so fed up he pitched his tent in the covered shelter.

Next day we experienced the famous Dempster Highway mud, a slick couple of inches of loose clay and water on the surface that turns the truck into a hydrofoil liable to slide off the road into the ditch at the slightest wrong move. We passed one, then two, then three abandoned motorcycles. Southbound trucks were black with mud. We didn't dare stop to look for berries, though we saw lots of likely spots. It was like driving on sheer ice. After 80 tough kilometres we climbed up onto drier ground and the sun came out; we were close to a spot where Hector had picked cloudberries years before. He spied a familiar dip in the tundra at the base of a long curving hill, and we scrambled out to investigate. Same story: unripe berries, and not very many, among a sea of green leaves.

We drove through Eagle Plains, saw stranded leather-clad motorcyclists sitting in the lobby at the Eagle Plains Hotel, looking remarkably cheerful, and carried on to the Arctic Circle. Here we got out and stretched and gazed across the valley at the Richardson Mountains, blue and peaceful, and the beginning of a whole other adventure we weren't going to have, this time. We agreed: it was time to cut our losses and head back to Dawson. All along the road between Eagle Plains and the Arctic Circle we had stopped and found a few unripe cloudberries and tons of plants. We needed time, not just for the berries to ripen, but to camp and explore. We needed the time to stumble across the berries.

Here's the thing: when you're out looking for a new berry or plant, you have to re-learn the techniques you already have. When we pick cranberries near home, we know where we're likely to find them, but we also know that the first spot won't be the best, that we need to put in the time, and we have to observe, remember and compare, the three essential ingredients for knowledge acquisition, as Alexander Graham Bell wrote in the inaugural issue of *Reader's Digest*. On our Dempster trip, we didn't have time to put in the time, and hadn't accumulated enough observation to remember habitats and growing conditions and compare them to others we'd observed and remembered.

But in Dawson, we got lucky. We met John Lenart, proprietor of the Klondike Valley Nursery & Market Garden on the Klondike River, and we told him our cloudberry saga. He said, "Really? You're looking for cloudberries? I've got cloudberries on my property, and they're ripe right now!" He laughed. So did we.

Next day John ferried Hector and me and two visiting journalists in his canoe, in stages, across the river to his property. We toured his collection of greenhouses and gardens as he illuminated dark corners of horticulture such as grafting and root stock and overwintering. Finally he led us to the bog where the berries were, and shared a nugget of information we could add to our file of cloudberry observations: in this micro-climate on the river, the late, cold spring had delayed the growth of the plants enough that by the time they bloomed all danger of frost had passed. And so they thrived.

The five of us picked berries together until we collectively had about one litre. The others insisted we take all the berries. More generosity! So this jam is for John and for Lindsay Anderson and Dana VanVeller, the Edible Road Trip trippers.

Cloudberry Jam

Ripe cloudberries have significant amounts of ascorbic acid and benzoic acid, a natural preservative. This recipe makes an almost candy-like jam that is pure cloudberry; no added lemon juice necessary. Some say the flavour of cloudberries is similar to baked apples, others find it almost meaty, still others say it's a combination of apricots and honey. I tend to agree with the last group.

4 cups (1 L) cloudberries

2 cups (475 mL) sugar

1. Pick through berries, wash them and gently shake dry in a sieve. Transfer to a saucepan; gently stir in sugar and leave to sit in a cool place for 2 to 3 hours.

2. Bring berries and sugar to a simmer over medium-low heat and cook until thick, about 20 minutes. The juice and sugar will develop into a clear, golden syrup and the berries will take on a translucent look.

3. Pour into sterilized jars and process in a boiling water bath, adding 2 minutes per 1,000 feet (305 m) above sea level.

Makes three to four 1-cup (250-mL) jars.

Cloudberry Salsa

Think of the almost pungent taste of dried mango; this salsa lives in that neighbourhood, brightened up by lime and jalapeno. Cilantro would seem to be a no-brainer here, but I left it out because it tends to dominate the other flavours.

1 cup (250 mL) fresh or frozen and thawed cloudberries, roughly chopped

½ cup (125 mL) chopped white or purple onion

½ medium jalapeno pepper, chopped

Juice of ½ lime

1. Two hours before you're ready to serve, combine all ingredients in a small bowl and chill.

Makes about 1½ cups (350 mL).

Soapberry Jelly

When I first moved to the Yukon I found soapberries (*Shepherdia canadensis*) impossibly bitter. I tried the traditional First Nations treat of soapberries whipped into a solid foam and sweetened with sugar, and I just didn't get it. But over time my palate changed, and now I enjoy the taste of the berries right off the bush, and even look for that hit of bitterness at the end.

Around where I live, the soapberries usually come into season in mid-July and are pretty much done by the end of August. But the summer of 2013 was so hot that the berries grew as fat as small grapes and were extra sweet. The hot summer turned into a warm fall, and the berries were still on the branches after the leaves had fallen off, which made for easy picking.

This jelly is almost a jam; you press some but not all the berries through a sieve. Though soapberries are high in both pectin and acid, I used some Pomona's Universal Pectin in this recipe because I didn't want to add a whole lot of sugar or cook the jelly down too much and reduce the yield; we had only picked 6 cups (1.4 L). The jelly retains a slightly bitter aftertaste and goes best with wild meats and creamy cheeses.

Caution: Soapberries are best eaten in moderation. Those same saponins that cause soapberries to foam up when they're whipped can irritate the digestive system when eaten in large quantities, sometimes causing acute distress.

6 cups (1.4 L) soapberries

1 cup (250 mL) sugar

2 tsp (10 mL) Pomona's Universal Pectin powder

2 tsp (10 mL) calcium water, prepared according to package directions

2 Tbsp (30 mL) lemon juice

1. In a 13-cup (3 L) saucepan crush about 2 cups (475 mL) of soapberries to release their juices, add remaining berries and bring to the boil over medium-low heat. Simmer for 15 to 20 minutes, stirring occasionally to bring down the foam.

2. Press 2 cups (475 mL) of berries through a sieve to make a purée, extracting as much pulp as possible. Add the purée back to the pot of berries.

3. Mix pectin powder with the sugar and set aside. Add the calcium water and lemon juice to the berries and bring to the boil over medium heat. Add the sugar-pectin mixture, boil for two minutes and remove from heat.

4. Pour into sterilized jars and process in a boiling water bath, adding 2 minutes per 1,000 feet (305 m) above sea level.

Makes three to four 1-cup (250-mL) jars.

Simple Redcurrant Jelly

Wild redcurrants (*Ribes triste*) grow throughout the Yukon; I've found them along the 9th Avenue Trail in Dawson and in Kluane National Park near Haines Junction (though I didn't pick them there; picking is strictly forbidden in a national park). The City of Whitehorse has taken to planting cultivars in public places throughout the city (so great!) and they're appearing more and more in downtown backyards. We came across bushes thick with white, red and blackcurrants in Jämtland and Norrbotten in Sweden, and wished we could have brought some home with us.

4 cups (1 L) redcurrants

3–4 cups (710 mL–1 L) water, or enough to cover

2 Tbsp (30 mL) lemon juice

1 cup (250 mL) sugar

1. Crush about 2 cups (475 mL) of redcurrants in the bottom of a saucepan to release the juices, add rest of currants and just enough water to barely cover. Bring to the boil, reduce heat and simmer until the currants are pale, from 20 to 30 minutes.

2. Strain into a bowl through a jelly bag or a strainer lined with cheesecloth.

3. Measure juice; there should be about 3 cups (710 mL). Return juice to the pot and bring to the boil, skim, and add sugar and lemon juice.

4. Cook over medium-high heat, stirring frequently, until jelly reaches the gelling point. Start testing after about 15 minutes (see page 204 for testing methods).

5. Pour into sterilized jars and process in a boiling water bath, adding 2 minutes per 1,000 feet (305 m) above sea level.

Makes about three 1-cup (250-mL) jars.

Simple Wild Raspberry Jam

Wild raspberries can appear anytime from mid-July to early August in the back lanes and alleys in downtown Whitehorse and I've picked them as late as early September on the South Canol Road. Wild raspberries tend to be more crumbly than the backyard version; the drupelets can come apart in your fingers as you pick. Raspberry jam is the perfect solution.

4 cups (1 L) raspberries, picked over and rinsed

1 Tbsp (15 mL) lemon rind

1 Tbsp (15 mL) lemon juice

2–3 cups (475–710 mL) sugar

1. Crush the bottom layer of raspberries in a medium saucepan. Add the rest of the berries, the lemon rind and juice and 2 cups (475 mL) of sugar. Bring to the boil over medium-high heat, stirring frequently, and taste for sweetness. Add more sugar if necessary.

2. Turn heat to medium and cook until the gelling point is reached—start testing after 15 minutes. Remember to stir often to keep the bottom layer from scorching.

3. Pour into sterilized jars and process in a boiling water bath, adding 2 minutes per 1,000 feet (305 m) above sea level.

Makes three to four 1-cup (250-mL) jars.

Lowbush cranberries in gorgeous profusion.

Redcurrant and Port Jelly

This classic is a great accompaniment to strong cheese, makes an excellent glaze for duck or grouse breasts and contributes a tart-sweet note to reduced sauces for wild meats such as moose or caribou.

4 cups (1 L) redcurrants

3–4 cups (710 mL–1 L) water, or enough to cover

2 Tbsp (30 mL) lemon juice

1 cup (250 mL) sugar

2 Tbsp (30 mL) port

1. Crush a layer of redcurrants in the bottom of a saucepan; add remaining currants and water to barely cover. Bring to the boil, reduce heat and simmer until the currants are pale, from 20 to 30 minutes.

2. Strain into a bowl through a jelly bag or a strainer lined with cheesecloth.

3. Measure juice; there should be about 3 cups (710 mL). Return currant juice to the pot, bring to the boil, and add sugar and lemon juice.

4. Cook over medium heat, stirring frequently until jelly reaches the gelling point. Start testing after about 15 minutes (see page 204 for testing methods).

5. Remove from heat and stir in the port.

6. Pour into sterilized jars and process in a boiling water bath, adding 2 minutes per 1,000 feet (305 m) above sea level.

Makes three to four 1-cup (250-mL) jars.

Lowbush Cranberries

The Swedish lingonberry (*Vaccinium vitis-idaea*) is the same species as our lowbush cranberry, but unlike in the Yukon, the Swedish berries grow in great abundance thanks to the warming effect of the Gulf Stream. You can buy lingonberries in Swedish supermarkets, which caused us much amazement when we first arrived. In Sweden there is this wonderful custom called *allemansrätten*; any person has the legal right to roam in any wood, meadow or field to pick berries, mushrooms, flowers or herbs, except vulnerable or endangered species. There are basic rules, such as not harming animals or property, not picking close to houses, and not picking from cultivated areas. The Swedish are proud of this right and were eager to tell us about it.

Hector and I picked lingonberries and blueberries every time we waited for a bus; if we were in a rental car we stopped en route to our destination and walked into the woods straight off the highway, picked a litre or so, then hopped back into the car and drove on. We felt very much at home, and were appreciative of this ability to participate in the Swedish landscape.

Last year's highbush cranberries glow like beacons in the early spring forest.

Lowbush Cranberry and Rosehip Jam

In this jam the rosehips almost take on the flavour of strawberries.

2 cups (475 mL) rosehips

2 cups (475 mL) water

4 cups (1 L) wild lowbush cranberries (lingonberries) or substitute cultivated cranberries

1½ cups (350 mL) sugar

Juice and zest of 1 Meyer lemon

1. In a medium saucepan bring rosehips and water to the boil at high heat, reduce to medium-low and simmer for 20 minutes. Press through a sieve into a bowl and measure the juice; it should be about 1½ cups (350 mL).

2. Pour the juice into a clean saucepan, add cranberries, sugar and lemon juice and zest and cook over medium heat, stirring frequently, until the mixture reaches the gelling stage, from 10 to 15 minutes.

3. Pour into sterilized jars and process in a boiling water bath, adding 2 minutes per 1,000 feet (305 m) above sea level.

Makes four to five 1-cup (250-mL) jars.

HIGHBUSH-LOWBUSH JAM

To make this variation of **Lowbush Cranberry and Rosehip Jam**, substitute an equal quantity of **highbush cranberries** for the rosehips.

Quick Lowbush Cranberry Condiment

Our friend Anna Sanders, one of my sister-in-law Tina's sisters, taught us this method in the kitchen of her small, pretty house near Åre.

1 cup (250 mL) wild lowbush cranberries (lingonberries), fresh or frozen (substitute cultivated cranberries)

2 Tbsp (30 mL) sugar, or more to taste

1. In a blender or food processor, or with a hand-held immersion blender, grind cranberries and sugar together until they have the rough texture of horseradish. Taste and add additional sugar if desired.

2. Serve at room temperature as an accompaniment to cheese or wild meat. We had ours with smoked reindeer heart.

Makes just over 1 cup (250 mL).

Rosehip Syrup

Green rosehips of the prickly wild rose (*Rosa acicularis*) start to appear around the middle of July, and by mid-August are full-sized and turning a rosy red. The jury's out on whether or not to wait for the first frost before picking rosehips. I've picked both before and after a frost, and haven't noticed a difference in taste, just in texture. The later rosehips are softer and mushier. Some people clean the hairy seeds from the hips with the tip of a small spoon; this is important if you want to use whole rosehips, because the seeds can irritate the digestive tract. I haven't yet found the patience to do this, and tend to enjoy rosehips best in jellies, jams, soups and in this simple syrup. In Sweden you can buy packets of dried rosehip soup, a popular breakfast food. I've become a fan of a hot rosehip drink made with a couple of spoonfuls of rosehip syrup and a cup of boiling water. It's great on a chilly winter afternoon.

4 cups (1 L) fresh or frozen and thawed rosehips, flower ends removed

6 cups (1.4 L) water, divided

1–2 cups (250 –475 mL) sugar

2 Tbsp (30 mL) lemon juice

1. Bring rosehips and 4 cups (1L) water to the boil in a medium saucepan, reduce heat to medium-low and simmer, covered, until rosehips have disintegrated and mixture is thick.

2. Press juice through a sieve into a medium bowl, reserving skins and seeds. Return skins and seeds to the saucepan, add remaining 2 cups (475 mL) of water, bring to the boil, reduce heat and simmer for 15 minutes. Press mixture through a sieve into the bowl containing the rosehip juice.

3. Transfer the mixture to a clean saucepan, bring to the boil over medium-high heat, stirring often, and add 1 cup (250 mL) sugar and the lemon juice. Stir until sugar is dissolved. Reduce heat to medium-low and simmer, stirring often. Taste after 5 minutes and add more sugar until you're satisfied with the level of sweetness.

4. Cook for another 10 minutes. Syrup should be fairly thick but still fall in a single drop from the spoon. Pour into sterilized jars and process in a boiling water bath, adding 2 minutes per 1,000 feet (305 m) above sea level.

Makes about four 1-cup (250-mL) jars.

Spiced Crabapple Jelly

1 Tbsp (15 mL) spruce tips

1 Tbsp (15 mL) juniper berries

4 cups (1 L) crabapple juice

1½ cups (350 mL) sugar

1. Tie spruce tips and juniper berries in a piece of clean cheesecloth to make a spice bag.
2. Bring juice to the boil over high heat; skim if necessary.
3. Add spice bag and sugar, reduce heat and cook to the gelling stage. Start testing after 15 minutes (see page 204 for testing methods).
4. Remove spice bag, pour into sterilized jars and process in a hot water bath for 10 minutes, adding 2 minutes per 1,000 feet (305 m) above sea level.

Makes two to three 1-cup (250-mL) jars.

CRABAPPLE SYRUP

To make a syrup with the flavours of **Straight-Ahead Crabapple** Jelly, stop the cooking when the mixture falls from a spoon held over the pot in a slow, steady drip. Can and process as for jelly.

Crabapple Chili Sauce

1 Tbsp (15 mL) butter

1 each red, orange and yellow peppers, finely chopped

1 serrano pepper, seeded and chopped

1½ cups (350 mL) apple cider vinegar

5 cups (1.2 L) crabapple juice

1½ cups (350 mL) sugar

1 Tbsp (15 mL) crushed red pepper

1 tsp (5 mL) coarse sea salt

1. Melt butter in a cast iron frying pan over medium heat. Sauté peppers, including serrano (don't touch your lips or eyes!) until soft but not browned, about 10 minutes. Set aside.
2. In a wide saucepan over medium-high heat, reduce the apple cider vinegar to 1 cup (250 mL). Add crabapple juice and bring to the boil. Add sugar, boil for 2 minutes, and add sautéed peppers, crushed red pepper and salt.
3. Cook over medium-high heat, stirring frequently, until the mixture is thick and syrupy, but not gelled, anywhere from 15 to 25 minutes.
4. Pour into sterilized jars and process in a hot water bath for 10 minutes, adding 2 minutes per 1,000 feet (305 m) above sea level.

Makes about four 1-cup (250-mL) jars.

Straight-Ahead Crabapple Jelly

5 lbs (2.3 kg) crabapples, stems removed

5 cups (1.2 L) water, or enough to cover

2–3 cups (475–710 mL) sugar

2 Tbsp (30 mL) lemon juice

1. Place crabapples in a large, heavy-bottomed pot and add just enough water to cover. Bring to a boil, reduce heat to medium and simmer for 15 to 20 minutes.
2. Strain through a jelly bag, or a layer of cheesecloth placed in a strainer and suspended over a bowl. Let drip for 2 hours.
3. Measure the juice—there should be about 5 cups (1.2 L).
4. Transfer juice to clean pot, add 2 cups (475 mL) sugar and lemon juice and bring to the boil over medium-high heat, stirring regularly. Taste and continue to add sugar until sweet enough for your taste.
5. Continue to boil until the gelling stage; start testing after 15 minutes (see page 204 for testing methods).
6. Pour into sterilized jars and process in a hot water bath for 10 minutes, adding 2 minutes per 1,000 feet (305 m) above sea level.

Makes three to four 1-cup (250-mL) jars.

Glassing for moose on a fall hunt.

Liqueurs and Aquavits

Making homemade liqueurs and aquavits is an area of life-long learning. I've only been at it for a couple of years, inspired by Stan Suchan of Seattle, Washington, a gourmand and keen home cook who gave me a tour of his basement shelves where jar upon jar of experimental concoctions stood in pretty rows. Since then, and since subsequent travels in Scandinavia, I've become a passionate amateur. Please treat these ideas as starting points, and if you get hooked, explore the excellent resources out there for making your own creations. See the Selected Biography (page 242) for more information.

Crabapple Aquavit

Crabapples make a beautiful, pink aquavit that over time changes to light amber in colour. Of all the homemade aquavits I've tried so far this one is the mildest and sweetest.

3 cups (710 mL) crabapples, washed, stemmed and quartered	3 cups (710 mL) good quality, 40 percent alcohol vodka

1. Place prepared apples in a sterile 4-cup (1-L) glass jar with a screw-top lid. Pour vodka over top. Shake to distribute.

2. Store in a cool, dark place for 3 to 6 weeks, turning every few days. Strain through a sieve and then through a coffee filter. Transfer to a new, sterile jar and store for 3 months.

Makes 3 cups (710 mL).

Artemisia Tilesii or Labrador Tea Infused Vodka

These two aquavits are quite bitter on their own, so I tend to use them as flavourings in place of vanilla. Try a teaspoon of Labrador tea vodka in the Smoked Labrador Tea Shortbreads on page 168, for example. Experiment with combining these aquavits with small amounts of Spruce Tip Syrup (page 209) or Rosehip Syrup (page 220). For a great primer on how to build your own bitters recipes by combining different herb-infused alcohols, *see* Magnus Nilsson's book, *Fäviken*.

¼ cup (60 mL) dried Labrador tea leaves or *Artemisia tilesii* leaves

2 cups (475 mL) good quality, 40 percent alcohol vodka

1. Place dried herbs and vodka in a sterile, 2-cup (475-mL) glass jar with a screw-top lid. Store in a cool, dark place for 3 weeks, shaking daily. Strain through a sieve and then through a coffee filter.

2. Transfer to a sterilized 2-cup (475-mL) glass jar and store for 3 months before using.

Makes about 2 cups (475 mL).

Rowanberry Aquavit

Rowanberries, or mountain ash berries, reside on the bitter end of the spectrum, especially in their aftertaste, but the upfront flavour is warm and spicy, reminiscent of apple, cloves and cinnamon. Others don't share my love of their flavour, but I offer this recipe here for fans of bitters as an after-dinner digestif. Pick rowanberries after the first frost and store them in the freezer for two to three weeks to reduce bitterness.

1 cup (250 mL) rowanberries, picked over, washed and dried

3 cups (710 mL) good brandy or cognac

1. Combine berries and liquor in a dry, sterilized, 4-cup (1-L) glass jar with a screw-top lid. Store in a cool, dark place for 3 weeks. Shake the jar gently once every few days.

2. Strain through a fine-mesh sieve and then a coffee filter. Transfer to a dry, sterilized glass jar and store in the cupboard for 2 to 3 months before sampling. If the flavour is truly too bitter for you, the Rowanberry and Rhubarb Liqueur recipe (page 224) describes how to change the aquavit into a liqueur.

Makes 3 cups (710 mL).

A note on equipment: I've purchased a Finnish stovetop steam juicer called the Mehu Liisa, and have found it the greatest boon in the kitchen for making fruit or berry juice destined for jams and jellies or simply for storing in the fridge for a hit of fresh, northern nutrition. The Mehu Liisa eliminates the step of straining the fruit to collect the juice, and produces a clear liquid after about an hour of steaming. For information on where to purchase, see the Products section, page 243.

RHUBARB JUICE

This recipe assumes you don't have a Mehu Liisa but are making juice in the usual way.

4 cups (1 L) chopped fresh or frozen rhubarb

2 cups (475 mL) water

1. Combine rhubarb and water in a medium saucepan. Bring to the boil over medium-high heat, reduce to medium-low and simmer until the rhubarb is soft, about 10 minutes.

2. Strain through a sieve lined with dampened cheesecloth or spoon into a jelly bag. Suspend over a bowl until the mixture stops dripping, about 2 hours. Reserve the rhubarb for muffins or a topping for porridge. Transfer the juice to a sterilized jar with a screw-top lid. Store in the refrigerator and consume within a week.

Makes about 2 cups (475 mL).

Rowanberry and Rhubarb Liqueur

Combining Rowanberry Aquavit (page 223) with Rhubarb Syrup produces a slightly astringent, bittersweet liqueur with a complex flavour.

1 cup (250 mL) Rowanberry Aquavit, recipe on page 223

¼–½ cup (60–125 mL) Rhubarb Syrup

1. This is more a roadmap than a recipe. Start by combining Rowanberry Aquavit with ¼ cup (60 mL) of Rhubarb Syrup. Mix and taste.

2. If it's to your liking, stop here; if not, continue adding Rhubarb Syrup until the mixture has reached the right balance of bitter and sweet. Store for 3 months to allow flavours to combine and mellow.

Makes about 1½ cups (350 mL).

RHUBARB SYRUP

1½ cups (350 mL) rhubarb juice

1 cup (250 mL) sugar

1. Combine juice and sugar in a small saucepan. Bring to a boil over high heat, stirring to dissolve sugar. Reduce heat to medium and cook for 2 minutes, skimming off the foam.

2. Remove from heat and cool to room temperature. Store in a sterilized glass jar in the refrigerator. Will keep for 2 to 3 weeks.

Makes about 1½ cups (350 mL).

Highbush Cranberry Vinegar

The wild, pungent flavour of highbush cranberries combines well with apple cider vinegar, and birch syrup softens the sour edges. This is a great vinegar for winter coleslaws or salads of raw kohlrabi, Belgian endive, daikon and other clean-tasting, crisp vegetables. For a warming winter drink stir 2 tablespoons (30 mL) of highbush cranberry vinegar into a cup of boiling water.

3 cups (710 mL) fresh or frozen highbush cranberries (or substitute organic commercial cranberries)

2 cups (475 mL) apple cider vinegar

2 Tbsp (30 mL) sugar

2 Tbsp (30 mL) birch syrup (or substitute maple syrup)

1. Combine ingredients in a medium saucepan. Bring to the boil over high heat, cover, reduce heat to low and simmer for 5 minutes.

2. Remove from heat and let sit, covered, for 30 minutes. Pour into a sieve lined with dampened cheesecloth or spoon into a dampened jelly bag. Suspend over a bowl and let drip without squeezing or pressing the fruit.

3. Once the dripping has stopped return the vinegar to a clean pot and bring to the boil.

4. Pour into sterilized jars and process in a boiling water bath for 10 minutes, adding 2 minutes for every 1,000 feet (305 m) above sea level.

Makes three 1-cup (250-mL) jars.

Blueberry Vinegar

Cooking the blueberries, especially wild blueberries, releases their flavour. I've found this method results in a much more flavourful vinegar than a simple infusion.

3 cups (710 mL) fresh or frozen wild blueberries

1 Tbsp (15 mL) dried Labrador tea leaves (or substitute dried rosemary)

2 cups (475 mL) red wine vinegar

2 Tbsp (30 mL) brown sugar

2 Tbsp (30 mL) birch syrup

1. Combine ingredients in a medium saucepan. Bring to the boil over high heat, cover, reduce heat to low and simmer for 5 minutes.

2. Remove from heat and let sit, covered, for 30 minutes. Pour into a sieve lined with dampened cheesecloth or a dampened jelly bag. Suspend over a bowl and let drip without squeezing or pressing the fruit.

3. Once the dripping has stopped, return the vinegar to a clean pot and bring to the boil.

4. Pour into sterilized jars and process in a boiling water bath for 10 minutes, adding 2 minutes for every 1,000 feet (305 m) above sea level.

Makes three 1-cup (250-mL) jars.

Flocks of Bohemian waxwings move through Whitehorse in early winter, a welcome visitation.
They load up on mountain ash berries to fuel the long ride south.

Pickled Spruce Tips

Pickled Spruce Tips are a great accompaniment to smoked salmon or Lake Trout Gravlax
page 46, playing the same role as capers, but with a distinctive evergreen flavour. Try substituting Pickled Spruce Tips for capers in salsa verde, or remoulade sauce, or tuck them into a corned beef sandwich.

¾ cup (180 mL) fresh or frozen and thawed spruce tips, brown husks removed

½ cup (125 mL) rice vinegar

½ cup (125 mL) water

1½ tsp (7.5 mL) coarse sea salt

1 tsp (5 mL) sugar

1. Place spruce tips in a sterilized 1-cup (250-mL) glass jar with a screw-top lid. Combine remaining ingredients in a small saucepan, stir to dissolve salt and sugar, and bring to a rolling boil.

2. Remove from heat and pour over spruce tips. Allow to cool to room temperature, screw lid shut and refrigerate. Allow spruce tips to season for 3 or 4 days before sampling. Store in refrigerator and use within a month.

Makes one 1-cup (250-mL) jar.

Mustards

There are several ways to make mustard (here we explore three) and one important rule of thumb: homemade mustard takes at least 24 hours to lose its bitterness, and this is especially true when the mustard seeds haven't been soaked in advance for two days. It can be difficult to assess the flavour as you're working. You almost have to train yourself to taste the seasoning underneath the bitterness. However, you can always adjust the salt or sugar after the fact. If you don't want to go the distance with the full amount of salt, refrigerate the mustard, taste two or three days later, adjust seasonings, then bring to the boil again before canning.

Dijon-Style Grainy Mustard with Labrador Tea

Here the mustard seeds are soaked for 48 hours in a combination of wine and wine vinegar, for a simple Dijon-style mustard that provides a good base for experimenting with flavours of your own choosing. In this version the Labrador tea isn't discernible on its own but intensifies the heat and astringency of the mustard. One taster thought this mustard would be great with strongly flavoured meat such as braised game. Another was instantly reminded of the healing qualities of Labrador tea, saying, "I can see wanting this mustard if I had a cold." If you don't have Labrador tea on hand, try dried wild sage or rosemary, adding 1 teaspoon (5 mL) at a time until you reach the level of herb intensity you enjoy.

3 Tbsp (45 mL) yellow mustard seeds

3 Tbsp (45mL) black mustard seeds

⅓ cup (80 mL) white wine vinegar

⅓ cup (80 mL) dry white wine

½ tsp (2.5 mL) coarse sea salt

2 Tbsp (30 mL) birch syrup

1 Tbsp (15 mL) Labrador tea leaves

1. Combine mustard seeds, vinegar and wine in a small bowl. Cover and let sit for 48 hours at room temperature.

2. Grind soaked mustard seeds in the bowl of a food processor until thick but still grainy, from 3 to 5 minutes. Add salt and birch syrup and pulse to combine.

3. Chop Labrador tea leaves with a sharp knife—you really do have to do this part by hand. Add to the mustard mixture and pulse again to thoroughly combine. Pour into a dry, sterilized screw-top jar and refrigerate. Use within two months.

Makes one 1-cup (250-mL) jar.

Rhubarb Mustard

¾ cup (180 mL) yellow mustard seeds

½ cup (125 mL) black or brown mustard seeds

1 tsp (5 mL) fenugreek seeds

3 cups (710 mL) fresh or frozen rhubarb, diced

½ cup (125 mL) brown sugar

½ cup (125 mL) birch syrup

1¾ cups (415 mL) apple cider vinegar

2 tsp (10 mL) coarse sea salt

1. Grind mustard seeds in a food processor; this could take from 5 to 7 minutes for a coarse grind. As the bottom layer turns to powder it tends to cake and cling to the bowl; stop the machine and scrape this up with a spoon periodically.

2. Combine ground mustard seeds with remaining ingredients in a medium saucepan. Stirring frequently, bring to the boil over high heat. Reduce the heat to medium-low and simmer for 30 minutes, stirring often, until the rhubarb is thoroughly broken down. (Some rhubarb stalks will break down more quickly than others.)

3. Purée with an immersion blender, if you'd like a smoother texture, or leave the chunks.

4. Pour into sterilized jars and process in a boiling water bath for 10 minutes, adding 2 minutes for every 1,000 feet (305 m) above sea level.

Makes 4½ cups (1.1 L).

Finnish Black Bread (page 235), whey cheese and homemade mustard make a great, Nordic midday snack.

Cranberry Mustard

In this recipe cranberries and birch syrup are cooked and then added to the soaked, ground mustard seeds. Cooking mellows the tartness of the berries and brings out their deeper, richer flavour. The quantities here are intended for one household's use. If you want to make the leap and give this mustard as a gift, simply double or triple the ingredients and boil for 1 minute before transferring to sterilized jars and processing in a boiling water bath.

3 Tbsp (45 mL) yellow mustard seeds

3 Tbsp (45mL) black mustard seeds

⅓ cup (80 mL) white wine vinegar

⅓ cup (80 mL) dry white wine

½ cup (125 mL) wild lowbush cranberries (lingonberries) or substitute cultivated cranberries

2½ Tbsp (37.5 mL) birch syrup, divided

1 tsp (5 mL) coarse sea salt

1. Combine mustard seeds, vinegar and wine in a small bowl. Cover and let sit for 48 hours at room temperature.

2. Combine cranberries and 2 tablespoons (30 mL) birch syrup in a small saucepan. Bring to the boil over medium-high heat, reduce heat slightly and cook until the cranberries have burst and the mixture resembles a thick jam, about 5 minutes. Let cool to room temperature.

3. Grind soaked mustard seeds in the bowl of a food processor until thick but still grainy. Add cooled cranberry mixture, the remaining ½ tablespoon (7.5 mL) birch syrup, and salt. Pulse until combined. Transfer to a sterilized glass jar and refrigerate. Consume within 2 months.

    Alternatively, mix ground seeds with cranberry mixture, syrup and salt in the saucepan; bring to the boil, can, seal and process in a boiling water bath for 10 minutes, adding 2 minutes for every 1,000 feet (305 m) above sea level.

Makes about one 1-cup (250-mL) jar or two ½-cup (125-mL) jars.

Infused Oils

The important thing to be aware of when infusing oils is the danger of botulism. The bacterium *Clostridium botulinum*, commonly present in soil and dust, can multiply under moist, anaerobic, low-acid conditions, producing a deadly toxin as a by-product. Any water clinging to the material you are putting into oil provides an ideal breeding ground. It's important to store oil infused with fresh herbs in the refrigerator and consume it within a week. Dried herbs pose less of a safety risk, since the moisture has evaporated, but it's still important to err on the side of caution. I'm far too nervous to make infused mushroom oil with anything but dried mushrooms.

Refrigerate your infused oil made with fresh spruce tips and use it within 10 days. Or use dried spruce tips for a longer shelf life.

Shaggy Mane Oil

I've experimented with infusing oil with both dried morel mushrooms and dried shaggy manes, and found that shaggy manes work best. Shaggy manes have an intense flavour when dried that is rivalled only by dried porcini; try dried porcini if you don't have shaggy manes. If you aren't satisfied that the mushrooms you want to use are completely dry, spread them on a parchment-lined baking sheet and place them in a 200F (95C) oven until they are dry enough to snap when you bend them.

Substitute shaggy mane oil in any recipe that calls for truffle oil; drizzle the oil on thin-crusted mushroom pizza when it comes out of the oven, for example, or toss with oven-roasted French fries. Like Spruce Tip Oil, Shaggy Mane Oil loses its oomph when heated and is best used as a finishing touch.

1 oz (30 gr) dried shaggy mane mushrooms
2 cups (475 mL) olive oil

1. Combine mushrooms and oil in a dry, sterilized 2-cup (475-mL) jar with a screw-top lid. Store in a cool, dark place for 3 days. Strain through a fine-meshed sieve, then through a coffee filter that has been pre-moistened with canola oil. Decant into a sterile 2-cup (475-mL) jar.

2. Store in the refrigerator and use within 1 month.

Makes about 2 cups (475 mL).

Spruce Tip Oil with Fresh Spruce Tips

Spruce Tip Oil is best used as a condiment rather than in cooking, in simple preparations that allow the bright, forest flavours to express themselves fully without dominating the dish. Experiment with uncomplicated recipes first, and as you grow more accustomed to the oil, try out new flavours. The oil pairs well with Mediterranean herbs such as cilantro, sage and oregano, and is a natural with lemon and juniper berries. My brother likes to spread Spruce Tip Oil on crostini and layer smoked salmon on top. Spruce Tip Oil is a great dipping oil for crusty country bread and excellent in salad dressings and mayonnaise. Have fun!

1 cup (250 mL) fresh spruce tips, husks removed

1 cup (250 mL) extra-virgin olive oil

1 cup (250 mL) canola or sunflower oil

1. Wash spruce tips and pat them dry with a tea towel. Spread out on a baking sheet lined with parchment paper and air-dry them for 24 hours away from direct sunlight. Since you're going to refrigerate the oil, the spruce tips don't have to be desiccated, just dry to the touch.

2. Combine spruce tips and oils in a medium saucepan and heat gently to 180F (82C); this will take about 8 minutes over low heat. Remove from heat. Strain oil through a fine-meshed sieve and then through a coffee filter that has been soaked in canola oil. Pour strained oil into a dry, sterilized 2-cup (500-mL) screw-top jar. Use within a week to 10 days.

Makes about 2 cups (475 mL) oil.

Try dipping Spruce Tip Focaccia in Spruce Tip Oil and highbush cranberry vinegar.

Spruce Tip Oil with Dried Spruce Tips

The disadvantage of this method is you'll need a greater proportion of spruce tips to oil, but the advantage is a longer shelf life. It's best to dry spruce tips when they're fresh; once frozen and dried they lose both colour and flavour.

3 cups (710 mL) fresh spruce tips

1½ cups (350 mL) extra-virgin olive oil

1½ cups (350 mL) canola or sunflower oil

1. To dry spruce tips, remove their brown husks, wash them, pat dry with a tea towel and spread in a single layer on parchment-lined baking sheets. Dry away from direct sunlight in an area where there's plenty of circulation. It can take from 3 to 4 days for spruce tips to dry completely.

2. Combine dry spruce tips and oils in a dry, sterilized 4-cup (1-L) jar. Shake gently. Place in a cool, dark cupboard and allow to infuse for 3 days. Strain through a fine-meshed sieve and then a coffee filter that has been moistened with canola oil. Decant into a dry, sterilized jar. Store in the refrigerator and use within a month.

Makes about 3 cups (710 mL) oil.

Mayonnaise

Homemade mayonnaise is so much better than store-bought, no matter how expensive and high-quality, that once you've sampled the from-your-own-hands version, it's really hard to go back. The barrier to venturing forth for many of us is the fear of adding oil too fast and curdling the mayonnaise, and the fear of salmonella in raw egg yolks.

Regarding the former, I was recently liberated by Chef James Peterson, who, in his book *Sauces*, suggests adding oil to the egg yolk mixture 1 tablespoon (15 mL) at a time. Until that day I had painstakingly drizzled the oil into the mix one drop at a time, got bored in the middle, said to hell with it, added oil with reckless abandon and came a cropper. Now I follow the Peterson method and am crowned with success.

Regarding salmonella: properly handled, a raw or lightly cooked Canada Grade A egg is safe for healthy individuals. However, due to the small risk of contamination, eating raw eggs may not be appropriate for everyone, including very young children, the elderly or pregnant women.

Basic Mayonnaise

Make mayonnaise in small batches you know you'll use quickly; it's best when fresh. And, a food safety note, the older it is the more chance of spoilage. Aim to finish a batch in 4 days.

2 egg yolks at room temperature
¾ cup (180 mL) oil; try half olive oil and half canola oil
1 tsp (5 mL) lemon juice or apple cider vinegar
½–1 tsp (2.5–5 mL) coarse sea salt
1 tsp (5 mL) Dijon mustard

1. Whisk egg yolks by hand or in a food processor until thick and creamy. Add oil, 1 tablespoon (15 mL) at a time, beating continuously. Make sure oil is thoroughly incorporated before the next addition.

2. When all the oil is incorporated, which takes a good 7 to 10 minutes if you're beating by hand, whisk in lemon juice or vinegar. This tends to change the texture and appearance of the mayonnaise from stiff and shiny to smooth and satiny. Whisk in salt and mustard. Transfer to a dry, sterilized jar, store in the refrigerator and use within 4 days.

Makes just under 1 cup (250 mL).

Spruce Tip Mayonnaise

¼ cup (60 mL) **Spruce Tip Oil**, recipes on page 230

¼ cup (60 mL) **extra-virgin olive oil**

¼ cup (60 mL) **canola or sunflower oil**

2 Tbsp (30 mL) **chopped fresh or frozen spruce tips**

2 **egg yolks at room temperature**

1 tsp (5 mL) **lemon juice or apple cider vinegar**

½ tsp (2.5 mL) **coarse sea salt**

½ tsp (2.5 mL) **dried juniper berries, finely ground with a mortar and pestle (optional)**

1. In a small bowl, combine the three oils. If you're using frozen spruce tips, thaw and press dry between layers of paper towel or a tea towel.

2. Whisk egg yolks by hand or in a food processor until thick and creamy. Add oil, 1 tablespoon (15 mL) at a time, beating continuously. Make sure oil is thoroughly incorporated before the next addition.

3. When all the oil is incorporated, which takes a good 7 to 10 minutes if you're beating by hand, whisk in lemon juice or vinegar. This tends to change the texture and appearance of the mayonnaise from stiff and shiny to smooth and satiny. Whisk in spruce tips, salt and juniper berries, if using. Transfer to a dry, sterilized jar and refrigerate for several hours before serving to allow flavours to develop. Store in the refrigerator and use within 4 days.

Makes just under 1 cup (250 mL).

Morel Mushroom Mayonnaise

This mushroom mayonnaise is a great accompaniment for *Gravad of Beef* or *Moose* (page 24), in cold grilled or baked salmon sandwiches or drizzled over fresh green spears of romaine lettuce.

2 oz (60 gr) **dried morel mushrooms**

1 Tbsp (15 mL) **olive oil**

1 clove **garlic, minced**

1 Tbsp (15 mL) **cognac**

¼ cup (60 mL) **Shaggy Mane Oil**, recipe on page 229

¼ cup (60 mL) **extra-virgin olive oil**

¼ cup (60 mL) **canola or sunflower oil**

2 **egg yolks at room temperature**

1 tsp (5 mL) **lemon juice or apple cider vinegar**

½ tsp (2.5 mL) **coarse sea salt**

1. Soak dried morel mushrooms in boiling water to cover until soft, about 15 minutes. Strain through a sieve into a bowl. Squeeze excess water from mushrooms into bowl. Reserve liquid.

2. Chop mushrooms finely. Heat olive oil in a cast iron pan over medium heat until it shimmers. Add morel mushrooms and sauté, stirring often, for 2 to 3 minutes. Add chopped garlic and cook for another 2 minutes. Add reserved mushroom water, leaving the silt behind, turn heat to high and sauté until liquid has evaporated. Add cognac and cook until the sharp aroma has subsided. Remove from heat and cool to room temperature.

3. Combine the three unused oils in a small bowl. Whisk egg yolks by hand or in a food processor until thick and creamy. Add oil, 1 tablespoon (15 mL) at a time, beating continuously. Make sure oil is thoroughly incorporated before the next addition.

4. When all the oil is incorporated, which takes a good 7 to 10 minutes if you're beating by hand, whisk in lemon juice or vinegar. This tends to change the texture and appearance of the mayonnaise from stiff and shiny to smooth and satiny. Whisk in cooked morel mushrooms and salt. Transfer to a dry, sterilized jar and refrigerate for several hours before serving to allow flavours to develop. Store in the refrigerator and use within 4 days.

Makes about 1 cup (250 mL).

Flavoured Butters

Butters

If you intend to spread butter on bread or crackers, remember to bring it to room temperature first.

To make butter pats, wrap the mixture in waxed paper, form a log and refrigerate until thoroughly chilled. Cut chilled butter into ¼-inch (0.6-cm) slices and place on hot steaks, salmon fillets or roasted vegetables just before serving.

To make butter curls, you'll need a butter curler (yes, there is such a thing!) I've tried with a potato peeler but it just doesn't have the same effect. Shape your butter into a rectangle, and allow the chilled butter to warm slightly before you start. Note that butters containing bigger pieces of spice or nuts will not curl as easily.

Birch Butter

¼ cup (60 mL) birch syrup

½ cup (125 mL) salted butter, softened

1. Whisk butter and syrup together until light and fluffy. Store in a covered container in the refrigerator. Will keep for about 2 weeks. Try on Finnish Pancakes (page 11), or spread on toasted Finnish Black Bread (page 235).

Makes about ¾ cup (180 mL).

Lemon-Spruce Tip Butter or Lemon-Caper Butter

¼ cup (60 mL) salted butter, softened

1 tsp (5 mL) Spruce Tip Oil, recipes on page 230

2 Tbsp (30 mL) fresh spruce tips, finely minced (substitute 1 Tbsp/15 mL chopped capers)

2 tsp (10 mL) grated lemon zest

1. Whisk all ingredients together. Store in a covered container in the refrigerator. Will keep for about 1 week.

Makes about ⅓ cup (80 mL).

Juniper Butter

Try this on Edna Helm's Best Bannock (page 71) with smoked salmon. Letting the juniper berries sit uncovered overnight allows the volatile oils to evaporate and the berries lose some of their bitter edge. I learned this trick from Ryan Cumming, a chef and instructor in the culinary program at Yukon College in Whitehorse.

1 Tbsp (15 mL) juniper berries

¾ cup (180 mL) salted butter, softened

½ tsp (2.5 mL) freshly ground black pepper

1. Grind the juniper berries in a mortar and pestle. Transfer to a medium bowl and let sit at room temperature for 8 hours or overnight.

2. Whisk together berries, softened butter and pepper until light and fluffy. Store in a covered container in the refrigerator and for optimum flavour, use within 2 weeks.

Makes ¾ cup (180 mL).

Clarified Butter

Clarified Butter is butter in which both water and milk solids have been removed through a process of slow cooking over low heat. Clarified Butter has a higher smoking point than regular butter so it's great for sautéing at higher temperatures; steak or mushrooms sautéed in clarified butter are wonderful. Clarified Butter is also used in sauces like hollandaise and Béarnaise, where the water in regular, melted butter could cause the sauce to break. Because it's pure butterfat, Clarified Butter will keep longer in the fridge. Finally, the flavour is wonderful; sweet and faintly nutty. When herbs, mushrooms or aromatics like ginger or turmeric root are heated slowly in Clarified Butter, the butter takes on their flavour and is transformed into a beautiful addition to starchy foods like rice, potatoes, parsnips and squash.

Start by clarifying half a pound (225 gr) until you're sure you will use it, but know that you will very probably graduate to preparing a pound (455 gr) at a time.

8 oz (225 gr) unsalted butter cut into 1-inch (2.5-cm) cubes

1. Place the butter in a heavy-bottomed saucepan and set it over medium-low to low heat.

2. Once it has melted the butter will start sputtering—this is the water evaporating. At the same time, the white milk solids will start to rise to the top. This phase should last about 5 minutes.

3. When the sputtering has stopped and the milk solids seem to have stopped rising to the top, remove butter from the heat. Spoon off as much of the milk solids as you can, reserving them in a bowl for use in muffins or pancakes, in mashed potatoes, in soups or in stews.

4. Strain the butter into a bowl through a sieve lined with clean cheesecloth. This will remove the remaining milk solids.

5. Allow the Clarified Butter to cool to room temperature, cover and refrigerate. Will keep for 3 to 6 months in the refrigerator.

Makes about 6 oz (170 gr).

One Bread and Two Crackers

Finnish Black Bread

We ate fabulous black bread in Finland, bought at the herring fair in Helsinki, in the Old Market Hall on the Market Square waterfront, and devoured in our hostel room. This recipe is adapted from Jeffrey Hamelman's *Bread: A Baker's Book of Techniques and Recipes*, and comes very close to that remembered Finnish flavour. The bread takes two and a half days to complete so plan accordingly.

For more information and resources on working with a sourdough starter see the Sources and Suppliers section on page 242.

RYE SOURDOUGH STARTER

To build the rye sourdough starter you will need an all-purpose sourdough starter that has been refreshed with flour and water and is actively bubbling.

1 Tbsp (15 mL) active all-purpose flour sourdough starter

¾ cup (180 mL) whole grain rye flour, divided

¾ cup (180 mL) warm water, divided

1. Combine starter, 2 tablespoons (30 mL) rye flour and 2 tablespoons (30 mL) water in a small bowl, cover and let sit in a warm place for 8 to 12 hours, at which time small pinprick-sized bubbles should have formed on the surface, and the surface will appear bumpy and uneven.

2. Transfer to a larger glass or plastic bowl and add remaining 10 Tbsp (150 mL) rye flour and 10 Tbsp (150 mL) warm water. Mix thoroughly. To measure the growth of the starter, put a piece of clear tape on the outside of the bowl and draw a line even with the top. Write the time beside it. Let sit, covered, for 8 to 12 hours.

3. By this time the starter should have doubled in size and should be filled with large and small bubbles when viewed from the side. Reserve ½ cup (125 mL) and store in the refrigerator. You'll be left with 1 cup (250 mL) active starter, ready to use in any recipe that calls for active starter.

4. To feed your starter in future, remove it from the fridge and measure it. Add whole grain rye flour and warm water to the starter at a ratio of 2 parts flour and 2 parts water to 1 part starter. Stir to combine. The starter will be active and ready to use after 8 to 12 hours. Remember to always reserve a portion and return it to the fridge for future use.

SPONGE

continued on next page

Finnish Black Bread continued

1 Tbsp (15 mL) rye sourdough starter, instructions on page 235 (use either active starter, or straight from the fridge)

½ cup (125 mL) warm water

1¼ cups (300 mL) whole grain rye flour

1. Stir together starter, water and flour in a medium bowl. Cover and let sit for 12 to 14 hours in a warm place.

SOAKED STALE BREAD MIXTURE

¾ cup (180 mL) stale rye or whole wheat bread, about 2 thick slices, toasted and cut into cubes

3 Tbsp (45 mL) espresso powder

1 Tbsp (15 mL) canola oil

¾ cup (180 mL) hot water

1. Combine ingredients in a small bowl and mix thoroughly. Cover and let sit for 12 to 14 hours.

DOUGH

1 cup (250 mL) whole grain rye flour

1¼–1⅓ cup (300–330 mL) all-purpose flour

2 tsp (10 mL) coarse sea salt

1 tsp (5 mL) instant dry yeast

Soaked stale bread mixture

Sponge

1. Stir together all ingredients with a wooden spoon in a large mixing bowl until the dough forms into a rough, sticky lump.

2. Dust the countertop with rye flour, turn the dough out and knead for 7 to 9 minutes, dusting with rye flour as necessary. The finished dough will be firm, dense and slightly tacky to the touch.

3. Place in a clean bowl, cover with plastic wrap and a tea towel and allow to rest for about 45 minutes.

4. Gently shape into a round loaf and transfer to a baking sheet lined with parchment paper. Cover with a tea towel and let rise for 60 to 80 minutes.

5. Fifteen minutes before baking, preheat oven to 450F (230C). Before baking, place a baking pan of boiling water on the bottom shelf.

6. Bake bread for 10 minutes, reduce heat to 400F (205C) and bake for 35 to 40 minutes longer.

7. Cool on a rack, then store in a brown paper bag. This is a great bread to serve with Solstice- or Vodka-Cured Lake Trout Gravlax (page 47) and Beet and Blueberry Borscht (page 186).

Makes one round loaf.

Rice Crackers

I experimented with several rice cracker recipes before finding the one that worked best. The trick is to get the rice crackers as thin as you can and flip them halfway through baking. This is another of those recipes it's good to prepare with a friend or a junior member of the family who will enjoy squashing the small rounds of dough with the bottom of a glass. (I tried rolling the crackers out into two big sheets, but it doesn't work nearly as well.)

2 Tbsp (30 mL) flaxseeds

1 cup (250 mL) plus 2 Tbsp (30 mL) water, divided

½ cup (125 mL) short-grain brown rice

2 Tbsp (30 mL) sesame seeds

½ cup (125 mL) brown rice flour

1 tsp (5 mL) soya sauce

1 tsp (5 mL) coarse sea salt

2 Tbsp (30 mL) canola oil

1. Combine flaxseeds and 2 tablespoons (30 mL) of water in a small bowl and soak overnight.

2. Combine rice and remaining 1 cup (250 mL) water in a small saucepan, bring to the boil over high heat, reduce to low and simmer until rice is cooked but not mushy, about 15 minutes.

3. Combine cooked rice, prepared flax seeds and remaining ingredients in a food processor. Pulse until the dough congeals into a firm mass.

4. Line four or five baking sheets with parchment paper. Pinch small pieces of dough and roll them into balls about the size of marbles. Place dough balls on the prepared baking sheets 2 inches (5 cm) apart.

5. Preheat oven to 375F (190C). Find a flat-bottomed jar, ramekin or glass about 2 inches (5 cm) in diameter. Press down on each dough ball, making a very thin round. You may have to do some twice.

6. Bake for 15 minutes, flipping the crackers halfway through. Transfer to a rack and cool to room temperature.

7. Store in a cookie tin. Crackers will keep for several weeks, but they tend to be eaten by the handful, so they don't last long.

Makes about 90 to 100 crackers.

From top to bottom, left to right: It's important to let the dough rest after shaping into balls. The notched rolling pin makes it easier to get flatbread really flat. In the old days, women used bundles of chicken feathers, quill ends down, and pricked the dough rapidly with both hands. It's a great workout for the biceps. A stack of crispy, thin rye flatbreads. Kerstin Hylén's house near Östersund, with a few of Sweden's hundreds of lakes in the long view. The ski hill and tow in Kerstin and Gustav's back yard.

Rye Flatbread

This recipe comes from Kerstin Hylén, who has a small bakery in Revsund, not far from Östersund in Jämtland, Sweden. Kerstin gave me a baking lesson one afternoon, and we rolled out about 30 of these paper-thin crackers with a special rolling pin covered in pockmarks that I immediately coveted. (I spent the next five weeks scouring second-hand stores for one as we travelled through Sweden, and finally found one in the ICA supermarket in Jokkmokk.) Kerstin's husband, Gustav, used to play with the folk rock band Hoven Droven, and performed at Salmon Arm Roots & Blues Festival in 2009. Kerstin and Gustav had their own tiny ski tow in the backyard, where their girls learned to ski, and we wished we were there in winter to see it in operation.

The idea with these flatbreads is to roll them as thin as you possibly can and cook them at high heat, using a baking stone if you have one. Kerstin used 25 grams (just under 1 ounce) of fresh yeast, but I've adapted this recipe for the more readily available dry yeast.

2 tsp (10 mL) dry yeast

¾ cup plus 1 Tbsp (200 mL) warm water

½ tsp (2.5 mL) salt

1 Tbsp (15 mL) fennel seeds

1¼ cup (300 mL) whole grain rye flour

1¼ cup (300 mL) all-purpose flour

3½ Tbsp (55 mL) canola oil

1. Sprinkle yeast over warm water and let sit until it blooms, about 10 minutes.

2. Combine dry ingredients in a large bowl and make a well in the centre.

3. Pour oil and yeast mixture into the well and whisk to combine without incorporating dry ingredients. With a wooden spoon, stir dry ingredients into wet, beating well until the dough is a rough but cohesive mass.

4. Tip onto a floured countertop. The dough is very wet at this stage and best manipulated with a scraper and floured hands. Knead for 8 to 10 minutes, dusting minimally with flour just to keep from sticking.

5. Transfer to a clean bowl, cover with plastic and refrigerate overnight.

6. Next day, allow the dough to come to room temperature, about 1 hour. Tip onto the counter and knead gently. Cut the dough in half and roll each half into a long cylinder. Cut each cylinder into 15 pieces. Roll each piece into a ball, and let rest for 30 minutes under a clean tea towel.

7. Fifteen minutes before baking, preheat oven to 450F (230C). If you have a bread stone, place it in the cold oven on a rack in the upper third of the oven. Alternatively, use two baking sheets and put them in the hot oven for 5 minutes before you start.

8. Working with 2 to 4 balls at a time (depending on baking method), roll out each one to a diameter of about 6 inches (15 cm), getting the dough as thin as you can. If you're using a baking stone, open the oven door, pull the rack with the baking stone out and transfer 1 or 2 rounds to the stone. Bake for 1 minute, flip each round and bake for another 1 to 2 minutes. Repeat with the remaining rounds.

   If you're using baking sheets, bake 4 rounds at a time. Set the timer for 1 minute; remove from the oven, flip each round and bake for another 1 to 2 minutes.

9. Cool on a wire rack and store in a large cookie tin.

Makes 30 × 6-inch (15-cm) round flatbreads.

Sockeye or Coho Salmon Roe

Wild fish roe is a pure gift, rare and precious. We were lucky enough to be in Sweden when the famous Kalix vendace roe was in season in September and October and enjoyed this exquisite treat from Stockholm to Kalix, where we visited a local processing plant late one night after the boat had come in. It seemed the whole village was there, or about 35 people anyway, dressed in coveralls, kerchiefs and rubber boots, hard at it until the early hours of the morning, processing the roe quickly while it was fresh. At one station men and women separated the males from the females, at another they made small slits in the bellies of the females, and women at long tables the length of the room squeezed the roe out into big plastic containers. Then the roe was whizzed with a giant immersion blender, to break the membrane, rinsed with water and stored in the fridge before being packed into containers destined for high-end food shops.

Vendace (*Coregonus albula*) are small salmonid fish, about the size of sardines, that return to the waters of the Bothnian Bay in the Baltic Sea at spawning time. The roe is mild and almost sweet, and is as different from canned or jarred lumpfish caviar as fresh, wild salmon is from commercially canned. Kalix *Löjrom*, as the roe is known, is famous throughout Scandinavia and often featured on the menu for royal dinners or Nobel Prize banquets. It's that special.

In the summer and fall of 2013 I lucked into a couple of windfalls that were just as special. One of our local fish suppliers brought in wild sockeye salmon roe from Haines, Alaska, and gave me a quick lesson on how to process it. Hector went to the hardware store to find a wire screen with holes just bigger than the eggs. I placed the screen over a bowl in the sink and pressed the skeins of roe against the screen, leaving as much of the connective membrane behind as possible. I then rinsed the roe in fresh water and brined it for 15 minutes in a 10 percent brine solution, drained it and vacuum packed about half of the eggs. We ate the rest over the next few days, on toast, in scrambled eggs, in a cream sauce over pasta and on rice crackers spread with chèvre and topped with chopped green onion.

I thought that was it for wild salmon roe that summer, and felt lucky to have had the experience. Then my neighbour and friend Lyn Fabio called in late September. "I have about 20 pounds of fresh coho roe," she said. "Can you help me?" Our local picture framer's father-in-law had returned from Haines with a huge harvest of fresh coho. The family didn't have time to process the entire yield and offered the heads, bones and eggs to Lyn, who had just arrived with some work to be framed. Lyn couldn't bear to refuse.

She parcelled out the fish heads and eggs to a few friends, and we spent the weekend processing the bounty. I went to her house and found her with a sinkful of salmon heads, cleaning out the blood with her fingers under cold running water. There was a propane burner on the back porch and a huge pot of stock bubbling away. I left with several pounds of fish roe. Phone calls flew back and forth. "How long are you brining the eggs?" "Do you think we can make botargo?" "I'm going to smoke some." "Will you smoke some for me too?" "I've smoked all of it. Now I'm going to dry a portion of the smoked." And so on. Two weeks later we convened at our friend Jen Jones's house for a Thanksgiving dinner of roast mountain goat, roast local lamb, and appetizers of smoked coho roe on tiny blini. It was incredible.

Salmon Roe

1. Press fresh roe through a screen into a bowl of fresh water in the kitchen sink, removing as much membrane as possible. This is a finicky process and there's no way around it. Don't worry too much about small pieces of membrane left among the roe. Rinse cleaned roe in a fine-meshed sieve under running water.

2. Make a 10 percent brine solution by mixing 6⅔ tablespoons (100 mL) of coarse salt per 4 cups (1 L) of cold water, whisking vigorously to dissolve salt. Pour roe into brine and leave for 15 minutes. Drain through a fine-meshed sieve. Store in a covered container in the fridge for up to 2 weeks.

Smoked Salmon Roe

For smoked roe it's best to leave the skeins intact.

1. Rinse whole skeins of salmon roe under cold running water. Make a 10 percent solution brine by mixing 6⅔ tablespoons (100 mL) of coarse salt per 4 cups (1 L) of cold water, whisking vigorously to dissolve salt. Pour roe into brine and leave for 15 minutes. Pat skeins dry with paper towel and arrange on a mesh rack set over a baking sheet to catch the drips. Refrigerate for 8 hours or overnight, uncovered, so that a pellicle (hard, tacky surface) forms.

2. Cold-smoke over alder chips with the vent open for two to three hours. If there's no temperature control on your smoker you have no choice but to hot-smoke, but you can mitigate the heat by placing a bowl of ice on the bottom shelf.

3. Store in the refrigerator for up to 2 weeks. Will keep, vacuum-packed, in the freezer for 6 to 8 months.

Sources and Suppliers

SELECTED BIBLIOGRAPHY

Cookbooks

Aidells, Bruce, and Denis Kelly. *Bruce Aidells' Complete Sausage Book: Recipes from America's Premier Sausage Maker*. Berkeley: Ten Speed Press, 2000.

Berriedale-Johnson, Michelle. *Festive Feasts Cookbook*. London: The British Museum Press, 2003.

Dufresne, Francine. *Cooking Fish and Game, French Canadian Style*. San Francisco: 101 Productions, 1975.

Fireweed Community Market Society. *Celebrate Yukon Food: Keeping the Harvest*. Whitehorse: Fireweed Community Market Society, 2011.

Fireweed Community Market Society. *Celebrate Yukon Food: Seasonal Recipes*. Whitehorse: Fireweed Community Market Society, 2006.

Grigson, Jane. *The Mushroom Feast: A Celebration of all Edible Fungi—Cultivated, Wild, and Dried Varieties—with more than 250 Recipes in which the Mushroom is the Occasion for the Feast*. New York: Alfred A. Knopf, 1975.

Hamelman, Jeffrey. *Bread: A Baker's Book of Techniques and Recipes*. Hoboken: John Wiley & Sons, Inc., 2004.

Hornmalm, Erik, ed. *Arctic Norrbotten A La Carte*. Haparanda, Sweden: A La Carte Böcker, 2008.

Hornmalm, Erik, ed. *Norrbotten A La Carte*. Haparanda, Sweden: A La Carte Böcker, 2005.

Hornmalm, Erik, and Manne Stenros, eds. *Vilt A La Carte*. Haparanda, Sweden: A La Carte Böcker, 2010.

Jonsson, Susanne. *Västerbottensost*. Stockholm: Prisma, 2008.

Katz, Sandor Ellix. *The Art of Fermentation: An In-Depth Exploration of Essential Concepts and Processes from Around the World*. White River Junction, VT: Chelsea Green Publishing, 2012.

McClellan, Marisa. *Food in Jars: Preserving in Small Batches Year-Round*. Philadelphia: Running Press Book Publishers, 2011.

Nilsson, Magnus. *Fäviken*. London, New York: Phaidon Press Limited, 2012.

Ojakangas, Beatrice. *Scandinavian Feasts: Celebrating Traditions throughout the Year*. Minneapolis: University of Minnesota Press, 1992.

Peterson, James. *Sauces: Classical and Contemporary Sauce Making*. Hoboken: John Wiley & Sons, Inc., 2008.

Rombauer, Irma S., and Marion Rombauer Becker. *Joy of Cooking: The American Household Classic Newly Revised and Expanded with Over 4500 Recipes and 1000 Informative Illustrations*. New York: Scribner, 1995.

Ruhlman, Michael, and Brian Polcyn. *Charcuterie: The Craft of Salting, Smoking and Curing*. New York: W.W. Norton & Company, Inc., 2005.

Scherber, Amy, and Toy Kim Dupree. *Amy's Bread*. Hoboken, : John Wiley & Sons, Inc., 2010

Schloss, Andrew. *Homemade Liqueurs and Infused Spirits: Innovative Flavor Combinations, Plus Homemade Versions of Kahlúa, Cointreau, and Other Popular Liqueurs*. North Adams, MA: Storey Publishing, 2013.

Wolfert, Paula. *The Slow Mediterranean Kitchen: Recipes for the Passionate Cook*. New Jersey: John Wiley & Sons, Inc., 2003

Wong, Tama Matsuoka, with Eddy Leroux. *Foraged Flavour: Finding Fabulous Ingredients in Your Backyard or Farmer's Market*. New York: Clarkson Potter Publishers, 2012.

Foraging, Field Guides and Reference

Andre, Alestine, and Alan Fehr. *Gwich'in Ethnobotany: Plants Used by the Gwich'in for Food, Medicine, Shelter and Tools*. Tsiigehtchic, NT: Gwich'in Social and Cultural Institute, 2001.

Arora, David. *All That the Rain Promises, and More…: A Hip Pocket Guide to Western Mushrooms*. Berkeley: Ten Speed Press, 1991.

Arora, David. *Mushrooms Demystified: A Comprehensive Guide to the Fleshy Fungi*. Berkeley: Ten Speed Press, 1986.

Gibbons, Euell. *Stalking the Wild Asparagus*. Chambersburg, PA: Alan C. Hood & Company, Inc., 1962.

Gray, Beverley. *The Boreal Herbal: Wild Food and Medicine Plants of the North, A Guide to Harvesting, Preserving and Preparing*. Whitehorse: Aroma Borealis Press, 2011.

Henry, J. David. *Canada's Boreal Forest*. Washington: Smithsonian Institution Press, 2002.

MacKinnon, Andy, Jim Pojar, and Ray Coupé. *Plants of Northern British Columbia*. Edmonton: Lone Pine Publishing, 1992.

MacKinnon, Andy, Linda Kershaw, and John Arnason. *Edible and Medicinal Plants of Canada*. Edmonton: Lone Pine Publishing, 2009.

Schalkwijk-Barendsen, Helene. *Mushrooms of Northwest North America*. Edmonton, Lone Pine Publishing: 1994.

Thayer, Samuel. *The Forager's Harvest: A Guide to Identifying, Harvesting, and Preparing Edible Wild Plants*. Birchwood, WI: Forager's Harvest Press, 2006.

Turner, Nancy J, and Adam F. Szczawinski. *Edible Wild Fruits and Nuts of Canada*. Ottawa: Fitzhenry and Whiteside, 1988.

Useful Websites

The best source for spruce tip ideas remains Alaskan cook Laurie Helen Constantino's blog:
Mediterranean Cooking in Alaska
medcookingalaska.blogspot.ca

For sourdough advice and inspiration, visit:

The Fresh Loaf
www.thefreshloaf.com

Sourdoughs International
www.sourdo.com

Wild Yeast
www.wildyeastblog.com

For the pH of common foods visit:

U.S Food and Drug Administration Bad Bug Book:
pH Values of Various Foods
**www.fda.gov/Food/
FoodborneIllnessContaminants
/CausesOfIllnessBadBugBook/ucm122561.htm**

For information on safely infusing oils visit:

The University of Maine: Safe Homemade Flavored and Infused Oils
www.umaine.edu/publications/4385e/

Colorado State University: Flavored Vinegars and Oils
www.ext.colostate.edu/pubs/foodnut/09340.html

PRODUCTS

Birch Syrup
Uncle Berwyn's Yukon Birch Syrup
P.O. Box 1735, Dawson City, YT Y0B IG0
uncleberwyn@yukonbirch.ca
www.yukonbirch.ca

**Kitchen equipment, including
Mehu-Liisa Steamer/Juicer**
Lee Valley Tools Ltd.
P.O. Box 6295, Station J
Ottawa, ON K2A 1T4
1.800.267.8767
customerservice@leevalley.com
www.leevalley.com

Lavender Products
Sledding Hill
714 Riverview Rd., RR 1
Bear River, NS B0S1B0
(902) 467.0196
sleddinghill@sleddinghill.ca
www.sleddinghill.ca

Matryoshka Dolls, Unpainted
Golden Cockerel
1651 NC Hwy. 194 N
Boone, NC 28607 USA
1.800.892.5409
service@goldencockerel.com
www.goldencockerel.com

Russian Crafts
Russia, 198330
St .Petersburg, P.O. Box 182
Terletsky Mikhail
+7.921.963.8086
eshop@russian-crafts.com
www.russian-crafts.com

Pectin
Bernardin No Sugar Needed Pectin
Bernardin c/o Jarden Branded Consumables Canada
845 Intermodal Drive
Brampton, ON L6T 0C6
www.bernardin.ca

Pomona's Universal Pectin
Harvest Plus
200 Crabapple Crescent
Parksville, BC V9P 2P7
(877) 706.8493
info@pomonapectin.com
www.pomonapectin.com

Sea Salt and Fleur de Sel
Vancouver Island Salt Co.
4235 Telegraph Road
Cobble Hill, BC V0R 1L3
250.882.4489
islandsalt@gmail.com
www.visaltco.com

**For information on Northern Jellies, Jams,
Mustards, Syrups and farm products**
Fireweed Community Market
P.O. Box 20228
Whitehorse, Yukon Y1A 7A2
(867) 393.2255
fireweedmarket@yahoo.ca
fireweedmarket.yukonfood.com

Yukon Agricultural Association
203-302 Steele Street
Whitehorse, YT Y1A 2E5
1.867.668.6864
admin@yukonag.ca
yukonag.ca

For dried herbs and other products from the boreal forest
Aroma Borealis Herb Shop
504-B Main St.
Whitehorse, Yukon
Y1A 2B9
(867) 667.HERB (4372)
aromaborealis.com

Etre Boreal, Coopérative forestière de Girardville
3103, route industrielle
Girardville, Québec
Canada, G0W 1R0
(418) 258.3451 ext. 222
(418) 258.3675
info@doriginca.com
dorigina.com

CULINARY TRAVEL

Scandinavia
Sweden Culinary Experiences
**www.visitsweden.com/sweden/Featured/Sweden
-the-new-culinary-nation/Culinary-experiences**

Norwegian Foodprints
www.visitnorway.com/foodprints

Taste of National Tourist Routes
www.matlangsnasjonaleturistveger.no

Aitojamakuha.fi
www.aitojamakuja.fi

The Yukon
Tourism Industry Association of the Yukon
www.tiayukon.com

Yukon: Larger than Life
travelyukon.com

Canada
Keep Exploring: An official site of the Canadian Tourism Commission
caen-keepexploring.canada.travel

Index